Malcolm X,
African American
Revolutionary

Malcolm X, African American Revolutionary

DENNIS D. WAINSTOCK

McFarland & Company, Inc., Publishers
Jefferson, North Carolina, and London

ALSO BY DENNIS D. WAINSTOCK

*The Decision to Drop the Atomic Bomb:
Hiroshima and Nagasaki August 1945* (2008)

Truman, MacArthur, and the Korean War (1999)

*The Turning Point: The 1968 United States
Presidential Campaign* (McFarland, 1988)

LIBRARY OF CONGRESS CATALOGUING-IN-PUBLICATION DATA

Wainstock, Dennis D., 1947–
   Malcolm X, African American revolutionary / Dennis D. Wainstock.
      p.   cm.
   Includes bibliographical references and index.

   ISBN 978-0-7864-3934-8
   softcover : 50# alkaline paper

   1. X, Malcolm, 1925–1965.   2. Black Muslims—Biography.
3. African Americans—Biography.   I. Title.
BP223.Z8L5779   2009
320.54'6092—dc22   [B]   2008037040

British Library cataloguing data are available

Cover images: Malcolm X, 1963, United Press International photo,
New York World-Telegram & Sun Collection, Library of Congress.

Manufactured in the United States of America

*McFarland & Company, Inc., Publishers
   Box 611, Jefferson, North Carolina 28640
   www.mcfarlandpub.com*

To African Americans in
their continuing struggle
for freedom and justice.
And ... to Barbara Allen,
friend and colleague.

Contents

Preface

This book is a biography of Malcolm X's life. Although it touches on his early life, it concentrates on his last years in the Nation of Islam, his conflict with Elijah Muhammad and the Chicago leadership, and his last eleven months from his break with the Nation of Islam on March 8, 1964, to his assassination on February 21, 1965.

The sheer quantity of material was daunting, but the research was rewarding. It was filled with colorful and outstanding personalities and dramatic action. The study raised a number of questions. How accurate was Malcolm's portrayal of himself as a street hustler? How much of a role did John Elton Bembry play in Malcolm's prison conversion? Did Malcolm decide to leave the Nation of Islam before his suspension by Elijah Muhammad? Was Malcolm seeking martyrdom? Just how great a role did government agencies play in Malcolm's death?

My research owes much to the trail-breaking contributions by scholars who have written biographies, general studies, and monographs on Malcolm X, Elijah Muhammad, the Nation of Islam, and the Civil Rights Movement. I am grateful to my colleague Dr. Larry Zbach and librarian, Phyllis Freeman of Salem-International University, for providing me with helpful advice and assistance during my research and writing. Also, my thanks go to Barbara Allen, who cheerfully typed numerous versions of my manuscript.

INTRODUCTION

The Early Years

An upsurge of racism marked the post World War I period of American history. In 1919, lynchings of blacks, which were declining before the war, rose to seventy and vigilante mobs burned another fourteen. Race riots broke out in over twenty northern cities. In Chicago alone, thirty-eight people died and over five hundred injuries occurred before the National Guard restored order.

The postwar social climate led to a revival of the Ku Klux Klan, whose platform distrusted blacks, Jews, Catholics, foreigners, unions, and liberals. By 1923, it claimed a total of five million members. Although it had relatively little appeal in the large metropolitan areas of the northeast, it found support both in the south and in the middle sized cities and small towns in midwestern and western states. In Indiana, for instance, the organization boasted of having 350,000 Klansmen, which represented ten percent of its population.[1]

Despite the wartime slogan "to make the world safe for democracy," black veterans came home to a democracy not reserved for them. In many areas of the country, whites deprived blacks of political rights, including the right to vote. Southern "Jim Crow" laws forced them into segregated schools, restaurants, hotels, barbershops, dentists, and churches. In the north, although "Jim Crow" laws did not officially exist, whites discriminated against blacks in employment, housing, and schools. They faced discrimination, in effect, in every area of their lives because of the color of their skins.

The postwar upsurge of racism generated massive black support for Jamaican born Marcus Garvey's Universal Negro Improvement Association (UNIA). Founded by Garvey in 1914, it soon grew into a worldwide organization with branches throughout the United States and over forty other countries. Based in Harlem, its program advocated the long range goal of pan-Africanism or "back to Africa." Until that time, however, the UNIA called for blacks to control the political, economic, and social institutions of their communities.

Referred to as black nationalism, in Harlem, the UNIA owned grocery stores, laundries, restaurants, hotels, factories, a publishing house, a university, and a steamship company, the Black Star Line. To influence politics, it formed the Negro Political Union, the Universal African-Legion, the Universal Black Cross Nurses, the Universal African Motor Corps, and the Black Flying Eagles.

In Africa, the Republic of Liberia, under President Charles D. B. King, agreed to provide for the settlement of about a hundred thousand of Garvey's followers in his country. But Britain and France, fearing that King's deal would threaten their colonial holdings which surrounded Liberia, persuaded him to lease the lands promised Garvey to the Firestone Rubber Corporation. Calling Garvey an "agitator," Britain's press then praised King for "putting his foot down firmly on such misguided movements."[2]

Likewise, the U.S. government looked upon Garvey's movement as a threat to American interests. In 1919, a U.S. Department of Justice report portrayed him as a dangerous agitator and referred to his newspaper, the *Negro World*, as seditious. At the same time, Edwin P. Kilroe, New York City's assistant district attorney, kept Garvey's movement under constant surveillance and the National Association for the Advancement of Colored People (NAACP), an integrationist organization, accused the UNIA of being "impractical, visionary, and ridiculous" and misleading "poor, ignorant Negroes."[3]

Knowing that he was under government surveillance, however, did not stop Garvey from breaking the law. When his shipping company, the Black Star Line, went bankrupt, he continued to sell its stocks. As a result, in 1922, the government indicted him for using the U.S. mails to defraud the public. He was found guilty and a federal judge sentenced him to five years in Atlanta Federal Penitentiary. In 1927, after President Calvin Coolidge commuted Garvey's sentence, the government deported him back to his native Jamaica. Without his "fiery leadership," the UNIA, which at one time numbered two million members, fell into disarray, and Garvey soon slipped into obscurity.[4]

The Little Family

Described at various times as tall, slim, pretty, intelligent, and proud, Louise Helen Norton Little was born on the Caribbean island of Grenada, ninety miles northeast of Trinidad. Ashamed of her light skin, because her father was white, she would teach her children the value of their blackness and favor the darker-skinned ones over the light-skinned Malcolm. Shortly after immigrating to North America in 1917, she met Earl Little, who was divorced with three children, at a Marcus Garvey convention in Montreal, Canada, and two years later they married.

From Reynolds, Georgia, dark skinned and with one eye, Earl Little, at six-foot four, was a formidable presence. The fact that four of his six brothers had died violently, three of them killed by white men, including one by lynching, influenced his decision to become a dedicated Garveyite. Pushing Garvey's message, Earl tried to instill in blacks a sense of self-dignity and convince them to seek independence from the white man by striving for economic self-sufficiency, and to prepare for a return to Africa someday.[5]

After a short stay in Philadelphia, Pennsylvania, the Littles settled down in Omaha, Nebraska. While Louise wrote articles for the UNIA's *Negro World*, Earl traveled around the state preaching Garvey's ideas. As a means to win over converts, Earl often spoke from behind the pulpits of black Baptist churches, but he made no claim to being a minister.[6]

Earl's Garveyite preaching got the attention of Nebraska's Ku Klux Klan, which considered him a troublemaker. Consequently, late one night in December 1924, horse riding klansmen surrounded his house, shouting for him to come outside. Opening the door a crack, Louise, who was pregnant with Malcolm, told them that her husband was away preaching. After warning her that Earl better leave town, the klansmen galloped around the house and broke every window with their gun butts.[7] Despite their threats, however, he would keep his family in Omaha until after Louise gave birth to Malcolm, their fourth child. The first three were Wilfred, Hilda, and Philbert; and Reginald, Yvonne, and Wesley came after Malcolm.

Born in Omaha on May 19, 1925, Malcolm was the seventh of his father's ten children, including three by a previous marriage: Ella, Earl and Mary. According to Malcolm, his parents were nearly always "at odds," harboring conflicting views on almost everything. Because Louise had more education than her husband, she had a tendency to correct him, and this behavior of hers only sparked counter-arguments by him to protect his pride. Another sore spot was that Louise did not approve of "soul food," such as pork and rabbit, which he loved.[8]

Naturally, the Littles raised their children on Garvey's views, which carried over throughout their lives. Reading to them from the Garveyite newspapers, Louise taught them self-reliance and to call themselves black, not Negroes. After leaving Garveyite meetings, said Wilfred, "You'd be proud that you were black."[9] Similarly, Malcolm described his father at those meetings as "intense," "intelligent," and "down to earth," and that "made me feel the same way."[10]

Yet, despite Earl's pride in his blackness and African heritage, of all his children, he preferred his lightest skinned child, Malcolm, described by some as "marigny," a dull yellowish skin, pale enough to freckle, pale eyes, and reddish coppery hair.[11] Although Earl was a fierce disciplinarian who had so many rules that, according to his children, "it was hard to know them all," he rarely laid a hand on Malcolm.[12] Nearly all of Malcolm's whippings, in fact, came from his mother. In contrast to her husband, she treated Malcolm as her least favorite child because of his light skin. Often scrubbing his face and neck violently, she told Anna Stohrer, a white neighbor, "I can make him look almost white if I bathe him enough."[13]

Shortly after Malcolm was born, the Littles moved to Milwaukee, Wisconsin, where Louise continued to write for the *Negro World* and Earl became president of the Industrial Club, a Garveyite self-help group. In August 1927, after Louise gave birth to Reginald, the Littles moved from Milwaukee to Albion, Michigan, and then to the northwestern outskirts of Lansing, purchasing a two-story farmhouse in a semi-rural, all white area. In Lansing, Malcolm's younger sister Yvonne and his brother Wesley were born.

Resenting their presence and Garveyite views, the Littles' white neighbors referred to them as "uppity smart niggers." Soon, the Littles came to the attention of the Black Legion, a Ku Klux Klan splinter group, whose members wore black instead of the Klan's traditional white robes and whose reputation in the Lansing area was even more sinister and violent than the Klan itself.[14]

When Earl bought his house, the realtor did not mention that the deed contained a racial exclusion clause. Consequently, not long after he moved his family into it, his white neighbors initiated legal proceedings against him and the court ordered him to move "forthwith."[15] Posting an appeals bond, his lawyer served notice that he would appeal the ruling to the Michigan Supreme Court. Before it went through, however, in the early morning hours of December 8, 1929, the Black Legion set fire to the Littles' home. "Everybody was asleep," said Wilfred later, when "all of a sudden we heard a big boom ... fire was everywhere."[16] But his parents snatched their children up and everybody got out safely.

Some discrepancy existed as to whether Lansing's firemen responded to the fire. Malcolm said that when they arrived, none of them made any effort to put it out.[17] According to Philbert, "No fire wagon came, nothing."[18] The official report said that Lansing's firemen had refused to respond because the

Littles' house was outside the city limits. Apparently, as spectators, some of them came "just to watch the house burn down."[19]

While friends temporarily housed and clothed his family, Earl, a carpenter by trade, built a new home on the outskirts of East Lansing. The property included a six-acre plot of farmland which enabled the Littles to grow most of their own food and sell it on the market. "This kept us more or less in an independent mode," said Wilfred.[20] "Self-sufficiency was very important for the Littles," added Philbert, because his father could not hold a job for long, refusing to "kowtow" to his white bosses "who would then let him go."[21]

Death and Disintegration

When Malcolm was six in September 1931, his father stormed out of the house after a bitter quarrel with Louise. At that instant, she had a vision that something bad was about to happen and she called to him before he was out of sight. Turning to her, he apologized for his anger by a hand signal and then waved goodbye.[22]

Later that night, Earl's body, nearly cut in half, was found on the trolley tracks near his home. While the police said that he had fallen under the trolley's rear wheels while trying to board it, the UNIA said that the Black Legion killed him and then placed his body on the streetcar's path to make his death appear accidental.

Left with seven children under twelve years of age to support, thirty-four year old Louise struggled to feed and clothe them amid the Great Depression. In Lansing, as elsewhere throughout the 1930s, loss of jobs for blacks was devastating. Like everyone else, she sought whatever employment she could find. According to Malcolm, whites would hire her for domestic work; then when they discovered she was half-black, they would let her go, and she would come home crying.[23]

The Littles were often hungry. Malcolm recalled that his mother would stand over the stove and stretch whatever little food they had to eat.[24] She would "boil a big pot of dandelion greens," he said, and "we would have oatmeal or cornmeal mush three times a day.[25] At other times, she would purchase stale surplus bread for five cents at the local bakery. According to Philbert, "She would take it and cut the mold and put sugar on it and put it in the oven and soften it with water."[26]

Although a proud woman, dire poverty forced Louise to violate her Garveyite philosophy of self-help and accept welfare. Yet, despite the increase of food from it, Malcolm, whose previous hunger had driven him to steal, continued to do it, leading to whippings from his mother. After neighbors told welfare agents that she was abusing her son, they placed him in the foster home of a black couple, Mabel and Thornton Gohanna.[27]

Louise's mental health suffered from the strain of trying to keep her family together. But after a relationship with a man failed because he did not want the responsibility of helping her care for her children, her psychological deterioration became more noticeable. He was a nice man, said Yvonne, and when his visits stopped, "she lost her glow."[28] Watching their anchor give way, said Malcolm, became "increasingly terrifying."[29]

On January 9, 1939, the courts, acting on her doctor's recommendation, judged Louise mentally unfit and committed her to the state mental hospital at Kalamazoo. While Malcolm continued to live with the Gohanna family and the two oldest, nineteen-year-old Wilfred and sixteen-year-old Hilda, stayed on their own in the four-room house that Earl had built for his family, the courts parceled out the rest of the children throughout the area. To Yvonne, being torn apart from her family at age nine was painful, and she was petrified.[30] Later, Malcolm blamed welfare, the courts, and Louise's doctor for giving his family the "one-two-three punch."[31]

Not long afterwards, because of some minor misbehavior, Malcolm wound up in a detention home waiting for transfer to reform school. Taking a liking to him, the Swerleins, a man and wife who ran the detention home, gave Malcolm his own room, the first in his life, and allowed him to eat dinner with them. In appreciation, he worked hard, sweeping, mopping, and dusting around the Swerleins' house. Impressed by his attitude, they blocked his transfer to reform school and enrolled him, instead, in Mason Junior High School, making him the first resident of the detention home to have that privilege.[32]

Malcolm, however, had mixed feelings towards the Swerleins. They "liked me," he said later, "not like a human being," but like one "likes a canary."[33] Driving through Lansing's black section with the Swerleins one day, Malcolm recalled that Mr. Swerlein told his wife that he could "not see how niggers can be so happy and be so poor," living in shacks but driving big, shiny cars. His wife replied that "niggers" were "just like that."[34] Malcolm never forgot that episode.

In 1939, during his seventh grade year, Malcolm rose to the head of his class, played sports, and became class president. But being the only black student at Mason Junior High School was not always pleasant for him. Both students and teachers referred to him as "the nigger"; older boys would accidentally elbow him as they passed by. At school dances, the boys gave him "psychic messages" that he better not dance with white girls. Since there were no black girls there, he would smile, stand around awhile, and then make some excuse to leave early.[35]

Just before the school year ended, Malcolm's half-sister, Ella Collins, whom he described as "jet black," "commanding," and "proud," arrived from Boston to take him and his siblings to visit their mother at the state hospital at Kalamazoo. Taken in by Malcolm's bright and inquisitive personality, before she left, she obtained permission from the Swerleins to have him visit her in Boston that summer.[36]

Later that summer of 1940, Malcolm, who looked country, got off the Greyhound bus at Boston carrying a cardboard suitcase and wearing a green suit. For the next two weeks, he explored Roxbury, Boston's black neighborhood where Ella lived. He had never experienced anything like it, savoring its neon lights, nightclubs, pool halls, bars, restaurants, jukeboxes and interracial couples strolling arm in arm. "I couldn't have feigned indifference if I had tried," he said.[37]

Upon returning to Mason and entering the eighth grade, Malcolm, who for the first time had experienced being part of his own people, no longer felt comfortable being around whites. When they asked him what was wrong, he said, "Nothing," knowing that they would not have understood the obvious. For him, continuing to live in a white detention home where he was treated as a pet canary had become intolerable, and going to a white school where everybody, though meaning well, referred to him as "nigger" was no longer acceptable.[38]

One day, according to Malcolm, his English teacher, Mr. Ostrowsky, asked him whether he had given any thought to a career. Since he had not, he said on a whim that he would like to become a lawyer. Ostrowsky, however, said that a lawyer was not a realistic goal "for a nigger" and told him to think about something attainable like a carpenter. To Malcolm, however, who was at the top of his class, "smarter than nearly all of those white kids," Ostrowsky's remark did not make sense, and in Malcolm's autobiography, he said that afterwards he began to turn away from whites.[39]

Although Malcolm talked about this incident throughout his life, he tended to exaggerate its importance. He had begun to draw away from whites after his visit in Boston with his half-sister Ella, not after Ostrowsky's remark. At this time, in fact, that he was as embittered against whites as he suggested in his autobiography was probably not accurate. He just wanted to live among his own people in Boston, not with whites in Mason.

Uncomfortable with Malcolm's continued "wall of silence," the Swerleins persuaded juvenile authorities to board him with a black family, Harold and Ivy Lyons, who already had five children. When that failed to work out, the court placed him in the home of Sidney Grayson, an elderly black resident of Mason. Unhappy there, in a letter to Ella, he pleaded with her to allow him to come live with her. Somehow, he never learned how, she convinced Michigan authorities to transfer his custody to her.

Boston

In February 1941, fifteen-year-old Malcolm arrived in Boston to live with Ella in her comfortable Harrishof Street home, located in the "Hill" section of Roxbury. In Boston's black ghetto, a sharp, social distinction existed among the Massachusetts born blacks of the middle-class Hill section and the southern newcomers living in the "Town" section. Feeling more comfortable with the Town section, with its grocery stores, walk-up flats, cheap restaurants, pool rooms, bars and pawn shops, Malcolm called the Hill section a "snooty, black neighborhood" whose residents "looked down their noses at the southern newcomers."[40]

Hoping to direct Malcolm into a respectable life, Ella wanted to find him a job on the Hill and enroll him in school. Instead, he would spend his days walking around the Town section, fascinated by its sharply dressed hustlers who hung out on the street corners, in the pool rooms, bars and restaurants, using words such as "stud," "chick," "cool," and "hip." At night, he would lay in bed turning these new words over in his mind.[41]

One day at a local pool hall, Malcolm met Malcolm Jarvis, nicknamed Shorty, a dark, stubby, conk-headed (hair straightened with lye) man, racking up balls for the pool players. Like Malcolm, Shorty was from Lansing and the two men became fast friends. A talented jazz trumpet player, he told Malcolm that he was working in the pool room to keep ends together until he could organize his own band.

As a shoeshine boy, Shorty got Malcolm a job at the Roseland State Ballroom where the big bands such as Count Basie, Lionel Hampton, Sonny Greer, Coatie Williams and Glenn Miller played when they came to Boston. To get tips, a boy named Freddie showed Malcolm how to shine "rag pop," like a firecracker, to offer hand towels or a whiskbroom to customers leaving the urinals, and to "Uncle Tom" a little. Also, for a tip, he would slip whites phone numbers of prostitutes or sell them marijuana, liquor, and condoms.[42]

Apparently, Malcolm was a complex personality. On the one hand, said Shorty, he was a "beautiful con-artist" who could "talk you out of your last two dollars, and you would give it to him with enthusiasm." On the other hand, said Shorty, the toughness that he portrayed was "just a camouflage to keep people from knowing how warm he really was."[43]

By this time, Malcolm began experimenting with alcohol, tobacco, marijuana, and gambling. Also, he bought himself a zoot suit. Originating in Georgia and just then coming in vogue in the northern black ghettos, it consisted of a brightly colored outfit, including pants that were very wide at the knee and cut very narrow at the bottom, with a long jacket, pinched at the waistline, and flared out at the bottom. Along with it, he wore a feathered, broad-brimmed hat and a gold plated chain.

To look the part of a zoot suiter, Malcolm needed to conk his hair. From a grocery store and a drugstore, he bought the necessary ingredients. These included a can of Red Devil lye, two eggs, two medium sized white potatoes, a large jar of Vaseline, a large bar of soap, a large toothed comb and a fine-toothed comb, a rubber hose with a metal spray head, a rubber apron, and a pair of gloves.

In his autobiography, Malcolm described his first conk, given to him by Shorty. After mixing the conk ingredients until it turned into a "jelly-like, starchy looking, pale-yellowish glop," he combed it into Malcolm's scalp. Gritting his teeth and feeling like his "head caught fire," he bolted for the wash basin, knees trembling, cursing Shorty until he looked in the mirror and saw the transformation of his hair from kinks to "as straight as any white man's." This, he said, was his "first really big step toward self-degradation," and he had joined the multitude of blacks who were brainwashed into believing in the superiority of whites.[44]

Meanwhile, leaving his job at the Roseland so that he could dance there when the big bands came to town, Malcolm floated through a number of jobs, including soda fountain clerk, factory worker, day laborer, and busboy. During his free time, he learned the Lindy, a lively swing dance nicknamed after aviator Charles Lindbergh. When Malcolm danced, he "astonished all the girls," said Shorty, with his pants "a floating balloon," and his coat "like a wing, flying around with that big ten gallon hat on and the chain flinging." The girls "were all after him."[45]

Along with women from the Town section, Malcolm dated Laura, whom he described as an educated Hill girl, not as snobbish as the other middle-class blacks in Ella's neighborhood. Equally important, although somewhat introverted, she loved dancing, which seemed to bring out another personality in her. "I can close my eyes right now and see it," said Malcolm later; she was "like a blurring ballet ... beautiful ... her lightness, like a shadow!"[46]

Yet, Malcolm's first long lasting relationship was with Beatrice Bazarian, a white woman, nicknamed Bea, whom he referred to as Sophia in his autobiography. While dancing with Laura one night at the Roseland, Malcolm noticed Bea, a blonde with shoulder-length hair, well-built, wearing expensive clothes, eyeing him levelly. Soon, he got loose from Laura and started dancing with Bea. Afterwards, she drove him to a deserted lane and made love to him in her car.

When Ella learned that Malcolm jilted Laura for a white woman, she was thoroughly disgusted with him. To her, Bea, like other white women who dated blacks, looked upon Malcolm as a way to fulfill her sexual fantasies with a black man.[47] Initially, perhaps, that may have been what drew her to him; and he, in turn, probably looked upon her as a status symbol, an attractive white woman who had money. With time, however, he came to care for her, and their relationship lasted for five years.

Later, Malcolm regretted hurting Laura, who was already going the wrong way and would eventually become a narcotics addict and prostitute. Blaming himself for this, he said that to have treated her as he did for a white woman "made the blow doubly heavy." But at that time, as he later said, he was "just deaf, dumb and blind."[48]

In 1941, eager to allure Malcolm away from Bea, Ella got a friend to obtain a job for him selling sandwiches on the Boston–New York run of the New York, New Haven and Hartford Railroad, making runs on the *Colonial* between Boston and Washington and on the *Yankee Clipper* to New York. On these runs, the cooks and waiters took a liking to Malcolm, treating him like a peer. "That grew me up real fast," he said later, "because in those days, railroad men were about the biggest people in town."[49]

Harlem

Malcolm knew that Ella got him the railroad job to get him out of Boston and away from Bea. But he took it, nonetheless, so that he could spend his layovers in New York City visiting Harlem. In this way, he discovered its nightspots, including Small's Paradise, the Savoy Ballroom, the Theresa Hotel, the Braddock Hotel bar, and the Apollo Theater. To him, Harlem was "seventh heaven," magnifying Lansing's and Roxbury's nightspots "a thousand times."[50]

Malcolm did not last long working as a sandwich man on the *Colonial* and *Yankee Clipper*. He would come to work high on liquor and marijuana, acting loud and wild. When the customers complained to the conductors, the New Haven Line fired him. He then got a job on the Seaboard Line's *Silver Meteor* from New York to St. Petersburg and Miami. But after he called the assistant conductor a "Florida cracker," the railroad's managers let him go.[51]

At this point, sometime in 1942, seventeen-year-old Malcolm obtained a waiter's job at Small's Paradise. From the professional hustlers who hung out there, he learned about Harlem's rackets, including numbers, pimping, selling drugs and robbery, and to never trust anyone outside of your own close-mouthed circle.[52]

When Ed and Charlie Small hired Malcolm, they told him never to hustle off customers, especially those in uniform. In early 1943, nonetheless, Malcolm gave a black soldier who appeared depressed the number of a prostitute living in his rooming house. Thereupon, he showed Malcolm his badge, but the undercover policeman let him go with a warning. The Small brothers had to fire Malcolm to protect their business.

Losing his job at Small's Paradise was not a problem for Malcolm. Known on the street as Detroit Red, he had already become a serious hustler. Doing a number of hustles simultaneously, he was a "steerer," an intermediary between prostitutes and their clients, ran numbers for Harlem's gangsters, and sold bootleg liquor, "hot" goods, and marijuana. He described himself as a "true hustler," living by his wits, "uneducated, unskilled at anything honorable," and exploiting any prey, knowing that if he ever slowed down, the other hungry wolves out thee would not "hesitate to make him their prey."[53]

Harlem was Malcolm's regular beat, but when the police were on his tail, he used his void New Haven railroad pass to travel until the heat died down. At other times, for psychological escape, he took drugs. Although he may have smoked marijuana regularly and inhaled cocaine on occasion, he was probably exaggerating his claims in the use of opium, hashish, Nembutal, Seconal, and Benzedrine. To be sure, whether he was actually addicted to any drug other than cigarettes or marijuana was unclear.

For several months, sometime in 1942 and 1943, according to Malcolm, he engaged in his most dangerous hustle, armed robbery. He did this either alone or with Sammy McKnight, a Harlem pimp. For street wear, he said, he carried a little, flat, blue steel twenty-five automatic, but when working, he used a bigger gun, either a thirty-two, a thirty-eight, or a forty-five. When his victims stared at the gun's "big black hole," he said, their "faces fell slack and mouths sagged open," and when he spoke, they "seemed to hear as though they were far away" and would do whatever he asked.[54]

On one occasion, in a holdup gone bad, Malcolm and Sammy split up, meeting later at their hideout. When one of Sammy's women, an olive-skinned Spanish prostitute, discovered that a bullet had scratched him, she blamed Malcolm for it. As she was about to attack him, he said later, he hit her in self-defense. Nonetheless, he had violated the hustler's code of never striking a pimp's woman, and Sammy drew his gun. His woman screamed, which distracted him long enough for Malcolm to make his escape. Although the two men made up, Malcolm never forgot the incident, reminding himself that living in a "hustler's jungle" meant that he could not fully trust anyone.[55]

Later, some contended that Malcolm was not as bad as he portrayed himself in his autobiography and in later interviews. To biographer Peter Goldman, Malcolm was "just a street kid ... overstating his criminality," since the "stuff he did was kind of petty."[56] "What he had done hadn't been that bad," said Philbert. "He was just trying to find a place."[57] He was not the "big time hustler that he had made himself out to be," added Spike Lee, film director of Malcolm X's life. "It was about trying to survive."[58]

To be sure, Malcolm never portrayed himself as a big time gangster, vice lord, or mob lieutenant. While his illicit activities of selling marijuana, running numbers and steering Johns to prostitutes was petty and fulfilled a public demand, he was more than just a street kid. Pointing guns at people in the commission of robberies was hardly kid stuff. As he later said, "No one who knew me, including myself, would doubt that I'd kill."[59]

In May 1943, upon reaching his eighteenth birthday, Malcolm, as required by law, registered at New York City's local draft board. Shortly thereafter, when he received his draft notice ordering him to report to an army induction center in Manhattan, he decided to portray himself as crazy. Hoping to get the attention of black army intelligence agents, who had saturated Harlem looking to keep soldiers on leave on their good behavior or to spot draft dodgers, he started dropping the word that he was a Japanese sympathizer and deliberately acted "high and crazy" in public places.[60]

On the day Malcolm reported to the induction office, he wore his wildest zoot suit, yellow knob-toe shoes and frizzled his hair into a reddish bush of conk. While waiting in line with the other inductees, he began running his mouth a mile a minute, acting like he was in a hurry to get into the military. Soon, a psychiatrist pulled him into a side room and wanted to know why he was so anxious to become a soldier. After a moment of silence, he whispered to him that he wanted to get sent down South, organize guns and kill "crackers."[61] With that, the psychiatrist, dropping his pencil, dismissed him. Soon thereafter, never bothering to ask why, the U.S. Army rejected him; he received a 4-F card in the mail.

Although Malcolm and Bea, who would occasionally visit him in Harlem, were still together, sometime in early 1944 she married a wealthy white Bostonian on leave from military service. Earlier, Sammy, trying to prepare Malcolm for this eventuality, told him that a white woman who liked blacks was still quite practical. While she went with a black man for forbidden pleasure, she married a white man for financial security.[62] On the surface, he appeared to have accepted Sammy's explanation, but how he really felt about Bea's marriage was difficult to know.

Serving in the Merchant Marine, Reginald, whenever his ship docked in New York City, would visit his brother. That Reginald admired Harlem's hustling life was obvious to Malcolm, and he persuaded Reginald to go AWOL (absent without leave) and stay. Malcolm found Reginald a safe hustle selling cheap watches and jewelry and acting as if he had stolen them to make them appear more valuable.[63]

Unlike Malcolm, Reginald was not attracted to white women. He was even cool around Bea, which tickled Malcolm. Instead, sixteen-year-old Reginald went for a black woman nearly twice his age; moreover, that he could get her to cook, wash, and buy clothes for him impressed Malcolm.

After the incident with Sammy over his Spanish woman, Malcolm said that the only person he could trust in Harlem was Reginald. To him, however, Malcolm was distant and would regard personal questions as unwelcome intrusions. "One never knew what he was thinking or feeling," said Reginald. "He could be talking with you, looking at you, yet off in some other world."[64]

Between October and December 1944, Malcolm returned to Boston. Rooming with Ella, he first obtained a job at a Sears Roebuck warehouse which lasted less than a month. Next, to get pocket change, he stole a fur coat from one of his relatives, pawning it for five dollars. When Ella found out, she called the police, and he received a three month suspended sentence. Then, traveling to Lansing, he worked for brief periods, dealt in stolen goods, and finally went back to Harlem in August 1945.

Shortly after returning to Harlem, Malcolm obtained a job delivering bootleg alcohol for Abe Goldstein, a Jewish nightclub owner. After work one night, two hoodlums, hired by a bar manager to track down a tall, light-skinned black man who had robbed him earlier that evening, kicked down Malcolm's door. That he was working that night did not totally convince them, but since they had other suspects to check out, they left. "That's all that saved me," said Malcolm.[65]

Shortly thereafter, the same holdup man robbed a group of Italian racketeers, and Malcolm was once again a suspect. This time mobsters cornered him in a barroom phone booth. Unarmed, he pretended to have a gun in his pocket. Just as they were about to call his bluff, however, a policeman inadvertently walked into the bar, which precipitated their retreat. "God must have been watching over me," said Malcolm later.[66]

Just as Malcolm escaped from one dangerous situation, another one developed. He learned that West Indian Archie, a numbers runner, was looking for him. Often, for customers like Malcolm who had established sound credit, Archie would, if they told him that a number they had bet had "hit," pay them himself and get reimbursed later by the numbers banker. Earlier, he had paid Malcolm three hundred dollars after he assured him that the number he had combinated had won, but when Archie checked the betting slip, he realized that Malcolm had combinated a different number.[67] That he would purposely do this was difficult to understand, since cheating an older, more experienced hustler was needlessly courting danger.

To save face, Archie could not allow Malcolm to get away with cheating him. When Archie found Malcolm with Sammy at their apartment hideout, Archie demanded his money. To emphasize his point, he took out his gun, a thirty-two twenty, bigger than a thirty-two, but not as big as a thirty-eight. Talking fast, Malcolm denied cheating him. Unconvinced, Archie gave him until noon the next day to pay up.[68]

Despite Malcolm's precarious position, that night he took a cab to one of his favorite nightspots, the La Marr-Cheri, a St. Nicholas Avenue bar. What's more, he foolishly tempted fate by sitting with his back to the door. Before long, Archie arrived, walked up behind him, and started cursing him loudly, floor-showing for the customers. But before Malcolm could react, Archie's friends stepped in between the two men and pushed Archie aside, working him back toward the rear, which allowed Malcolm to back out the door.[69]

Posturing by holding his hand in his pocket, Malcolm stood outside for about five minutes. When Archie did not show, Malcolm left. But nobody expected Archie, a professional hustler, to engage in a public shootout, and Malcolm knew it.

For the next several hours, Malcolm stayed high on a number of different drugs, including opium, Benzedrine, marijuana, and cocaine. Eventually, he passed out, sleeping through Archie's noon deadline, but nothing happened that day. Those who knew him, however, kept their distance, expecting a shootout. And Malcolm continued to stay high on drugs.

During this time, Malcolm got into a barroom fight with another young hustler. What started the fight was unclear, but after Malcolm busted him in the mouth, the hustler pulled a knife. Fortunately for Malcolm, several bystanders grabbed the hustler, who kept shouting that he was going to kill him. Meanwhile, as the police arrived, Malcolm slipped his gun to a friendly hustler standing nearby. After frisking him, the police let Malcolm go with a warning to leave town.

Just as luck seemed to be running out for Malcolm, Shorty, who had learned from Sammy that he was in trouble, had driven to Harlem and spotted him on the corner of Edgecombe and St. Nicholas Avenue. Seeing Shorty, Malcolm couldn't have been happier. After stuffing his clothes into the car's trunk, he told him to drive to Boston.

According to the hustler code, running from Archie meant that Malcolm had ruined his reputation as a hustler in Harlem, and that he could never regain the respect required of a hustler there again.

Burglary and Sentence

Back in Boston, both Ella and Shorty agreed that Malcolm had changed considerably. They noticed that he was more profane, with a working vocabulary of about two hundred words, cynical, and atheistic. He spent his time sleeping, smoking marijuana, sniffing cocaine, and playing records. "I was slightly out of my mind," he said later, viewing narcotics as most people regarded food, wearing guns as others wore neckties, and inviting death "in many, sometimes insane, ways."[70]

At first, obtaining money from Bea and staying at Shorty's apartment, Malcolm remained inactive, but he soon grew restless and bored and began looking for a hustle. After trying gambling for awhile, he formed a burglary gang, including Shorty, Bea, her younger sister Joyce, another white woman, Kora Marderosian, and a black man, Francis E. Brown, known as Rudy or Sonny.

In his autobiography, Malcolm said that he learned about burglary from the pros. A good burglary team, he said, included a finder, someone who located lucrative homes to rob and someone to case their physical layouts and determine the best means of entry and getaway routes. For this, the white women could case places where blacks would otherwise stick out like sore thumbs. He obtained a fence, someone who paid cash for stolen goods, and a base of operations, an apartment in Harvard Square.

According to Malcolm, his gang got burglary down to a science. First, under false pretenses, the women would enter the homes and mentally note their layout to sketch later. Then, while Rudy drove the getaway car, Malcolm and Shorty would break into them, using a passkey, jimmy, or lock pick. Afterwards, they would fence the goods for cash. And when the gang made a good score, they would lay low for awhile, nightclubbing and living it up.[71]

Much of Malcolm's account of his burglary gang may have been fictitious. They were not, said Louis DeCaro, one of Malcolm's biographers, as efficient, experienced, or seasoned as Malcolm had claimed in his autobiography.[72] "My hunch," he added, was that "the whole burglary thing described in his autobiography was stuff that he had learned from John Elton Bembry," a professional whom he would later meet in prison.[73]

According to another biographer, Bruce Perry, Malcolm's gang neither reconnoitered the homes that they broke into nor engaged in advance planning. Basically, they just drove around until they spotted an unlighted home, rang the doorbell to make sure nobody was home, and then smashed the back door lock with a hammer or jimmy or opened a window with a screwdriver or crowbar.[74]

Shorty's account of the burglaries reinforced DeCaro's and Perry's version of events. According to Shorty, the burglaries occurred over a two week period during the Christmas holidays in 1945. He said that the gang, "being young and adventurous," committed them for fun. "We certainly weren't doing this for money," he said. "We were making our own livelihoods in our own rights."[75]

One night shortly after Christmas, Malcolm walked into a nightclub and saw Joyce and Bea, who was sitting next to her husband's best friend. He could have been Bea's husband for all Malcolm knew since he had never seen him. Instead of leaving the club or ignoring the trio, he went to the table where they were sitting and called Bea "baby." Her face went "chalky-white" and the white man's "beet red." Although Malcolm later blamed his unwise move on a cocaine high, he knew that this kind of mistake, cocaine or not, was extremely dangerous. "I had gotten to the point," he said later, "where I was walking on my own coffin."[76]

Somehow, the friend of Bea's husband had gotten the key to the gang's hideout apartment. First he knocked, waited awhile, then used the key to open the door. Sensing that something was wrong, since every member of the gang had a key, Malcolm rolled under the bed, but he forgot to grab his gun, which was lying on the dresser. The intruder looked around, noticed women's clothes in the closet, and spotted him under the bed. He then left the apartment. "I had trapped myself under the bed without a gun," said Malcolm later. "I really was slipping."[77]

On January 7, 1946, Malcolm made a mistake that would cost him his freedom. He knew that the police arrested the majority of burglars trying to market their stolen goods, not at the scene of the crime, and that removing all identifying marks from each stolen item was a given. Yet, at Al Beeman's jewelry store in Boston, Malcolm pawned a stolen wedding band with the owner's initials on it and gave the jeweler a stolen watch to repair. Also, he wrote his real name and Ella's address down and promised to return for it. Consequently, when Beeman filed his daily police reports, detectives spotted the stolen items and set up a stakeout of his shop.[78]

To pick up the stolen watch, Malcolm returned to the jewelry store five days later. As he attempted to pay for it, Detective Stanley Slack came up from behind and placed him under arrest. At that moment, an innocent bystander, a black man, walked into the store. Instinctively, Slack turned to look, which gave Malcolm an opportunity to go for his gun; instead, he raised his arm, motioning for Slack to take it.

Unknown to Malcolm, two other detectives, hidden from view, had him covered. If he had gone for his gun, they would have shot him. While the detectives were taking him to the precinct to book him for carrying a firearm and larceny, Bea's husband was at Malcolm's apartment with a gun looking for him. "I have thought a thousand times," he said later, "about how I so narrowly escaped death twice that day.... Allah was with me even then."[79]

According to Malcolm, because he had not tried to kill Slack, the detectives did not beat him. Nonetheless, they did not have to treat him badly to get him to talk. To them, he acted more like a "friendless, scared kid" than a hardened criminal, and when they promised to drop the gun charge, he named his accomplices.[80] By this time, however, after searching his apartment and finding it loaded with stolen goods, they had enough evidence to charge him with breaking and entering.

Except for Rudy, who got the word and skipped town, the detectives rounded up the rest of the gang. While the court set bail low for Bea, Joyce and Kora, it asked for ten thousand dollars for Malcolm and Shorty, too high for them to pay. By using her property as collateral, Ella could have paid Malcolm's bond, but she regarded his getting into trouble with white women and Jarvis, whom she regarded as a bad influence on him, as a sign of disrespect. "As much as I cared for my brother," she said later, "I wasn't prepared to help him continue on a path to destruction."[81]

Although Malcolm had confessed, he pleaded not guilty along with the rest of the defendants. Since they had committed burglaries in two counties, they had two trials: the first on February 27, 1946, in Middlesex County Court and the second on April 10, 1946, in the Norfolk County Superior Court. While the three white women sat at the defense tables, Malcolm and Shorty, because they were unable to make bail, sat in locked courtroom cages.

During their first trial, Malcolm and Shorty soon realized that they were being tried more for their involvement with white women than for the burglaries. The court, moreover, considered the two men particularly reprehensible because the women were not so-called "tramps" but came from upper middle-class homes. What's more, they testified that Malcolm and Shorty had forced them to participate in the burglaries. "If we had you niggers down south," said a detective to the two men while they were sitting in the court-room cage, "we'd lynch you."[82]

Since the trial was going badly for Malcolm and Shorty, they changed their pleas to guilty, hoping for leniency. Although the average sentence for burglary was two to five years, Judge Allan Buttrick sentenced them to serve eight to ten years at Charleston State Prison. While Shorty grabbed the cage's bars shouting at the judge that he would rather die than get ten years, Malcolm just smiled.[83]

Later, Malcolm and Shorty attributed Judge Buttrick's harsh sentence to his bigotry over their relationship with white women. When he sentenced them, according to Malcolm, Buttrick said, "This will teach you to stay away from white girls."[84] He even asked them to "press rape charges against us," said Shorty, which they wouldn't do.[85]

At the second trial, where the women again testified against them, Malcolm and Shorty received from six to eight years in prison, which proved meaningless since their sentences in this trial ran concurrently with Judge Buttrick's sentences.

Predictably, the women received lesser sentences. While Joyce and Kora got suspended sentences, Bea received a sentence of from one to five years in the women's reformatory at Farmingham, Massachusetts. An appellate court, however, changed it to an indefinite period of time, which enabled her to get a parole in seven months.

In a racist society, said Malcolm later, going to prison for "a black youth here in America [was] really just about inevitable."[86] Nevertheless, unlike a professional hustler, who was trying to stay one jump ahead of the law in the end, he acted like a man who wanted to get caught. At that point, he may have realized that he was no longer able to control his destructive behavior, and that his choices had narrowed to either prison or death. He wisely chose the former.

CHAPTER 1

Imprisonment and Redemption

Entering prison at twenty-one years old, Malcolm Little would serve seven years of his eight to ten year sentence in three different Massachusetts state correctional institutions, which included the Charleston State Prison, the Concord Reformatory, and the Norfolk Prison Colony.

Charleston State Prison

In February 1946, handcuffed together, Malcolm and Shorty arrived at Massachusetts' antiquated Charleston State Prison, located in the southwestern part of Charleston, across the Charles River from Boston. Built in 1805 and modeled after the Bastille, its inmates lived in small six by twelve feet cells, had covered pails for toilets, and was crawling with rodents and white lice. Shorty described them as "unsanitary, unclean, and filthy."[1]

As a new inmate and in the thrall of drug withdrawal, Malcolm characterized himself as "evil-tempered as a snake," and to Ella, after her first prison visit, he appeared cocky, unrepentant, and without remorse.[2] Considering himself "beyond atheism," he took pride in being blasphemous toward God and the Bible, which earned him the nickname of "Satan." Later, he said, "I didn't see anybody living according to the religion that they were talking about so it lost its appeal to me."[3]

Malcolm portrayed his first year in prison as rebellious. It ran all together, he said, in a memory of "semi-drugs," of "cursing guards," of "throwing things out of my cell," and of "balking in the lines." He preferred the solitary confinement to which this behavior brought him, where he would "pace for hours," cursing aloud to himself.[4]

Just like Malcolm's description of himself as a skilled burglar, his characterization of himself as "an unyielding convict" may have been inaccurate. According to DeCaro, rather than being "explosive and vulgar," Malcolm's approach to prison authorities "was played out in low key rebellion."[5] To Perry, although Malcolm was "insolent to certain guards," he was neither a troublemaker nor did he spend more than his first day in prison in solitary confinement, which was routine procedure.[6] If, indeed, he had been an aggressive inmate, prison authorities would not have allowed him to transfer to a less restrictive correctional institution after only one year at Charleston.

During his seven years in prison, Malcolm underwent a great personality change. It began when he came under the influence of John Elton Bembry, a light, reddish-skinned African American who was a self-educated intellectual. During work breaks and in the prison yard, he would sit, surrounded by interested inmates and nearby guards, and discuss history, theology, and other subjects.

That Bembry could command total respect with words impressed Malcolm. In turn, Bembry sensed that Malcolm had the potential to make something of himself. The two men soon became friends. Then one day, "out of the blue," Bembry told Malcolm that he "had some brains" if he would only use them.[7] This was the kind of advice he was looking for. Consequently, he began his own self-education, which would transform his life.

In his autobiography, Malcolm understated Bembry's influence in the reprocess of his self-education, giving the most credit to Elijah Muhammad and the Nation of Islam. But Bembry, not Muhammad, was fundamental to Malcolm's quest for self-education, which was well underway before his family, Reginald, Philbert, and Hilda introduced him to the nation. Bembry, said Malcolm, "turned me from reading what you might call cowboy books, which was my diet at the time, into a higher level of reading."[8]

By using the prison library, correspondence courses, and a systematic study of the dictionary, Malcolm began his self-education program. Although Bembry inspired him to do it, according to DeCaro, Malcolm had already acquired the foundation values of learning from his family. To DeCaro, he reached for the dictionary because he had often seen his mother and elder brother Wilfred using it and had "internalized" its value for learning.[9]

Shorty soon joined Malcolm in self-study. At this time, however, neither man was doing it as an attempt at moral rehabilitation. Malcolm, for instance, continued his tough and cynical attitude and gambled, drank prison nutmeg, smoked marijuana and took Benzedrine drugs that guards and visitors had smuggled into the prison. "In our own way," they were out to rebel against society, said Shorty, and by cramming some knowledge into their brains, "we wouldn't have to worry about ever going back to prison — because we'd know too much and be too smart for that."[10] Or as Malcolm put it, they were going to become "smart bad niggers."[11]

Malcolm's Prison Transfers

In January 1947, without Malcolm's request, Charleston State Prison authorities decided to transfer him to Concord Reformatory, where he remained for the next fifteen months. If he kept his record clean, they informed him, he could reapply to another correctional center. But why they transferred him in the first place was unclear.

Sometime in 1948, in a series of letters to Malcolm, Wilfred, Philbert, Reginald, and Hilda wrote that they had joined the Nation of Islam, whose leader, Elijah Muhammad, "a small gentleman," sometimes called The Messenger of Allah, taught that black people were the original people, that God, called Allah, was black, and that blacks needed their own homeland "where they would be masters in their own land."[12] For blacks, then, they wrote, he had "the best program going."[13]

To his siblings' pleas to join the Nation, Malcolm's replies were blasphemous and insulting. Expressing their exasperation, Philbert admitted that Malcolm "had very low tolerance for religion."[14] But although discouraged, they refused to give up on him and agreed that Reginald, the latest convert and the closest to Malcolm, would best know how to approach him.

Meanwhile, in early 1948, to further his program of self-education, Malcolm wrote to prison officials asking them to transfer him to the Norfolk Prison Colony, which had excellent educational facilities. Since it was an experimental rehabilitation jail with comparatively good living conditions, transfer to it from other prisons often took outside political connections. Here, Ella, who had never given up on him, through the assistance of Shag Taylor, a Roxbury ward boss, succeeded in securing Malcolm's transfer in March 1948. He would remain there until March 1950.

Although Norfolk had twenty-foot high walls manned by armed guards, unlike Charleston or Concord, it had neither cellblocks nor iron bars. Prisoners lived in individual cells in one of six three-story dormitories, and each contained its own recreation room and showers, which prisoners could take at any time. Most important for Malcolm, state Senator Lewis Parkhurst, who had devoted his career to penal reform, had willed his extensively stocked library to the prison.

Shortly after Malcolm's arrival at Norfolk, Reginald visited him. Earlier, in a letter to Malcolm, he told him to neither eat any more pork nor smoke anymore cigarettes, and that he would show him how to get out of prison. But Reginald refused to hurry it. Instead, in an offhand manner, he talked about family and the situation in Detroit, building up the tension that something big was coming. Then, just as Malcolm was getting irritated at Reginald's indirection, he mentioned that God was a man named Allah, and that he had made himself known to Elijah Muhammad, informing him that the white man was the devil.[15]

Although Malcolm listened, he found the white devil theory puzzling. When he asked Reginald if this was without exception, he replied with emphasis, "Without exception." Thinking about it, Malcolm could not "make of it head, tail, or middle."[16] Reginald informed his siblings that Malcolm was becoming receptive to the Nation of Islam's message. Consequently, they stepped up their correspondence with him, explaining in depth Elijah Muhammad's teachings.

Receiving at least two letters every day from his siblings in Detroit, Malcolm learned that "the Original Man" was the black man, the primogenitor of all other races, including the white race, which was only six thousand years old, compared with the black man's coexistence with the creation of the earth. Blacks were the descendants of the planet, including the area which became the Holy City of Mecca in Arabia. Thus, they are, "whether they knew it or not," Muslims.[17]

Elijah Muhammad's mission was to bring Islam to American blacks to teach them that they are descendants from the tribe of Shabazz and therefore original and by nature divine, and that the time was approaching in which Allah would point out to the nations of the earth their rightful places.[18]

During this time, Malcolm received a visit from his older sister, Hilda, who introduced him to the Nation of Islam's central myth, called "Yacub's History." As a result of a genetic grafting project, Yacub, a black scientist, had invented the devilish white race. Once formed, they were predestined to oppress the black race, the "originals," for six thousand years. In 1931, in Detroit, Wallace D. Fard, "God in person" or "Allah in the flesh," had revealed himself to Elijah Muhammad and gave to him Allah's message to save the "Lost-Found" Nation of Islam, the so-called Negroes, here in "this wilderness of North America."[19]

At first Malcolm found the white devil theory difficult to accept. But after his readings in the prison library on slavery in the Americas and colonialism in Africa, it began to make more sense to him. Then, his thoughts turned to his eighth grade English teacher who had told him, despite his evident intelligence, that being a lawyer was not a realistic goal for a "nigger." He recalled the state welfare workers whom he blamed for causing his mother's breakdown and the racists who had previously burned down his family's home. And now, with Hilda telling him that God himself had told Muhammad that whites were devils, he said later, "My eyes came open on the spot."[20]

At Hilda's suggestion, Malcolm wrote Muhammad a letter. Apologizing in it for his poor grammar, he rewrote it about two dozen times. In a typed reply and enclosing a five dollar bill, Muhammad welcomed him into the "true knowledge" and explained how white society had forced blacks into lives of crime by keeping them ignorant and destitute. His reply, according to Malcolm, had "an electrical effect upon me."[21] Shortly thereafter he began his conversion to the Nation of Islam.

With his religious conversion, Malcolm's goal was to both increase his self-improvement program and to help spread Muhammad's message among the prison population. As part of this, he joined Norfolk's debating program, which was popular among the inmates. Whenever a debate took place, the prison theater's capacity of three hundred seats was filled. Usually, inmate teams debated each other, but at other times, debating teams came from nearby colleges and universities, including Harvard and Yale.

Through hard work, Malcolm became an accomplished debater. By listening to his hero, Paul Robeson, an outstanding black singer and well-known political speaker, on the radio, Malcolm learned about timing, delivery techniques, and cadence. Before every debate, he would read everything he could on the topic, and trying to anticipate his opponents arguments, he prepared himself to take both sides of the issue. Also, he may have inherited his love of "verbal battle and challenge" and some of his natural speaking talent from his father, Earl, who spoke often and well.[22]

Among the inmates, Malcolm became a popular speaker. "Most of the fellows would come over just to hear him speak," said Shorty .[23] "People listened," said fellow inmate Stanley Jones, and he got their attention.[24]

While debating had improved Malcolm's verbal skills, his writing ability was primitive. In trying to write simple English, he said, he was neither articulate nor functional.[25] To improve his writing skills and expand his vocabulary, he began leafing through the dictionary. Then, he wrote all of the words from its first page into a tablet and read them aloud. Most of them he had never heard of before, and learning new words so fascinated him that he eventually copied the whole dictionary.[26]

As Malcolm's vocabulary improved, he began an evangelistic letter writing campaign in an attempt to win Muslim converts. At first, after carefully crafting his letters to include Elijah Muhammad's teachings, he wrote people he had known in the hustling world. Since he did not know where they lived, he addressed their letters to their favorite hangouts in Harlem and Roxbury. Then, he wrote to a number of politicians, including President Harry S. Truman.

But Malcolm never received a single reply to his evangelistic letters. While the politicians probably never even read them, his hustling friends may have been too uneducated to write replies. To them, perhaps, he appeared to either have gone crazy or that he was trying some hype on prison authorities.[27]

Malcolm, nonetheless, was not discouraged by the lack of replies to his letters. Writing them was his way of learning to write. He enjoyed writing. Moreover, because he loved words, saying them aloud, defining them, and writing them. Also, writing was an emotional outlet for him, a way of articulating his new found beliefs, and letting the outside world know where he stood on them.

Although Malcolm had begun his reading program prior to his conversion to the Nation of Islam, his stated goal now was to read with the intent of validating the truth of Elijah Muhammad's teachings. This was, however, only half true. Like debating and writing, reading was crucial to his personal quest for self-education. Until then, he said later, "I never had been so truly free in my life."[28]

With the help of Norfolk's excellent library, Malcolm read in a wide variety of fields, including history, politics, philosophy, genetics, anthropology, literature, religion, and linguistics. He liked Shakespeare and Milton and favored the biographies of conquerors, rebels, and tyrants. Some of them included Hannibal, Haile Selassie, Ibn Saud, Karl Marx, Vladimir Lenin, Joseph Stalin, Adolf Hitler, Erwin Rommel, and Mahatma Gandhi. In philosophy, he read in Plato, Aristotle, Kant, Spinoza, Nietzsche, and Schopenhauer; and he absorbed himself in his story with the help of H. G. Wells' *Outline of History* and Will Durant's *Story of Civilization*.

From anti-slavery books and pamphlets, Malcolm read about the slave trade and slavery. He learned that European slave traders packed captive Africans below deck in rat-infested ships, allowing them little food, keeping them chained together, and preventing them from receiving fresh air for the three week voyage to the Western Hemisphere. Upon arrival, the slave traders sold their cargos to the America's slave holders, who used whips, chains, clubs, guns, and dogs against them. To Malcolm, incensed by all of this, if a real devil existed on earth, the white man was it.[29]

Sometime in 1949, Malcolm began to recruit among Norfolk's eighty black inmates. He would remind them that the authorities who kept them imprisoned, the judge who tried them and the officers who arrested them were white. If they had stolen from a white man, he said, that only meant that the white man had anything, and that they only got a fraction of what he owed them.[30] Within a short time, he had recruited about a dozen inmates, including Shorty, who would leave the Nation of Islam not long after his release.

During this time, Malcolm noticed that Reginald's appearance and personality had changed. When he had first began visiting him, Reginald was always dressed nicely and exuded a positive attitude. But now, his appearance had become dirty and shabby-looking, and he began to speak ill of Elijah Muhammad. In his autobiography, Malcolm would not specify the exact things Reginald said. According to Malcolm, they were "in the nature of implications," the pitch in Reginald's voice, and the way he looked rather than what he said.[31] To DeCaro, Reginald's negative comments may have been a foretaste of revelations many years later of Muhammad's adulterous behavior.[32]

Then, from Wilfred, Malcolm learned that Muhammad had suspended Reginald for having an illicit affair with the secretary of New York City's Temple Number Seven. Deeply shocked, in a letter to Muhammad, Malcolm appealed to him to restore Reginald's status in the Nation. Soon thereafter, as Malcolm lay on his prison bed, the vision of a light brown-skinned man with oily black hair appeared sitting in a chair beside him. For a few moments, their eyes met, neither spoke and then, the silent figure in the chair vanished.[33]

Among his biographers, Malcolm's vision experience generated different views. Eugene V. Wolfenstein called it a "hallucination, a moment of visually mediated auto-hypnotic experience."[34] Perry considered it evidence of psychological family weakness, because Malcolm's mother sometimes saw "visions from heavens."[35] Rejecting both interpretations, DeCaro regarded it as a metaphysical phenomenon that "should be respected, as testimony of an authentic religious experience."[36]

Later, with Elijah Muhammad's prodding, Malcolm concluded that the man in the vision was W. D. Fard, the Messiah who had appointed Muhammad as his messenger to blacks in North America, confirming the Nation of Islam's ideology. Still, at the time, Malcolm had no idea who the vision represented or what it meant. It was merely there. Of all the scenes in Malcolm's autobiography, in fact, his vision experience was the strangest and most mysterious of them all.

Not long afterward, Malcolm received Muhammad's reply concerning Reginald's fall from grace. "If you once believed in the truth," wrote Muhammad, "and now you are beginning to doubt the truth, you didn't believe in the truth in the first place." Thus, chastising him for doubting his word, Muhammad turned the issue back on Malcolm himself, and his doubts became his own responsibility.[37]

Muhammad's letter had the desired effect, relieving the confusion from Malcolm's mind. And if there was any lingering doubt, Reginald's commitment shortly thereafter to a mental hospital removed it. That, said Malcolm, was "Allah's chastisement" for going against Muhammad.

Back to Charleston

On March 23, 1950, Norfolk's prison authorities ordered Malcolm transferred back to Charleston State Prison. That he had refused Norfolk's standard typhoid inoculation, necessary because its well water was untreated, was their official reason. According to Malcolm, however, they wanted him transferred because of their anti-Muslim prejudice. Nonetheless, by refusing inoculation, he was aware that they would transfer him back to Charleston, which he may have desired, since he had run out of converts at Norfolk.[38]

Shorty and Osborne Thaxton, another Muslim convert, accompanied Malcolm back to Charleston. While there, Osborne's younger brother, Leroy, joined them. The four Muslims requested that prison authorities provide them with a non-pork diet, time off from work on Islamic holidays, facilities for communal worship, outside religious instruction and cells facing east towards Mecca. Although they gave similar privileges to Christian and Jewish inmates, they denied them to the Muslims.

Local newspapers, however, picked up the story and printed it on their front pages. Under heavy outside pressure, prison officials relented and gave the Muslims more religious freedom, including cells that faced East. They had won a victory, becoming a new force that prison officials could no longer deny.

In June 1950, the United States entered the Korean War. Most observers predicted that Washington would soon draft a large number of men. To those inmates eligible for parole in the immediate future, and Malcolm was among them, the rise in the possibility of being drafted was real. But except for a crusade against whites, he had no intention of donning a uniform.

CHAPTER 2

Elijah Muhammad
and Malcolm X

On October 7, 1897, in Sandersville, Georgia, Elijah Muhammad, one of thirteen children, whose father was a sharecropper and part time Baptist minister, was born Elijah Poole. As a child who had beautiful black eyes, he became the darling of both preachers and parishioners alike. Calling him baby Elijah, "The Prophet," his grandfather predicted that he would one day become one.[1]

In school, Elijah's goal was to learn to read the Bible. Unfortunately, his family was so poor that he had to drop out of school in the fourth grade to work full-time. For the next several years, he encountered racist employers and marginal wages, and he witnessed two lynchings which traumatized him, making him more susceptible to black separatist doctrines.[2]

On March 17, 1919, Elijah married Clara Evans, a petite woman with a deep brown complexion, who would have their first, named Emmanuel, of eight children in February 1921. Two years later, embittered by Georgia's virulent racism, Elijah moved his family to Detroit, Michigan. Upon arrival he found economic conditions for blacks, lacking job skills and social connections, not much better than in the south.

From 1923 to 1931, Elijah worked at low paying jobs, where he experienced frequent firings, layoffs, and walkouts. In 1929, with the Stock Market crash and its resulting mass unemployment, he spent his days beseeching employers for work. When that failed and his family was forced to accept public assistance, he turned to liquor for escape.

In 1930, in the guise of a peddler of clothes and silks, Wallace D. Fard appeared to Detroit's poverty-stricken blacks who lived in the city's over-

crowded ghetto. Identifying himself as a Muslim from the East, they listened
to his denouncements against the white race and the need for blacks to
understand their African past. He admonished them against eating pork,
offered advice to improve their physical health, and introduced them to
Islam's Holy Koran. Eventually, he won enough followers to join the organizational structure for his Nation of Islam.[3]

Fard's background was somewhat of a mystery. According to the Los
Angeles Police Department, he was born in either New Zealand or Portland,
Oregon, to parents of either Hawaiian, British, Syrian, or Polynesian descent.
In 1926, they reported a conviction for selling narcotics, for which he drew
a six-year term in San Quentin Prison. Released in 1929, he moved first to
Chicago and then departed for Detroit in 1930.[4]

In 1931, a year after Fard had arrived in Detroit, Elijah Poole started
attending his lectures. During one of them, although only he heard it, Fard
said, "I am God myself." When Poole asked him if it was true, he said, "Yes,
I am the One."[5] His answer apparently had instantly converted Poole, who
now learned that Fard was Allah "the All-Perfect One," who had come to
waken "the spiritually dead black lost-founds in America" and "to bring
judgment against their white slavemasters."[6]

Becoming one of Fard's most loyal followers, Poole said later that Fard
had taken him "out of the gutters in the streets of Detroit and taught me
knowledge of Islam."[7]

To restore blacks to their rightful heritage, Fard would replace his followers' slave surnames with "original" names, in which he would know intu-
itively because of the omniscient spirit of Allah dwelling in him. Elijah
Karriem became Poole's "original" surname. Later, Fard appointed him
Supreme Minister, giving him authority second only to his own. From then
on, according to Karriem, Fard's instructions to him included "things never
revealed to others."[8]

After several recruitment expeditions to Chicago, Fard and Karriem
established Temple Number Two. Despite Fard's claim of being a "brother
from the East," by naming the Nation of Islam's places of worship "temples," he exhibited a lack of knowledge of Islamic culture, which referred to
its sanctuaries as mosques.

By 1932, Fard's two temples, in Detroit and Chicago, had similar organizational structures. Each temple included a minister and his assistants,
appointed by Fard, the University of Islam, a combined elementary and secondary school, a Muslim Girls' Training Class, a course to train women to
become good housewives and mothers, and the Fruit of Islam (FOI), an elite
Muslim guard to provide security.

Nation of Islam members, in addition, lived under strict ethical and dietary codes. These included a ban on alcoholic beverages and tobacco products, dietary restrictions, including no pork, and prohibitions on both premarital and extramarital relations.

As Fard's influence increased among Detroit's black community, the police began a campaign of harassment against him. At the same time, on November 21, 1932, Robert Harris, who belonged to a Nation of Islam splinter group, in an act of human sacrifice, plunged a knife into the heart of his roomer, John Smith.[9] Although Harris' connection to Fard was vague, the police arrested him. During questioning, Fard denied any knowledge of the killing. The police, who hoped that banishment would demoralize his followers and weaken the Nation's strength, released him on condition that he leave the city.[10]

Once released, however, Fard stayed in Detroit. He tried to guide the Nation in hiding, but knowing that arrest was inevitable, he both transferred its administrative powers to Karriem and gave him a "better name:" Elijah Karriem, formerly Elijah Poole, became Elijah Muhammad.

On May 25, 1933, after arresting Fard and ordering him again to leave Detroit, the police emphasized "the severity of the consequences" if he failed to carry it out this time. In an emotional farewell, he told his followers that he would soon return to lead them "out of this hell."[11]

From Detroit, Fard first traveled to Chicago, where the police briefly detained him. Next, he traveled to the West Coast and then returned to Chicago before totally disappearing, which remained a mystery. Even so, rumors abounded that he left for Mecca; that he met foul play from either the Detroit police or Nation of Islam dissidents; or that Muhammad persuaded Fard to offer himself as a human sacrifice in order to become "Savior of the World." The Nation eventually celebrated his birthday, February 26, as "Saviour's Day."[12]

Shortly after Fard's disappearance, Elijah Muhammad began to deify him. Earlier, to Muhammad, he had presented himself as the incarnation of Allah, but to others in the Nation, he called himself the Prophet of Allah. With his disappearance, however, Muhammad identified Fard as Allah incarnate. As his former chief lieutenant, Muhammad now called himself "The Messenger of Allah." In this way, he established a direct connection with Allah. "I know Allah," he said, "and I am with him."[13]

But not all Muslims accepted Muhammad's claim as Fard's successor. On this issue, after a struggle for power ensued among the various ministers, the Nation of Islam split into different factions. Calling his faction the Temple People, Muhammad appointed trusted assistants to supervise Temple Number One in Detroit while he moved the movement's headquarters to the less hostile Chicago.

But the successor issue followed Muhammad to Chicago. Soon, a mutiny among his ranks diminished his followers from four hundred to thirteen. After receiving death threats, he decided to flee the city. Before he left, as in Detroit, he appointed trusted assistants to oversee the Temple People and left his wife, Clara, who would now depend on Muslim charity to hold her family together.

From 1935 to 1942, Muhammad lived as a leader in exile, traveling from city to city to spread the Muslim doctrine and using pseudonyms to protect his identity. When the Japanese attacked Pearl Harbor on December 7, 1941, Muhammad, who had just started another temple in Washington, D.C., was still eligible for the draft. But to his followers, he advocated non-compliance since they should not fight white men on behalf of other white men. When his turn came to register for it, on February 16, 1942, he failed to show up.

The FBI arrested Muhammad for refusing to register for the draft. Then, they added a sedition charge to it, charging him with advocating a Japanese victory.[14] Lacking evidence, however, the Department of Justice dropped its sedition charge against him, but it indicted him and sixty-six other Muslims for draft evasion. While most of them received three year sentences, he got five years in prison. On July 23, 1943, he entered the Federal Correctional Institution at Milan, Michigan, where he would stay until his release on August 24, 1946.[15]

With Muhammad and most of his male followers in prison, the Muslim women under Clara ran the Temple People. They supported themselves by recycling paper, iron, and clothing.

In prison, meanwhile, the authorities refused to accommodate Muhammad and his followers. They denied them a copy of the Koran, the Muslim bible, and refused to allow them time and space for Islamic ritual and worship. The prison, moreover, used pork products, especially for seasoning, forcing the Muslims to eat bread and potatoes. An inadequate diet and poor living conditions led Muhammad to develop bronchial asthma.[16]

On August 24, 1946, Elijah Muhammad walked out of prison. By this time, he was no longer the embattled Supreme Minister, the leader of the Temple People, a small splinter group of the Nation of Islam. His four years in prison had made him the movement's martyr. The competing factions united behind him as the Nation's undisputed leader, Fard's legitimate successor, the Messenger of Allah.[17]

When Muhammad returned to Chicago in 1946, the Nation of Islam's membership, through imprisonment and police and FBI intimidation, had fallen from its pre-war level of seven thousand to four hundred, and most of them were elderly. Determined to avoid further government censure and reprisal, he adopted a less activist, more conservative style of leadership. While the Nation's basic teachings would remain the same, racial separatism, white devilry, and the coming Armageddon, he encouraged his members to avoid past activities, such as courtroom brawls, protest rallies at police stations, and aggressive draft resistance, that had brought the law down on them.[18]

Malcolm Little Meets Elijah Muhammad

In August 1952, straight from prison, Malcolm Little arrived in Detroit to live with his brother Wilfred, the manager of a furniture store in the city's black ghetto. Malcolm, the former teenage hipster, with his zoot suit, knob-toed shoes, and conked fire-red hair, was now a twenty-seven year old conservatively dressed man. Standing six feet three, with close cut hair, he exhibited the straight up bearing of a soldier or a priest.

In Detroit's suburbs, Wilfred's family lived in a five room frame house. Having been without a family and a home for years, Malcolm found the warmth of his brother's home "a healing change from the prison cage."[19] Unlike his own upbringing, too, he noticed that no arbitrary rules existed, that the parents did not beat their children and that everybody treated each other with respect.

For a brief time, Malcolm worked as a salesman at the white owned cut-rate furniture store managed by Wilfred. But he resented the owner's unethical business practices of posting misleading advertisements, displaying shoddy merchandise, and charging high interest rates. Other white retailers in the ghetto did the same, he said, and its poor residents had little alternative but to buy their highly priced inferior products and pay exorbitant interest rates. The white man, said Malcolm, "went home every night with another bag of the money drained out of the ghetto."

During this time, Malcolm was attending meetings at Detroit's Temple Number One, which was only a storefront, located near a slaughterhouse, and the sounds of squealing hogs emanated into it during services. This did not disturb him, however, for he took in Minister Lemuel Hassan's "every syllable and gesture," expanding his knowledge of the Nation and becoming more comfortable with it.

Malcolm, noticing that many seats were empty, was anxious to increase the temple's membership. He blamed the temple's recruitment policy, which only recruited among family and friends, for the low membership. Instead, he wanted everybody to go into the streets to fish for new recruits. But his brothers, Philbert and Wilfred, counseled him to remain patient, for he would soon meet the Messenger, Elijah Muhammad himself.[20]

On August 31, 1952, riding in a small caravan of cars with other Muslims from Temple Number One, Malcolm journeyed to Chicago to hear Elijah Muhammad give a sermon. Throughout his life, he said later, he had never duplicated the "eagerness and excitement" that he felt that day in traveling to Chicago to hear him. According to Malcolm, "I experienced tingling up my spine."[21]

As Malcolm took his seat among the small gathering of about two hundred people at Temple Number Two, he was "totally unprepared" for Elijah Muhammad's "physical impact" upon his emotions.[22] As Malcolm sat riveted, Muhammad, to cheers and applause and flanked by Fruit of Islam bodyguards, entered the temple. Taking his place behind the lectern he was an unimposing man. He stood only five and a half feet tall and weighed less than one hundred-fifty pounds; his features, fair-skinned, thin lips, pronounced cheekbones, and deep set brown eyes gave him an oriental look. In his mannerisms, there was a fatherly quality about him.[23]

Touching on the Nation of Islam's standard themes, Muhammad talked about the white devil and how blacks' true knowledge of themselves would lift them up. Then, pausing in his speech and not looking directly at Malcolm, he called on him to stand up. Upon hearing this, he felt "an electrical shock" going through him. As Muhammad issued a challenge to him, he just stood silent, too stunned to speak, feeling the eyes of two hundred Muslims upon him. Muhammad said, "Well, now, our good brother Malcolm's hedge [prison cell] is removed, and we will see how he does."[24]

After the meeting, Muhammad invited the entire small Detroit contingent to dine at his eighteen-room home. Apparently, the invitation was more than Malcolm had expected. He was "so excited," said Wallace D. Muhammad. "When he met me, he kept repeating, 'This is the Messenger's son, the Messenger's son.' It wasn't about seeing me," added Wallace, "it was the Messenger's son."[25]

To other guests at dinner, Malcolm mentioned his concern over the empty seats during Temple Number One's meetings, and that his recruitment policy was too limiting, based as it was on family and friends. Then, during a conversation lull, he asked Muhammad what was the best way to get members. "Go after the young people," he said. "Once you get them, the older ones will follow through shame."[26] That was all Malcolm had to hear, for he was now determined to follow Muhammad's advice.

Malcolm X

In September 1952, shortly after Malcolm's first visit to Chicago, Elijah Muhammad replaced Malcolm's last name, Little, which was his slave name, with an X. As in algebra, representing the unknown, it symbolized Malcolm's African family name that he could never know. Sometimes, this was confusing. If more than one member of a particular temple had the same first name, an Arabic number dependent on the date of the person's conversion would precede the X. If Jack Johnson joined in April, for instance, and Jack Smith in June, Johnson would become Jack X and Smith, Jack 2X.[27]

Acquiring the "X" meant that Muslims were no longer "deaf, blind, and dumb." They had "woken up, cleaned up, and stood up," rejecting "all those things that were negative," including drinking, smoking, and fornicating.[28] In addition, according to the Nation of Islam's teachings, they had thrown off the white man's "three hundred years of systematic brainwashing." And with it, learned their true identity, gaining a realistic appreciation of their past accomplishments.[29]

During the winter of 1952, Malcolm X frequently visited Muhammad at his home in Chicago. Before this, they had mainly communicated through correspondence; but now, they personally got to know each other and bonded. Muhammad, who had six sons and two daughters, began to look upon Malcolm as his seventh son. For Malcolm, whose father had died when he was six years old, Muhammad became a father figure, loving him, seemingly, more than Muhammad did his own children.[30]

In between visits with Muhammad, Malcolm was leading an aggressive recruitment drive in Detroit's ghetto. Because of his persistence, energy, and knowledge of ghetto psychology, learned during his hustler days, he became a role model for Temple Number One's younger members.[31] Although most of the ghetto residents rebuffed him and his followers, their sustained efforts enabled them to triple Temple Number One's membership within a few months. This won Malcolm warm praise from Muhammad, who recognized his potential to the movement.[32]

Malcolm strictly abided by the puritanical rules of the Nation of Islam. He neither drank, smoked, gambled, danced, swore, or womanized. Along with neatness and cleanliness, he lived up to the Nation's strict dietary code, including fasting and restricting meals to one per day. To author Louis Lomax, Malcolm, who would not meet him at any place where liquor was sold, was the most puritanical man that he had ever met.[33]

In other ways, too, Malcolm was a disciplined man. He had less patience for someone who was "not time-conscious" than with anyone else. To him, the proper respect for time determined success or failure.[34] Likewise, although the Nation of Islam encouraged members to reduce the amount of time they spent sleeping, Malcolm got only about four hours a night, often less. According to his biographers, Alex Haley, he kept up that pace "day by day."[35]

Malcolm was only one of many whom the Nation rehabilitated. Its record of rehabilitation among drug addicts, alcoholics, prostitutes, and criminals was almost miraculous. To Elijah Muhammad, the "knowledge of self," the "truth about the white," and the "constructive program" of building the Nation was sufficient to "reclaim the most incorrigible."[36] The Nation completely re-educates the "so-called Negro," he said, making him feel proud, not ashamed of being a black man.[37] The Nation's record of rehabilitation, wrote newsman Alfred Balk, arose from its "tight disciple, dedication, and camaraderie."[38]

On May 25, 1953, for failing to register for the Korean War draft, an FBI agent pulled Malcolm off his job at the Gar Wood factory. Although his failure to register for the draft was deliberate, since he would not fight on behalf of the white man, he acted as if he thought being an ex-convict disqualified him from the draft. Apparently, the FBI agent accepted his explanation, telling him to register immediately.

At Detroit's local draft board, Malcolm told officials that he was a Muslim, a conscientious objector, and that he would not fight "to preserve the way the white man treated the black man in America."[39] Also, as he did before the New York City draft board, he may have staged a crazy act, for his psychiatric diagnosis concluded that he had "an asocial personality" with "pre-psychotic paranoid schizophrenic tendencies."[40] Consequently, the draft board categorized him as "Class 5-A," meaning that the military would not take him under any conceivable circumstances.

Malcolm X's Rising Star

In May 1953, after Massachusetts discharged Malcolm from parole, he quit his blue collar job to become Temple Number One's assistant minister. This allowed him to both give sermons and to spend more time fishing for converts on the streets of Detroit's black ghetto. After hours of fishing, he said later, "My head would reel with mingled anger and pity for my poor blind black brothers.... I couldn't wait for the next time our Minister Lemuel Hassan would let me speak."[41]

By December 1953, Malcolm had helped expand Temple Number One's membership by another two hundred, and Elijah Muhammad considered him the obvious choice to return to Boston to set up a temple there. That Malcolm might become a minister never occurred to him; he never felt "remotely qualified" to directly represent Muhammad and he would have been happy and willing to serve him in the lowliest capacity.

In Boston's Roxbury ghetto, where he had once hustled before his imprisonment in 1946, Malcolm, with help from Lloyd X, who allowed him to use his living room for meetings, began fishing for converts. By March 1954, he had recruited enough members to afford a small temple with rented chairs. Designated Temple Number Eleven, he appointed a local laborer, Ulysses X, as its minister.

During his recruiting drive, Malcolm had a friendly reunion with Shorty. Since his release from prison, however, he was not interested in joining the Nation. Malcolm had more success with his half-sister Ella, who came to the meetings and gave donations. Even so, since she was tough-minded and cautious about joining anything, he did not expect to recruit her. Among those he did recruit was a popular black calypso singer named Louis Walcott, who became Louis X and considered Malcolm both his teacher and friend.

In March 1954, shortly after Malcolm had started Temple Number Eleven, Muhammad moved him to Philadelphia, where he laid the foundation for Temple Number Twelve. Then, in June, Muhammad named him minister to New York City's Temple Number Seven. Thus, in less than two years, Malcolm had risen to become a minister in one of the Nation's biggest temples in Harlem, home to over a million blacks.

CHAPTER 3

Malcolm X's Ministry

In the 1950s, most of New York City's one million blacks lived in Harlem, which measured less than four square miles.[1] While in midtown and lower Manhattan, luxurious high-rises, electric garbage disposals, air purifiers, and air conditioners proliferated, in Harlem children played in streets filled with uncollected garbage, in filthy gutters crammed with shattered glass, or in the stairwells and hallways of overcrowded tenements, reeking with the stench of the urine of wandering vagrants.[2]

While the 1950s was a time for prosperity for most Americans, in Harlem, one man in three was either unemployed or underemployed; women worked as domestics for subsistence pay; the police patrolled in groups; one out of six persons was addicted to drugs; and the children sometimes disappeared or died.[3] Yet, on a good night, its streets would "crackle with excitement" as various religious groups would accost passersby looking for converts, peddlers selling tamales and hot dogs gathered, and music filled the air.[4]

In June 1954, Malcolm arrived in Harlem to assume command of Elijah Muhammad's Temple Number Seven. Although this was a great honor for Malcolm, expressing Muhammad's faith and trust in his abilities to do the job, since it was only a little storefront with a small membership, the task appeared daunting. He had to keep reminding himself, he said later, that all of Harlem's Muslims could not even fill up one bus, and that of the entire city's black population, not more than one in a thousand knew anything about the Muslims.[5]

From the temple, Malcolm drew a weekly salary of between one hundred twenty-five and one hundred fifty dollars, plus traveling expenses. Living frugally, he obtained a furnished room in a brother Muslim's house in East Elmhurst, Long Island. Interestingly, although he upgraded his housing, eventually moving out of his single room to three rooms in a two-family flat and, after he married and began having children, to a seven-room house, he never left East Elmhurst. Whether he stayed there from an attempt at upward mobility or from a refusal to make the symbolic commitment of the pastor to his parish by moving to Harlem was difficult to know.[6]

Armed with freshly printed leaflets, Malcolm would fish for converts on the corner of 125th Street and Seventh Avenue, the location of Louis Michaux's National African Memorial Bookstore and the center of activity among Harlem's black nationalist street orators. They were "making it tough for Mr. Muhammad's voice to be heard," said Malcolm.[7] Still, his Temple Number Seven's followers were an impressive group. Because of their "appearance and discipline," said William DeForest, a New York City policeman, "they were the best looking group you could find out there on the street."[8]

When not fishing for new recruits, Malcolm, an avid reader, would browse through the books at Michaux's bookstore and engage with him in long discussions on black nationalism, pan–Africanism, and Islam.[9] Malcolm, in fact, would often spend more time there, where he received phone messages and mail, than at Temple Number Seven.

With time, Malcolm realized that simply approaching people on the street was too limiting, so he began fishing on the fringes of black nationalist meetings and around the small, storefront Christian churches which proliferated throughout Harlem, composed mostly of Southern migrant people who loved "good preaching." By far, they became one of his best sources for new recruits.

On Sunday mornings, Malcolm's people would hand out leaflets at the entrances of the storefront Christian churches, inviting their members "to hear the truth" at Temple Number Seven's afternoon meetings.[10] During those, Malcolm would get "emotionally charged," tears would well up in his eyes, and he would lambaste Christianity as the white man's religion that taught blacks to wait until the "dreamy heaven-in-the-hereafter" to get justice. Instead, he said, Jesus Christ was a black man, not a blond, blue-eyed god.[11] Although he had not cried since he was a little boy, he added, he could not now help himself because of what the white man's religion had done to blacks.[12]

Likewise, since many storefront Christians who attended his meetings were women, Malcolm would often direct his appeals to them.[13] Referring to them as beautiful black women, he called upon black men to shelter, protect, and respect them. Meanwhile, he continued to fish among Harlem's drug addicts, alcoholics, gamblers, and hustlers.

Malcolm was a man of contrasts. On the platform, he displayed a "cold fury," and his eyes "burned behind horn-rimmed glasses," but in private conversation, he was "quiet, pleasant, articulate, and humorous."[14] "When you got to know him," said his friend, John Henrik Clarke, "he was kind of shy."[15]

To his followers, Malcolm's high degree of personal discipline and integrity was morally uplifting. "We changed," said Benjamin 2X Goodman, whose loyalty to him never wavered; "he helped us restore our self-esteem; and we understood what he meant when he said that Islam had given him wings."[16] "He literally became my mentor," said Louis X, who adopted Malcolm's speaking style and considered him one of the most disciplined men that he had ever known.[17] To Ella Collins, her half-brother not only talked about Islam but also lived it, visiting the sick, listening to people, and giving them advice; and as a result, Temple Number Seven "was a place that really worked."[18]

According to some, Malcolm's energy and commitment came from his strong religious convictions and in his absolute faith in Elijah Muhammad. To DeCaro, for instance, his zeal and enthusiastic defense of Muhammad were "really a religious expression [more] akin to the evangelistic programs and activities of religious organizations than to the activity of a political movement."[19] He never failed, said biographer Peter Goldman, "in his obeisance to his patron," and he would emphasize that he was only repeating what had been taught to him by the "Honorable Elijah Muhammad."[20]

Yet, in its white devil theory and black nationalist and separatist philosophies, the Nation of Islam was both a religious and a political movement, and Malcolm would integrate the two in his speeches.

As a public speaker, in fact, Malcolm was incomparable. Often, when he took the platform, his audiences would shout and clap for five minutes before he could speak. He could make them cry, bring them to the point of riot, and then quickly pull them back. "He played them," said Amina Rahman, a close associate, moving them close to the edge but "with just incredible control."[21] On a personal level, too, he knew how to deal with them. When Sonia Sanchez, a Harlem activist, told him that she liked only some of what he said, Malcolm, holding her hand in a very gentle manner, replied, "One day you will sister, one day you will."[22]

In his speeches, Malcolm called blacks "deaf, dumb, and blind" for failing to recognize the white man's satanic nature. Waking them up to this fact was his mission.[23] Neither poverty nor the white man was an excuse for ignorance, he said, and blacks must take responsibility for their own education.[24]

In November 1955, signaling increased enrollment, Malcolm's Temple

Number Seven opened up in a luncheonette nearby at 116th Street and Lennox Avenue. Most temples had their own restaurants where Muslim women, without violating Islamic laws, prepared dishes to satisfy its members' traditional eating habits. Most important, both the temple and its restaurant functioned as the center of their religious and social life.

Heading Temple Number Seven's Fruit of Islam (FOI), the Nation of Islam's defense arm, was Captain Joseph X Gravitt. Until a 1961 administrative decree would make Temple captains answerable to Chicago's Supreme Captain Raymond Sharrieff, Joseph was subordinate to Malcolm, as were the temple's assistant ministers. Joseph's duties included conducting military drills and calisthenics and training the temple's FOI contingent in combat techniques that did not employ weapons. He took new brothers, said Benjamin 2X, who had just left a secular society where they had been abusing themselves with drugs and alcohol, "reformed them" and "made of them the Fruit of Islam."[25]

Since Malcolm's prison days, when he wrote President Truman that he was a Communist, the FBI had been monitoring his activities. By 1955, however, it had placed him on both its security list and its special list entitled "Communist Sabotage."[26] Considering that he had neither sabotage training nor lived anywhere near a defense industry, the FBI was either acting stupidly or lacked an understanding of the Nation of Islam's ideology and program.

In early 1955, two FBI agents approached Malcolm at his home in East Elmhurst, Queens. They were hoping, apparently, to make him into an informant, which indicated how little they understood of the man. At the end of the interview, they wrote that the subject was "uncooperative." He refused, for instance, to furnish them any information concerning the Nation's officers, the names of its members, whether he would serve in the armed forces, or even if he considered himself a citizen of the United States.[27]

Although always seeking advice and instruction from Elijah Muhammad, Malcolm's unique abilities and tireless efforts were largely responsible for the Nation of Islam's expansion from seven temples in 1952 to twenty-seven by the end of 1955. At the same time, for example, that he was building the membership of New York, Philadelphia, and Boston temples, he was instrumental in founding Temple Number Thirteen in Springfield, Massachusetts, Temple Number Fourteen in Hartford, Connecticut, and Temple Number Fifteen in Atlanta, Georgia. Similarly, he played a part in organizing temples in Buffalo, Pittsburgh, Atlantic City, Newark, Jersey City, Miami, Cleveland, and Richmond.

Yet, Malcolm, who publicly referred to his mentor as "The Honorable

Elijah Muhammad," gave him full credit for the Nation's phenomenal growth. Muhammad, in turn, rewarded Malcolm's loyalty by appointing him the Nation's ambassador during its 1956 Southern "Goodwill Tour" and authorized Temple Number Seven to purchase and assign to him a new Chevrolet.[28] Years later, after their relationship soured, Malcolm said, "I was going downhill until he picked me up, but the more I thought of it, we picked each other up."[29]

The Hinton Johnson Incident

Although the Nation of Islam and the National Association for the Advancement of Colored People (NAACP) had serious differences over their respective philosophies of integration or separatism, they united against police brutality, which was rampant in the northern ghettoes. In their attacks against blacks, to be sure, white racist policemen did not discriminate among them on the basis of religion or politics.

As events turned out, however, the Nation of Islam would take the lead on the issue of police brutality in Harlem, and Malcolm would come out of the conflict with renewed stature among its blacks and generate anxiety within the New York City Police Department (NYPD) over his enhanced power over them.

The incident that catapulted Malcolm to prominence and got him NYPD attention occurred on April 14, 1957. At a Harlem street corner, a member of Malcolm's temple, Hinton Johnson, came upon two white policemen using their nightsticks to break up an argument between a young black couple. Butting in, Johnson told the policemen that they were not in Alabama. Incensed by his intrusion, they ordered Johnson to move on. When he refused, they split his scalp open with their nightsticks and then took Johnson, handcuffed and bleeding, to the Twenty-Eighth Precinct Station, located on 123rd Street, where detectives again beat him.[30]

Meanwhile, at Temple Number Seven's restaurant, word of the incident had reached Malcolm, who decided that the time had come for a show of strength. By using the temple's telephone tree, set-up for just such an emergency, he ordered his followers to immediately gather outside the Twenty-Eighth Precinct Station house. As a result, over eight-hundred Muslims assembled in formation outside of it, and a huge crowd of non–Muslims gathered behind them.[31] Inside, the police, who had never seen anything like this, were getting nervous and scared, fearing that the situation would "become explosive."[32]

To keep the crisis from escalating, Inspector William McGowan asked

James Hicks, the editor of the *Amsterdam News,* Harlem's weekly newspaper, to arrange a meeting between the police and Malcolm X.

At his newspaper office shortly thereafter, Hicks and Malcolm assembled with McGowan, Deputy Commissioners Walter Arn and Deputy Inspector Robert J. Mangum. After a moment of silence, Malcolm said that Muslims do not go looking for trouble, but when they find "something that is worthwhile getting into trouble about," they are "ready to die, then and there."[33] Taken aback, the police officials, emphasizing that they wanted to resolve the crisis peacefully, said that Malcolm should remove his followers from in front of the precinct station. He agreed on condition that they allow him to see Johnson, that Johnson receive medical attention, and that the police punish those responsible for his beating. Immediately acceding to Malcolm's requirements, they gave him their word that the police department would investigate the assault.[34]

At the precinct house, when Malcolm saw a semi-conscious Johnson, whose blood spilled over his "head and face and shoulders," he insisted that the police get him to the hospital. They called an ambulance. On its way to Harlem's Sydenham Hospital, about fifteen blocks away from the police station along Lennox Avenue, the Muslims and the crowd behind them followed it. Many others coming out of the shops and bars along its route joined them. By the time those following the ambulance assembled at the hospital, the police estimated the crowd at two thousand persons.[35]

Later that night, despite Johnson X's serious injuries, the police took him back to the precinct station and placed him in a cell. When the Muslims and the ever-expanding crowd of Harlemites standing outside of the hospital heard about this, they marched back to the precinct station. While they waited restively outside, Malcolm went inside to confer with McGowan and Mangum. After they reassured him that Johnson would continue to receive medical treatment and that the police department, as they had concurred to do earlier, would investigate the incident, Malcolm agreed to call off his followers.

As Malcolm reached the precinct's door, however, a police sergeant stepped in front of him and motioned to the Muslims outside to leave. "They are not going to move for you," said Malcolm, who then slowly walked over to them, stood quietly for a moment, "flicked his hands," and they "disappeared." Watching this with amazement, McGowan turned to his colleagues and said, "No one man should have that much power!"[36]

Later that morning, Malcolm, Charles Beaver, the Nation of Islam's attorney, John Ali, its national secretary, and James Hicks appeared at the Twenty-Eighth Precinct Station, paid Hinton Johnson's twenty-five hundred dollar bail, and waited by the door for the police to deliver him to them. Instead, staggering and bleeding, he came out alone. They immediately rushed him to Malcolm's doctor, Leona Turner, who took him directly to Sydenham Hospital, where doctors this time discovered a blood clot on his brain as well as internal bleeding.[37]

As Johnson fought for his life, the Muslims, joined by others from Boston, Hartford, Baltimore, and Washington, paraded outside the hospital. Soon, however, gun-toting teenagers joined the crowd, gathering behind the Muslims. When Malcolm heard of this, fearful of losing the initiative, he immediately dismissed his followers.

Meanwhile, while doctors were inserting into Johnson's head a sizeable silver plate to replace a major portion of the bone that the police had destroyed in battering his skull, a grand jury refused to indict him on police charges of disorderly conduct and resisting arrest. This paved the way for the Nation of Islam, on his behalf, to file a half-million dollar suit against the police department, accusing its officers of false arrest and imprisonment and malicious criminal prosecution.[38] An all-white jury eventually awarded him seventy thousand dollars, the largest award ever made by New York City in a police brutality case.[39]

To Harlemites, the Hinton Johnson incident made a hero of Malcolm X and enhanced their respect for the Nation of Islam. It was now a fact that the Muslims not only talked bad but backed it up with action. For days afterwards, said Benjamin 2X, "People were talking of nothing else."[40] As a result, Temple Number Seven's membership climbed from hundreds to thousands, and the incident itself became a Harlem folk story. Ironically, Malcolm himself could not accurately remember it. In his autobiography, for instance, he scrambled Johnson's name, which came out Johnson Hinton, and he misplaced the episode in time by two years.[41]

Throughout the country, black and white newspapers presented the Hinton Johnson incident as headline news. The Nation's membership soared; major universities invited Malcolm to speak on their campuses, and the *Los Angeles Herald Dispatch* granted him a weekly column entitled "God's Angry Men." The Muslims, he said later, had become a "hot copy."[42]

After the Hinton Johnson incident, Malcolm became a major focus of the NYPD's surveillance program, coordinated by its Bureau of Special Services (BOSS), which would, along with the FBI, monitor him throughout the rest of his life.[43] The NYPD, to be sure, greatly feared his rising power among Harlem's blacks. According to Mangum, if he could "wave his hand and disperse so many people," he could also "wave it and create any kind of disturbance he wanted to."[44]

Along with surveillance, BOSS's agents compiled a file on Malcolm's former police and prison records. They sent out letters to the Detroit Police Department, the Michigan Parole Commission, and the police departments of Lansing, Michigan, and Dedham and Milton, Massachusetts: the locations which had indicted him for criminal activities as a youth. In addition, they sent requests to the superintendents of Massachusetts' Concord Reformatory and Charleston State Prison.[45]

Before the year was out, from October 30 to November 2, 1957, Malcolm's exhausting schedule, along with eating only one meal a day and sleeping little, had landed him in Sydenham Hospital. While Wilfred X referred to his brother's condition as a combination of "stress, exhaustion and a cold," Malcolm, who had been experiencing palpitations in recent months, feared a coronary condition. The doctors, however, said he suffered from an inflammation around the ribs, indicating stress and exhaustion, which required him to spend several days of rest in the hospital.[46]

Marriage

The Nation of Islam had strict moral rules that governed the relations between men and women. Prohibiting premarital and extramarital sex were the main ones. But "to prevent temptation," singles were forbidden to touch, to sit together at temple meetings, or to remain alone with each other in the same room.[47] Practically their whole social life, as stated previously, centered around the temple and its restaurant.

Among the men, the Fruit of Islam (FOI) policed the Nation's moral rules. Infractions resulted in either suspension or expulsion for the worst offenses. Suspensions could occur from one month to a year, depriving a member of all contact with the Nation. To a Muslim whose life centered around it, suspension was a very painful punishment. If he behaved himself during it, however, the Nation would forgive his transgressions and he could once again regain his standing within it.

Enforcing the Nation's moral rules among the women was the Muslim Girls' Training and General Civilization Class (MGT-GCC). Headed by a female supreme captain, it acted as the women's counterpart to the FOI. Its duties included holding classes on cooking, sewing, and cleaning and instructing women on the proper role of a Muslim woman in the family and temple life.

The nation forbid dating. To match up men and women interested in marriage, the captains of the MGT-GCC and the FOI relayed to each of them the vital information — such as education, occupation, and personal habits of the other — necessary to make a decision. This would continue until they either arrived at a mutual agreement to marry or to discontinue the communication. If they agreed to marry, the captains would announce it in the temple several weeks prior to the ceremony, but the couple could not see each other without being accompanied by a chaperone until after their marriage. "Our community had its rules," said Benjamin 2X, "but in my seven years at Temple Number Seven [1957–1964], I remember only one divorce."[48]

In marriage, the Nation expected a man, as head of the home, to support his family, treat his wife with dignity and respect, live honestly and obey constituted authority. It expected a married woman to follow strict dietary rules, reject birth control, and attend classes on nutrition and child rearing held at their temples.[49]

In 1956, tall, lean, and muscular, thirty-year-old Malcolm, whose attractiveness only increased with age, was the Nation of Islam's most eligible bachelor. In his temple addresses, however, he often expressed a negative attitude toward women. Many of them, in fact, complained to Elijah Muhammad about Malcolm's grossly offensive statements about them. Describing them as tricky, deceitful, and untrustworthy, he blamed them "for the miserable condition of black men" and for holding them back from saving themselves.[50]

Long before his prison conversion to the Nation of Islam, of course, Malcolm had become convinced that women were inherently deceitful and untrustworthy. His experience as a hustler in Harlem and the views of his friend Sammy McKnight partly shaped them. But his often difficult relationship with Beatrice Bazarian Caragulian probably had more to do with forming them than anything else.

Nevertheless, Malcolm began to notice Betty Sanders, renamed Betty X, a recent convert to the Nation and a member of Temple Number Seven. Like him, she was tall, but darker, which appealed to him since he wanted to avoid any accusation of partiality towards light-skinned women.[51] While not as slender as Beatrice, he found her, with her brown eyes, attractive.

Reared by foster parents in Detroit and a graduate of Tuskegee Institute in Tuskegee, Alabama, Betty was studying nursing in New York when she started attending meetings at Malcolm's temple. Although she had experienced discrimination in segregationist Alabama, listening to his addresses was the first time she had heard anyone use the word racism in such an intelligent fashion. "I began to see why people did certain things," she said, "I began to see myself from a different perspective."[52]

Betty liked Malcolm's quick smile and, once off the podium, relaxed manner. Still, although interested, he kept a certain distance from her. But when she started teaching women's classes at night, he would drop in to advise her on what matters to emphasize; and she, in turn, began typing and correcting papers for him. Soon, they were having dinner together at the temple's restaurant. She knew, by this time, that he wanted to marry her. Meanwhile, she acted as if they were just friends, maintaining the relationship "on the same level that he did."[53]

Since Malcolm would not marry Betty without Elijah Muhammad's approval, he arranged, under another pretense, for her to meet him. Accordingly, after informing Malcolm that she would make a fine wife, knowing his ambivalence on the matter of marriage, Muhammad told him to make up his mind "to do it or not do it."[54]

On January 12, 1958, while driving to Detroit to visit his brother Wilfred, Malcolm stopped at a gas station and telephoned Betty. Either unwilling or unable to directly put the question of marriage to her, he asked "if she was ready to make that move." Knowing exactly what he meant, she dropped the phone and screamed "yes" at the top of her voice.[55]

Immediately flying to Detroit, Betty introduced Malcolm to her foster parents, and he, in turn, introduced her to Wilfred. Since they wanted a quick wedding, he suggested that they drive to Indiana, which had a short waiting period. But once they got there, they discovered it had lengthened its waiting period. Undeterred, on January 14, they drove to Philbert's house in Lansing, secured a marriage license, got married, and consummated it. For Malcolm, from the time that he had entered prison twelve years earlier until that night, Betty was the first woman he had touched.[56]

Back in New York City, Malcolm and Betty moved into a house in Queens with fellow Muslim John Ali, who later became national secretary, and his wife. In November 1958, with the birth of their oldest daughter, Attallah, named for Attila the Hun, the Nation purchased for them a seven room house in East Elmhurst, Queens. On Christmas day of 1960, Betty gave birth to another girl, Qubilah, named after Qubilah Khan. In July 1962, she had a third daughter, Ilyasah, which is Arabic for Elijah, and a fourth one, Amilah, in 1964. Finally, in late 1965, after Malcolm's assassination she had twins, again both girls.

Although Malcolm had access to the Nation's treasury, which paid his travel expenses and the cost of his home and car, he drew only one-hundred-fifty dollars a week from it for his salary. Except for books, he was not interested in acquiring material possessions. He loved reading, however, retreating nightly to his book-filled attic studio, containing a desk, tape recorder, prayer rug, and fold-out bed, to work and study. His varied reading interests consisted of the classics, anthropology, Africa, religion, and contemporary problems. As a result, he had developed amazing reading skill. According to Betty, he could read a difficult book in about three hours and easier ones in one or two hours.[57]

Malcolm and Betty's marriage was not without difficulty. Saving money was one issue between them. Fearing for her husband's life, she wanted him to increase his weekly paycheck so that they could put money away for their children. Because others might view it as self-aggrandizement, however, he refused to do it. Another issue was over whether she should stay at home and care for the children, which was his view, or, as she wished to do, continue with her nursing career. She left him three times over these issues. Yet, she always returned. "Over the years," she said later, "he had proven that he had my best interests at heart."[58]

Betty, moreover, disapproved of his non-stop schedule, which allowed little time for restaurants, movies, and plays, and found his negative attitude on romance annoying. He would criticize her for caring "too much" for "a lot of lovey-dovey words" and "dime-novel romantic talk."[59] Yet, she considered him "tender." When he left home for long periods, she said later, he would send her a letter telling her to look in some hiding place in the house, and there she would find some money or a love letter.[60]

In public, at least, Betty deferred to Malcolm's male chauvinism. She would, on many occasions, let him speak for her; when he called her "Girl," she referred to him as "Daddy."[61] In private, however, being a strong woman, she insisted on a more mutual exchange.[62] One time, after telling her what he expected of her as a wife, she, to his surprise, told him what she expected of him as a husband. The realization that he was not being fair to her, according to Betty, came as a shock to him.[63]

When Malcolm was in prison, to avoid eating pork products, he went for long periods of time eating little or purchasing bread and cheese in the commissary. As a result, he developed a persistent nutritional deficiency disorder. Fortunately for him, Betty, who was both a nurse and a home economics major, knew the nutritional value of foods and prepared a diet for him that included the basic essentials which cured his gastronomical problem.[64]

Despite his busy schedule, Malcolm put time aside to spend with his four girls. Although strict, he was a gentle and loving father.[65] After he read a book to them, said Betty, they would urge him to read it again, and each time he would give it a different ending.[66] To the girls, said Attallah later, while they looked to mother as a role model, Dad became their "buddy."[67]

Malcolm X's Achievements

From 1952, when Malcolm got out of prison, to 1959, the Nation of Islam's membership jumped from a few hundred into the thousands and its temples increased from several storefronts to more than thirty, located in fifteen states and the District of Columbia.[68]

That Malcolm was responsible for much of the Nation's growth was difficult to dispute. With about three hundred fifty members, Temple Number Seven was the Nation's fastest growing temple, and its annual income was 23,250 dollars, compared to Chicago Temple Number Two's 14,375 dollars.[69] Throughout the country, in fact, he spoke at temples, helped organize new ones, infused members with renewed spirit and encouragement, conducted fund raising campaigns, and served as both Muhammad's trouble-shooter and spokesman. "Thank Allah for my brother Minister Malcolm," said Muhammad.[70]

In 1958, Malcolm was living his life to the fullest. He was not only Muhammad's National representative but also a family man, a prolific reader, a skilled speaker and debater, and a popular figure in the movement. By this time, said Alex Haley, he had "tuned in to life in such a way that he didn't miss too much of it."[71] According to Malcolm, "I had every gratification that I wanted."[72]

As his achievements within the Nation increased, Malcolm relied less on Muhammad's opinions and began making more decisions on his own. In satisfying his love of knowledge, too, he no longer "assumed that the Muslims had it."[73] Muhammad, on the other hand, began to gently chastise him for pushing the Nation's members too hard.[74] At this point, however, tension between the two men was not noticeable.

First Overseas Visit to the Muslim World

In the late 1950s, Malcolm, who had an abiding interest in the Muslim world, convinced Muhammad that the Nation would benefit by building bridges into the Middle East and Africa.[75] To shore up his religious credentials, since the Muslim world did not recognize the Nation's teachings as authentic Islam, Muhammad announced his intention to make the annual hajj or sacred pilgrimage to Mecca, Islam's Holy City in Saudi Arabia.

In 1959, to pave the way for Muhammad's visit, Malcolm announced his intention to embark on a three-week tour of the Muslim countries; and that he, too, would visit Mecca, scheduling his visit to coincide with the annual hajj, on June 9, which all devout Muslims attempt to make at least once in their lives. Yet, for unexplained reasons, he did not leave until July after the hajj had ended. Nonetheless, he said, he was determined to visit Mecca.[76]

As Muhammad's ambassador, from July 5 to July 24, Malcolm visited Egypt, Saudi Arabia, Sudan, Nigeria, and Ghana. His longest stay, eleven days, was in Cairo, Egypt. Although President Gamal Abdel Nasser had scheduled a meeting with him, for reasons that were unclear, Nasser canceled it at the last minute. Some observers suggested that the Central Intelligence Agency (CIA) had persuaded Nasser not to meet with Malcolm, but its agents had little clout with Nasser. Since 1956, when the United States reneged on a promised loan to Egypt to build the Aswan Dam, unfriendly relations existed between the two countries.

Despite Nasser's failure to meet with Malcolm, he sent important Egyptian officials to accompany Malcolm throughout his visit. They introduced him to prominent people, took him to visit the great Sphinx and pyramids of Egypt, and allowed him to mingle with students at the University of Cairo and Al Azhar, a leading Islamic university. Aware of the Nation of Islam's "blasphemy" of Islam, its rectors "closed their eyes to it," listening politely to Malcolm's reiteration of the Nation's interpretation of Islam.[77]

From Egypt, Malcolm flew to Jedda, Saudi Arabia; upon arrival, he canceled his planned visit to Mecca. That he did so was difficult to understand since his visit would have been one of the high points of his religious life. Some orthodox Muslims believed the Saudis prevented it because the Nation's doctrines perverted Islam's teachings.[78] A few months later, however, they allowed Elijah Muhammad to visit Mecca. This indicated that they were not responsible for Malcolm's cancellation.

Deepening the mystery, Malcolm's reasons given for canceling his visit to Mecca continually changed. They included coming down with diarrhea from something that he had eaten in Cairo; scheduling problems with his plane reservation, which would have prevented him from continuing with his African tour; visiting Mecca before Muhammad's visit to it would have been inappropriate; and explaining that the whole thing was "the will of Allah."[79]

While traveling throughout Africa, Malcolm wrote letters to black newspapers back home. Hoping to instill in blacks a sense of pride in their heritage, he wrote that they would play a "key role" in Africa, which had replaced America as the "world of the future."[80] America's racial problems, he added, occupied the front pages of African newspapers, and Africans considered

America's treatment of its blacks "a good yardstick" to measure the sincerity of America's offer of assistance.[81]

While Malcolm knew that inconsistencies existed between Muhammad's teachings and orthodox Islam, his visit to the Muslim world better clarified them for him. Meeting racially tolerant white Muslims, he realized, if he had not already known, that the Muslim world was neither all black, as Muhammad depicted, nor racist. He continued, nonetheless, to outwardly adhere to the Nation's white devil theory.

From November 21, 1959, to January 6, 1960, accompanied by his sons, Akbar and Herbert, Elijah Muhammad, calling his trip "a friendly visit," traveled throughout the Middle East and Africa. While abroad, he left Malcolm, who wanted to go with him, behind to oversee the Nation.

Despite Muhammad's differences with orthodox Islam, Arab Muslim officials, hoping perhaps to convert him to their religious view, "warmly received him." Flattered by their attention, his goal, nevertheless, was to shore up his religious credentials at home. Besides, he was not about to assimilate orthodox Islam into the Nation of Islam. While Malcolm leaned towards the internationalization of Islam, Muhammad's view of it was nationalistic. To him, orthodox Islam was endemic to the Middle East and Africa and not viable to the American black experience.[82]

Unlike Malcolm, Muhammad and his sons visited Mecca. Since the pilgrimage season was over, orthodox Muslims referred to their visit as the "omra" or "the lesser pilgrimage." During the proper season, Muhammad himself never returned to complete the required hajj.

Back in the United States, the only thing Muhammad did differently to conform to Orthodox Islam was to change the name of his temples to mosques.

National Attention

In early 1959, Louis Lomax, a black journalist, informed Mike Wallace, a white reporter who put on controversial television programs, about the Nation of Islam, and said that it was sufficiently provocative to garner a large audience. After learning that "such a large and hostile organization" had somehow escaped the notice of the press, he became intrigued by the prospect of doing a documentary on it. If Lomax was "even half right," said Wallace, "it would make an extraordinary story," and "that kind of controversy was right up my alley."[83]

With Wallace's urging, Lomax approached Malcolm X with the idea of a television documentary on the Nation of Islam. Regarding it favorably, he, in turn, informed Muhammad, who was initially against it, fearing it would hurt the Nation. On the contrary, said Malcolm, it would benefit the Nation, and he continued to press the issue.[84] Eventually, Muhammad consented, but he did so only on condition that Lomax, not a white reporter, would do the interviewing.

Even so, Lomax used white cameramen, who began filming scenes of Muslims fishing for converts, attending classes, and praying at the Nation's mosques in New York City, Chicago, and Washington. Even though the Muslims were wary of them, Lomax's presence, armed with Muhammad's consent, allowed the cameramen wide discretion in filming.[85]

Between July 13 and July 17, on New York's Channel 13, Wallace presented a five-part documentary entitled "The Hate that Hate Produced" on the Nation of Islam. It was neither sensitive nor balanced in its portrayal of the Nation. The filmmakers underplayed its religious nature, de-emphasized its impact in cleaning up alcoholics and drug addicts and reforming criminals, and presented it, instead, as a hate group.

Wallace began his program by describing the movement as "black racism," "black supremacy," and "gospel of hate."[86] Similarly, his film makers edited Muhammad's speeches and interviews, seemingly, to emphasize his hostility to whites. Showing Muslim children attending Chicago's University of Islam, they said that their teachers taught them "to hate the white man."[87] That the Nation owned businesses to service Muslims and the black communities in which they lived was about the only positive statement that the film makers made about it. To Jack Gould, a *New York Times* television critic, Wallace's penchant "for pursuing sensationalism" was neither conscientious nor constructive.[88]

In the documentary, Malcolm X made the most dramatic impact on white New Yorkers, whom he described as devils. To them, unaccustomed to being called devils, he conveyed a "sense of menace," described by some as "palpable and riveting."[89] News commentators characterized him as an extremist, a hate monger, and a demagogue.[90] And to one Harlem resident, Sonia Sanchez, "that man is saying stuff we're not supposed to hear."[91]

The Nation's leaders expressed anger and dismay at Wallace's presentation of them. After the program finished, Malcolm sat there "just about limp."[92] He was embarrassed, said Captain Joseph, since Wallace did exactly what Muhammad said he would do.[93] "Does Mike Wallace classify truth as hate?" said Muhammad, and his son Wallace charged Mike Wallace with twisting his father's words to make him sound as if he was "plotting for the Muslims to overthrow the government."[94]

Instead of attacking Wallace's insensitive portrayal of a black organization, prominent civil rights leaders, Dr. Martin Luther King Jr., president of the Southern Christian Leadership Conference (SCLC), and Roy Wilkins, the NAACP's executive secretary, denounced the black racism of the Nation of Islam.[95] In response, Muhammad and Malcolm, referring to them as "Uncle Toms" who were "hungry for a place among the white race," charged them with having brought blacks to their present conditions.[96]

Almost overnight, Wallace's documentary, catching the Muslims by surprise, generated a media blitz which propelled them into national prominence. All three national networks, the weeklies, *Life, Look, Newsweek, Time, U.S. News and World Report,* the monthlies, including the *Reader's Digest,* with a worldwide circulation of twenty-four million, began reporting on them. The Muslims, quipped black comedian Dick Gregory, had been around for thirty years, "but nobody knew it until the white man put them on television."[97]

Similarly, two full length studies came out of the Nation of Islam. First, black scholar C. Eric Lincoln wrote *The Black Muslims in America,* a sociological study of the Nation of Islam. To the chagrin of its members, the name Black Muslims, which he used to describe them, stuck. The Nation's members, said Malcolm, were black people who practicized Islam, "not Black Muslims."[98] Then, E. U. Essienudom, a Nigerian scholar, came out with *Black Nationalism: A Search for an Identity in America,* a cultural study which complemented Lincoln's work.

While the two authors wrote good scholarly studies, they only added to the outcries against the Nation, because reviews often quoted only those sections which emphasized the Nation's anti-white attitudes.

With the national media attention came an increase in membership. Estimates varied between 20,000 to 250,000, and mosques expanded to about fifty, located in twenty-two states.[99] But to questions about membership rolls, Muslim officials refused to disclose them. Expressing a typical response, Malcolm said, "Those who know aren't saying, and those who say don't know."[100]

Malcolm X and Fidel Castro

In September 1960, the leader of Cuba's 1959 revolution, Fidel Castro, and his delegation arrived in New York City to attend the United Nations (U.N.) General Assembly, where it would admit Cuba and thirteen newly independent African nations to the world body.

So that they would not have to eat tainted poultry, Castro's delegation carried live chickens with them. As a result, Manhattan's Shelburne Hotel would not honor their reservations unless they made a deposit of ten thousand dollars as a guarantee against damages. Rather than pay it, Castro said that his delegation would stay in tents at the U.N. gardens. Inadvertently saving U.N. officials embarrassment, Love B. Woods, the black owner of Harlem's Theresa Hotel, located on 125th Street and Seventh Avenue, offered them rooms for twenty-one dollars a day, which Castro immediately accepted.[101]

When Castro's delegation arrived at Harlem's Theresa Hotel, hundreds of Harlemites, proud to host Cuba's revolutionary leaders, cheered them. As one eyewitness reported, the crowds surrounded the hotel day and night, and whenever anyone showed themselves at Castro's window, a cheer would go up.[102] For Harlemites, said one commentator, it was an event in the development of community consciousness.[103]

On September 20, as a member of the Twenty-eighth Precinct Committee Council, formed to greet prominent U.N. members, Malcolm accepted Castro's invitation to the council to send someone to meet with him at the Theresa Hotel.[104] During their thirty minute visit, Malcolm wanted to know Castro's views concerning America's race situation and his attitude towards black Cubans, whom previous administrations had discriminated against. Somewhat evasively, he told him that while he had no intention of becoming involved in America's "race situation," in Cuba, he was "fighting against discrimination everywhere."[105]

To reporters afterwards, Malcolm, ignoring Castro's evasiveness, referred to him as a "humble, sincere, peaceful man" who had taken a "more open stand" than previous regimes for black Cubans' civil rights.[106]

Meanwhile, Elijah Muhammad was furious with Malcolm for not contacting him before meeting with Castro. Yet, he had initiated it, not Malcolm. Since Malcolm was on the committee to greet foreign dignitaries visiting Harlem and the only member on it available at the time to meet with Castro, he may not have considered obtaining Muhammad's permission necessary.

Nonetheless, because Washington suspected Castro of being a Communist, Muhammad feared that Malcolm's visit with him would lead the FBI to link Communism with the Nation of Islam, and that this would generate a government crackdown on it similar to the one that had occurred after the Japanese had attacked Pearl Harbor on December 7, 1941.[107]

Justifying Muhammad's fears, shortly thereafter, FBI agents visited Malcolm at Harlem's mosque to inquire about Castro's affiliation with Communism. Without sufficient knowledge to comment on it, Malcolm said that Muslims believed in God, "not atheistic Communism."[108]

Dealings with the Ku Klux Klan and the Nazis

By early 1961, the Ku Klux Klan's growing power in the south, as a result of the white backlash against the Civil Rights Movement, threatened the Nation of Islam's southern base. Since opposition to integration was their common ground, Muhammad hoped that this might act as a catalyst for a truce between them. To set it up, he sent Malcolm to Atlanta, where the local Muslim minister, Jeremiah X Pugh, arranged to have him meet with the Klan.

At a secret location, Malcolm and Jeremiah X met with members of the Klan on the night of January 28. According to an FBI informant, the Klansmen offered to sell them a county-sized parcel of land, about twenty-thousand acres, hoping by this action to make the Nation's separatist program more attractive to blacks. The Klansmen, moreover, agreed not to interfere with the Nation's affairs in the south on condition that its members would not aid the Civil Rights Movement there.[109] With this understanding, then, the Nation made its truce with the Klan. But whether the land deal between them went through was not entirely clear.

To one of Malcolm's biographers, negotiating with Klansmen generated a "maturing realization" within Malcolm that the Nation was evolving into "something he could not justify."[110] But although he never went back south again to meet with them, at this juncture, whether he disagreed with Muhammad on the probability of negotiating with the Klan was difficult to know.

Along with the Klan, the leader of the American Nazi Party, George Lincoln Rockwell, sympathized with Muhammad's separatist philosophy. The two men, in fact, may have worked out an "agreement of mutual assistance," which Malcolm may not have known about.[111] He knew, however, that Muhammad encouraged Rockwell and his Nazi storm troopers to attend the Nation's rallies, using them as "a sort of bugbear" to scare blacks into the Nation.[112]

On one occasion, at the Nation's annual Saviour's Day Rally, on February 25, 1962, Rockwell, taking the floor mike, addressed over twelve thousand people gathered at Chicago's International Amphitheater to celebrate Fard's birthday. Praising Muhammad separatist philosophy and calling him "the man to solve the race problem," Rockwell promised him that when the Nazis get power, they will not integrate.[113]

Later, when critics asked Malcolm about the probability of allowing Rockwell to speak at a Saviour's Day Rally, he called him "no different than any other white man" and, in fact, better than the liberals, who "think the same thing that Rockwell thinks only they speak a different talk."[114]

On the Public Circuit

A tall, commanding figure, Malcolm evolved into one of the most dynamic speakers of his time. Political observers described him as "charismatic," "magnetic," and "self-assured."[115] "You didn't want to take your eyes off him," said writer Maya Angelou. "He had that energy."[116] "More than anyone else," said civil rights activist James Baldwin, "he articulated black people's suffering."[117] He was our hero, said comedian Dick Gregory, "who didn't take nothing from nobody [and] had the best lines."[118]

Malcolm had the psychic ability to both adapt his speaking to fit a particular audience and set the rhythm necessary to play them so as not "to put people to sleep."[119] According to reporter Charles Wiley, he could speak in the "emotional language of the Harlem streets, shift gears en route to the studio, and carry on a cool logical debate before television cameras."[120]

For his speeches and debates, Malcolm would retire to his attic library to prepare for them. He would rehearse his opponent's position, making sure he understood it so that he could better deflect it.[121] At times, too, he would consult experts in the field, including historians, political scientists, and sociologists.

Described by some as "whip smart," Malcolm was an expert at "rational calisthenics." In debating politicians, he would say that he had never met any sincere ones, but he hadn't, adding with a smile, met all of them. And to a hostile interviewer who asked him if he would accept aid from Communists, he related the parable of a man trapped in a wolf's den, "who'd take whatever help he could get." When the interviewer pressed him to acknowledge that this was a "yes," he replied, laughing, that he was only talking about wolves.[122]

Most civil rights leaders, including Dr. King, refused to debate with Malcolm. If they appeared on the same platform with him, they feared alienating their white supporters. "He was saying some pretty rough things about whites," said activist Ossie Davis, "and we wanted to keep peace with the white world."[123] To Malcolm, however, who called integration "a dream," he had nothing to debate with civil rights leaders anyway.[124]

Although often not recognized, he also had considerable writing ability, which he had developed during his prison years by studying the dictionary and writing letters. Throughout the 1950s in fact, both Muhammad, under "Mr. Muhammad Speaks," and Malcolm, under "God's Angry Men," were writing editorial columns for black newspapers. Yet, both men recognized the need for the Nation to have its own newspaper.

In 1960, after the Nation failed in this endeavor twice with *The Mes-*

Malcolm X addresses a rally in Harlem, New York City, on June 29, 1963 (AP/ Wide World Photos).

senger Magazine and *The Islamic News,* Malcolm, working alone in his base-ment, created its first successful newspaper, naming it *Muhammad Speaks.*[125] To produce it, he obtained technical advice from Louis Lomax. He observed, during organizational drives in Los Angeles, how the editor of the city's black newspaper, the *Los Angeles Herald Dispatch,* put it together. He could do this, he said later, because he was "a quick study," learning how to do it dur-ing his street hustling days when "quick picking up" was "probably the num-ber one survival rule."[126]

Throughout the early sixties, Muhammad, who lacked Malcolm's ora-torical abilities, encouraged him to become the bridge between the Nation and the news media. Knowing that his "fiend like" reputation got him into print, he promoted it. In his fiery, forceful manner of speaking, the "balled fist," the "jaw militantly clenched," the grimace, and the snarl, he created an image of a villain, which became familiar to white Americans watching the evening news.[127]

Malcolm became the master of saying something to the news media in a dramatic manner that would take less than thirty seconds, called the sound byte. "There have been few public men," said newsman Murry Kempton, "whose message fit so snug and yet so lively into a two minute segment of a news broadcast."[128] Peter Goldman called him a media genius who understood media politics before "white elected politicians figured it out."[129] Yet, to Captain Joseph, Malcolm was "becoming intoxicated with the cameras and microphones."[130]

By 1961, next to Senator Barry Goldwater of Arizona, who became the Republican nominee for the 1964 presidential election, Malcolm became the most sought after speaker on college and university campuses. Unintentionally, many professors had generated his popularity by making Eric Lincoln's book, *The Black Muslims in America,* required reading in their courses; and *Playboy* magazine, which had the greatest circulation among college students, printed a candid interview of him by Alex Haley.[131]

Speaking at colleges and universities, Malcolm was the model of civility. He acted more professional than pugnacious, yet his continued condemnation of whites stirred controversy. To describe student reactions to him, observers used such words as "indignation," "hostility," "rage," and "enthusiasm."[132] And he frightened college and university administrators, who sometimes tried to prevent him from speaking at their institutions. In 1961, for instance, the officials of New York's Queens College barred him from speaking there. This precipitated student demonstrations on his behalf, leading to a reversal of their decision.[133]

Similarly, that same year, the administrators of Howard University, a renowned black school, reneged on the campus NAACP's invitation for Malcolm to speak there. Apparently, because the university's charter grew out of reconstruction's Freedman's Bureau, which Congress oversaw, they feared its reaction if Malcolm spoke there. Because of student pressure, however, they gave in as long as he debated an integrationist speaker.[134] Eventually, he debated Bayard Rustin, a member of the Fellowship of Reconciliation and a civil rights activist.

Within the spirit of searching minds, Malcolm found students "amazingly open-minded." For him, sessions with students were "exhilarating," for "they never failed," he said, in helping him to further his own education.[135] Also, impressed by the sincerity of white students to find a solution to the race problem, he began to modify his views towards them. While the older generation was "hopeless," he told reporters, young people were incensed over racism and "filled with an urge to eliminate it."[136]

Still, Malcolm stubbornly held onto his anti-white prejudices. At one New England college, for example, his speech so upset a woman student that she caught the next plane behind his to new York City. She found him at the Muslim restaurant having coffee with Benjamin 2X, Captain Joseph, and Louis X. When she asked Malcolm what she could do to help, he said "nothing." With that she "burst into tears," ran out of the restaurant, and disappeared into a taxicab.[137]

After the college woman had gone, the conversation between Malcolm and his Muslim brothers "took a heavy turn," and he seemed to be lamenting his response to her. "When you realize that you're wrong," he said to Benjamin 2X many months later, "admit it, even if it is against yourself."[138]

Nonetheless, Malcolm's enthusiasm for white students concerned Muhammad, who feared that by praising them, Malcolm was "losing his spirit" for the Nation of Islam's white devil theory. Lacking his intellectual and oratorical abilities, too, he may have been jealous of all the attention Malcolm was getting from students.[139]

CHAPTER 4

The Developing Rift

By the late 1950s, the Nation of Islam had established three mosques in California. These included Mosque Number Twenty-Six in San Francisco; Mosque Number Twenty-Six-B in Oakland; and Mosque Number Twenty-Seven in Los Angeles with over a thousand members, the biggest in the state.

With ties to the right wing John Birch Society and the Christian Anti-Communist Crusade, William H. Parker headed the Los Angeles Police Department (LAPD). He divided the city into two camps: one consisted of "conservative, patriotic Americans" and the other of "Communist-inspired disloyal Americans," with the Nation of Islam in the latter.[1] In 1962, a secret LAPD report on it concluded that its members were dangerous and fanatic, willing to both die for their cause and take a "Caucasian," preferably a police officer, with them.[2]

On April 27, 1962, after an early evening meeting at the Los Angeles mosque, Monroe X Jones invited Fred X Jingles to his parked car nearby to purchase some used clothes, which he had obtained as a delivery driver for a dry cleaning company. Just as Monroe X opened his trunk and Fred X began inspecting the clothes, officers Frank Tomlinson and Stanley Kensic, suspecting a crime in progress, pulled their squad car over to them. Almost immediately, a scuffle broke out between the policemen and the two Muslims. Other Muslims standing nearby descended upon the policemen and in the ensuing melee, someone shot Tomlinson in the elbow with the service revolver taken from his partner.[3]

By this time, tipped off by an off-duty policeman, reinforcements arrived from three police divisions. While some policemen converged on the scene of the incident, others, including Donald Weese and Richard Anderson, went to the mosque located a block away.

What happened next was unclear. According to the Muslims, the police stormed the mosque with their weapons firing. They, in contrast, said that the Muslims attacked first, hitting Anderson in the head with his own night-stick and a five gallon bottle. At that point, said Weese later, he told Anderson's attackers to freeze. When they refused, he and another policeman opened fire. Then, Ronald X Stokes, the mosque's secretary, jumped on Weese's back and began choking him. As another policeman pulled him off, Weese, who said later that Stokes raised his hands "menacingly," shot and killed him.[4] In the Muslim version, however, Stokes had raised his hands to surrender, not to attack Weese.[5]

Besides killing Stokes, the police wounded six other Muslims, including William Rogers, whom they shot in the spine, paralyzing him from the waist down.[6]

The police shootings and Stokes' death shocked Elijah Muhammad. In the Nation of Islam's thirty-one years, he had never lost a Muslim at the hands of law enforcement officers. He immediately ordered Malcolm X to fly to Los Angeles to assist the Muslims there. Like Muhammad, Stokes' death had shaken Malcolm, who wept upon hearing of it.[7]

Meanwhile, Mayor Sam Yorty and Chief Parker portrayed their police officers as "victims of a savage attack" by the Muslims, whose goal was "the destruction of the Caucasian race."[8]

The LAPD, said Mayor Sam Yorty to reporters, had been watching them for "a long time" and expected "trouble from them."[9] The nature of their teachings, added Chief William Parker, means "such clashes as occurred the other night are bound to reoccur and will become more frequent."[10]

Immediately upon arrival in Los Angeles, on April 18, Malcolm went on the offensive, calling Sam Yorty "a professional liar" and referring to Stokes' death as "a brutal and cold-blooded murder" by Chief Parker's "well armed storm troopers."[11]

Throughout his week's visit, Malcolm spent much time countering Mayor Yorty's and Chief Parker's version of the incident. To reporters, he said that he had questioned the wounded men and other eyewitnesses, and that the Muslims provoked them was contrary to fact. Obeying the law, he said, Muslims were never the aggressors; instead, the police "went wild," acting like maniacs.[12]

Having both founded the Los Angeles mosque and helped recruit Stokes only intensified Malcolm's bitterness towards Chief Parker's LAPD. Along with other Muslims, he was ready for retaliatory action against them. Throughout the country, in fact, Muslims were phoning the Los Angeles mosque to express their willingness to come out there for the coming battle.[13] Yet, knowing that Mayor Yorty and Chief Parker held the upper hand in Los Angeles and fearing that a battle there would again bring the federal government down on the whole movement, Muhammad refused to sanction revenge attacks.[14]

Back in Harlem, Malcolm, following Muhammad's instructions to defuse the conflict, encouraged his followers to trust in Allah, who "gives justice in his own way."[15] Still, Malcolm was dissatisfied with the way Muhammad handled the whole affair. To Malcolm, in the face of beatings and shootings, Muhammad's call for discipline and trust in God contradicted the Nation's themes of retribution, justice, and redemption. What's more, that some Harlemites began describing the Muslims as "talk only" troubled Malcolm.[16] From then on, said Philbert later, his brother began speaking less of God bringing justice to blacks and more of them getting it for themselves.[17]

In the Stokes case, on May 14, despite Weese's acknowledgment of shooting an unarmed man, an all white coroner's jury delivered a ruling of justifiable homicide. The courts, on the other hand, found guilty and sentenced to prison eleven of the fourteen Muslims whom the LAPD had arrested during the incident and charged with assault.[18]

In June, two months after the Los Angeles shootings, one-hundred and twenty Americans from Atlanta died in a plane crash near Paris, France. At the time, Malcolm, speaking at a Muslim rally in Los Angeles, announced that Allah, by "dropping an airplane out of the sky with over a hundred people on it," had brought justice upon those responsible for the lynching of Ronald Stokes. As the crowd cheered, wrote newsmen, he said that "God got rid of them in one whoop," and "we hope that every day another plane falls out of the sky."[19]

To political observers, who described him as "fiend" and a man with a "depraved mind," Malcolm defended his plane crash statements as only right that a black man should manifest joy when his God, Allah, inflicted pain on his enemy.[20] Nor did Muhammad consider Malcolm's statements extreme enough to render him a censure.[21] Later, however, Malcolm expressed regret for making them to the writer of his autobiography, Alex Haley.[22]

Wealth and Power

By 1961, as the Nation's chief spokesman, Malcolm's eloquence and charisma had brought him greater name recognition than Elijah Muhammad. Because Malcolm was in the news every day, said civil rights activist Gordon Parks, not to think of him as the Nation's central figure was "impossible."[23] After covering a Harlem rally, newsman Pete Hamill noticed "how impressive Malcolm had been and how feeble Elijah Muhammad had seemed beside him."[24]

Except for Wallace, minister of Philadelphia's Mosque Number Twelve, and Akbar, a student at Cairo, Egypt's El-Azhar University, Muhammad's children were jealous of Malcolm's power and prestige in the movement. They included Herbert, editor of *Muhammad Speaks*, Elijah, Jr., the FOI's assistant supreme commander, and Ethel, the MGT-GCC's supreme instructor. Less in conflict with Malcolm than the others were Lottie, who supervised Chicago's University of Islam, and Emanuel, a dry cleaner.

Siding with Herbert, Elijah Jr. and Ethel against Malcolm were John Ali, the Nation's national secretary, and Raymond Sharrieff, the FOI's supreme captain and Ethel's husband. All of them resided in Chicago and made up the Nation's national leadership.

The Chicago leadership, considering Malcolm a threat to their domain, started a campaign to turn Elijah Muhammad against him. They spread rumors that Malcolm was promoting himself over Muhammad and that he had stacked the Nation with a nucleus of ministers primed to aid a "succession coup."[25]

Inadvertently, by attacking Malcolm, the Chicago leadership was giving the FBI more leverage in its ongoing attempts to destabilize the Nation of Islam. Reporting to headquarters in Washington, Chicago's special agent in charge wrote that "future disruption plans may well play the fact that Malcolm is the heir apparent," and that he "may have already taken over the organization."[26]

Upon Malcolm's recommendation, Elijah Muhammad had appointed John Ali, Mosque Number Seven's former secretary, to national secretary, whose job was to oversee all of the Nation's financial interests. In his new position, however, unlike Malcolm, who practiced thrift and simple living, Ali adopted a lavish lifestyle, purchasing a new car, a large home, and tailor-made suits.[27] Soon, Malcolm concluded that Ali's sole purpose as national secretary was "to steal as much money as he could from the Muslim treasury."[28]

As Muhammad's right hand man, in his position as FOI's supreme captain, Sharrieff, like the others, was jealous of Malcolm's rapid rise in the movement and fearful, too, that he would use his growing power to challenge the Chicago leadership's control of the Nation's wealth and power.[29]

Within New York's Mosque Number Seven, the Chicago leadership found a ready ally in Captain Joseph, described by some as "a man not to be played with."[30] Once close to Malcolm, Joseph had helped him build the

Boston and New York mosques, but by 1961, friction arose between them. According to Herman Ferguson, a later follower of Malcolm, Joseph's thinking was narrow and limited, and once the Chicago leadership had "planted something in his mind against Malcolm," it would fester and grow because of his "dogmatic nature."[31]

Another disciple to turn against Malcolm was Louis X, minister of Boston's Mosque Number Eleven. Like Captain Joseph, his reasons for siding with the Chicago leadership were unclear. But as some suggested, Malcolm's "stern, authoritarian manner" may have played a role in alienating the two men from him. His "sense of command," said Goldman, meant "maintaining distance."[32] He could be difficult said Benjamin 2X. "When he fixed his eyes on you," they became "piercing like ice."[33]

Although Muhammad had not named a successor, fellow Muslims considered his son Wallace, described by them as a man of faith, honest, and humble, the likeliest to succeed him.[34] His integrity, said Benjamin 2X, "had always set him outside the circle of power in Chicago."[35] Even FBI agents, in their reports to headquarters, acknowledged that he was less interested in money than the other children.[36]

In the early sixties, however, Wallace was not in a position to take over from his father. On March 23, 1960, a federal court sentenced him to serve three years in prison for evading the draft. After a series of unsuccessful appeals, on October 30, 1961, his twenty-eighth birthday, he entered federal prison at Sandstone, Minnesota.

Although Wallace had doubted his father's interpretation of Islam, he never really studied the Koran, the orthodox Muslims' Bible, until he went to prison. After studying it, he concluded that many of the Nation's teachings contradicted Islam's scriptural doctrines. The Koran, for instance, neither mentioned Fard nor supported Elijah Muhammad's claim as Allah's messenger.[37]

After winning parole on January 10, 1963, Wallace resumed his position as minister of Philadelphia's Mosque Number Twelve. While he kept his doubts about his father's teachings to himself, he did share with Malcolm his concern that the Chicago leadership was taking advantage of his father's worsening bronchial asthma condition to gain more authority over the Nation's operations.[38]

Without the Chicago leadership's prodding, whether Elijah Muhammad would have eventually turned against Malcolm was unclear. Yet, along with them, his rising prominence and growing power within the Nation concerned Muhammad, too. To counter these trends, he took over Malcolm's weekly column in New York's *Amsterdam News* and instructed Herbert, as editor of *Muhammad Speaks,* to give Malcolm as little coverage as possible.[39] Soon, said Malcolm later, "there was more in the Muslim paper about integrationist Negro leaders than there was about me."[40]

Ironically, Malcolm had made Herbert's job as editor of the Nation's newspaper possible. He had, earlier, noticed that Elijah Muhammad's children worked at menial jobs. To Malcolm's thinking, however, by holding administrative jobs and forming a cadre around their father, they could better serve the Nation. Through a fund-raising drive, he raised the money necessary to accomplish this. Unwittingly, said Betty later, her husband had "set up his own doom through the very people he had helped."[41]

In 1961, when Muhammad's illness got worse, Malcolm became aware of negative remarks directed against him. To his close associates, he denied "taking credit for Muhammad's teachings" or trying to take over the Nation; and to reporters, he described himself as nothing compared to Muhammad, who had no equal on earth.[42] Still, regarding his teachings, said Benjamin 2X, Malcolm no longer slavishly followed them because his intellect "had begun to outgrow the nation's doctrine," and he felt impelled "to move where his mind took him."[43]

Along with the Nation's business and real estate, an important source of the Nation's income came from the sales of its newspaper, *Muhammad Speaks.* From a small newsletter published out of Malcolm's basement, it had grown to become a weekly tabloid with its own printing press in Chicago. At wholesale price, the Nation required all Muslim men to purchase forty-four dollars worth of each edition. Theoretically, then, they could make a profit, but they rarely sold their weekly quotas and payments for them became "a burden."[44]

For the Nation, another source of income was from donations by its members. Working Muslims contributed twelve dollars a week to the Nation, and on Saviour's Day, February 26, it required them, whether they attended the rally or not, to donate another one hundred dollars. At Sunday services, too, the Nation's ministers encouraged their congregations to fill the donation baskets with money. After deducting expenses, they sent the balance to the Chicago leadership, and because of the Nation's tax-exempt status as a religious organization, they did not have to account for it.

While the Chicago leadership publicly said that only blacks donated money to the Nation, a white Texas oilman, Haroldson L. Hunt, who sponsored conservative and right wing causes, was an exception. Apparently, because he agreed with the Muslims' separatist program, he donated considerable sums of money to them.[45]

A sizeable amount of the Nation's donations went to support Elijah

During a black Muslim rally in New York City, August 6, 1963, Malcolm X holds up a paper for the crowd to see (AP/Wide World Photos).

Muhammad and his family. As a result of them, he was able to acquire a large home in Chicago and Phoenix, drive expensive cars, hire bodyguards and servants, and hold titles to large amounts of property, including two apartments, a bakery, a grocery store in Chicago and a one-hundred and sixty acre farm in Michigan. He obtained these luxuries, according to an FBI report, "at the expense of his followers," who were, for the most part, extremely poor and continually harassed by the Nation's officials for greater contributions.[46]

Encouraged by Muhammad, the Chicago leadership wore expensive clothes, drove big cars, and lived in fancy neighborhoods.[47] Thus, he set the trend among them to corrupt the Nation's religious ideals, which began with him to benefit their acquisitiveness.[48]

The rise in the possibility of Wallace taking over the Nation was anathema to the Chicago leadership since they feared that he would align with

Malcolm against them. If that happened, said Herman Ferguson, they knew that their "exorbitant lifestyles would come to a screeching halt."[49] All that they could expect from Malcolm, added Benjamin 2X, was "a thorough house cleaning."[50]

Like Wallace, Malcolm's non-materialist lifestyle contrasted vividly with that of the Chicago leadership's extravagance. After becoming a Muslim, he said that money was "the last thing" to cross his mind.[51] From the Nation's funds, in fact, he allocated to himself only about one-hundred and seventy-five dollars a week for living expenses. He "didn't give a damn about making money," said Peter Goldman.[52] And an FBI report conceded that Malcolm was "extremely sincere in his efforts to promote the Nation of Islam," and that he "had very little interest in personally accumulating money."[53]

By 1962, although Malcolm had said that he thought and acted through Muhammad's mind, his restless nature and knowledge of the world, combined with the ongoing civil rights struggles, was too great for him not to eventually question the Nation's doctrines. He had "outgrown Muhammad," said associate Yuri Kochiyama, and "found his ideology too narrow."[54]

Most important, with blacks battling for civil rights in the streets, Muhammad's nonengagement policy of waiting for divine intervention to bring justice now appeared outdated to Malcolm. "We talk about our people being brutalized in the civil rights movements," he told his associates, but "we haven't done anything."[55] In his public addresses, increasingly, he began to talk more of political action than of divine intervention, sounding to some more like a sociologist than a representative of the Nation of Islam.[56] Keeping himself in check was becoming hard for him, said his brother Wilfred, and "it was gonna get worse."[57]

But whether the nonengagement issue, on its own, would have compelled Malcolm to break with the Nation was uncertain. Although he had become increasingly convinced that the Nation could play a more activist role, said Malcolm X scholar Paul Lee, he "would not have pushed that to the point of breaking with it."[58] On the contrary, he was too affected by the ongoing civil rights struggle to passively accept the Nation's nonengagement policy indefinitely.

Malcolm's shift from religion to politics did not go unnoticed by Elijah Muhammad. If the Nation abandoned its nonengagement policy, he feared that the government might lift its tax-exempt status as a religious organization.[59] The Nation, said Peter Goldman, had become "a quiet organization" whose members "regarded white people as a race of devils, and that it was too dangerous to provoke them."[60]

The Autobiography

In 1939, as a young black man, Alex Haley dropped out of college and joined the U.S. Coast Guard, where he would spend the next twenty years. While in the service, he made money writing personal letters, often love letters, for less literate white shipmates. After leaving the Coast Guard, he embarked on a second career as a freelance magazine writer. In 1960, he wrote an article for the *Reader's Digest* on the Nation of Islam that Muhammad liked. This helped position him to do an interview of Malcolm X for *Playboy* magazine in 1963.

After the *Playboy* interview, Haley's agent, interested in the idea of an autobiography of Malcolm X, brought the writer together with the editors of a leading publishing firm. Soon thereafter, Haley asked Malcolm if he could write an "as told to" autobiography on his life. Uncertain at first, he eventually agreed to it on condition that all of the profits go to the Nation. He viewed it, moreover, as a way both to spread the Nation's message and to recruit new members. "My life story," he told Haley, "may help people to appreciate better how Mr. Muhammad salvages black people."[61]

But first, to obtain Muhammad's permission to write the book, Haley flew to Phoenix. If Muhammad seemed unsettled by Haley's request to write Malcolm's autobiography and not his own, he did not show it. Instead, he told Haley that "Allah" approved of his request and that Malcolm was one of the Nation's most outstanding ministers.[62] Clearly, despite the festering tension between the two men, Muhammad still trusted Malcolm enough to present his autobiography in a way that would further the Nation's program.

From 1963 to early 1964, Haley conducted almost daily interviews with Malcolm. Often late at night, Malcolm would drive to Haley's working studio in Greenwich Village after work. While Haley typed, Malcolm would pace nonstop, talking about Elijah Muhammad and the Nation of Islam, but he would not talk about himself. Whenever Haley reminded him that the book was about him, Malcolm's "hackles would rise."[63]

Then one night, "nearly out on his feet from fatigue," Malcolm arrived at Haley's studio exhausted. For two hours, he paced the floor talking against Muhammad's black critics. Finally, out of sheer frustration, Haley asked him to talk about his mother. He quit pacing, shot Haley a glance, and slowly began talking about his mother. Haley's chance question had the effect of opening him up. "I must have caught him so physically weak," he said later, "that the defenses were vulnerable."[64]

In the end, Malcolm's autobiography was a story of redemption and rebirth. It "wove a dramatic metaphor for the miracle of Islam," said Benjamin 2X.[65] It was "a powerful teaching tool" to win converts to the Nation, said Peter Goldman: "I was this low, and Muhammad raised me up, raised me from the grave."[66] To Paul Lee, however, it was "a propagandistic vehicle," very similar to *Muhammad Speaks*.[67]

For most of the book, interestingly, as Malcolm gradually disclosed his life, he gave no inkling to Haley of the tensions that were developing against him by Elijah Muhammad and the Chicago leadership.

CHAPTER 5

The Rift Deepens

Beginning in 1955, perhaps earlier, Elijah Muhammad had been frequently committing adultery, a serious offense in the Nation of Islam, with a number of young Muslim women employed as his personal secretaries. Seven of them would later claim to have given birth to a total of thirteen children by him.

To seduce his secretaries, Muhammad used a similar story. Allah had revealed to him, he said to each woman, that if she slept with him, she would become a modern day variant of Khadijah, the wife of Muhammad, the original prophet. Sleeping with Elijah, then, was her religious duty. By claiming access to the divine, according to later critics, his sexual conquests became "acts of religious exploitation."[1]

By engaging in extramarital relations, Muhammad was risking both his leadership and marriage. While his reasons for them were difficult to know, the fact that he knew that the FBI was monitoring the Nation and could use them against him made his behavior both irresponsible and dangerous to the movement. According to an FBI report, moreover, his wife and children knew about them but would not act against him because he was their only source of support.[2]

Since 1955, Malcolm had heard rumors of Muhammad's infidelities. But as Malcolm said later, he simply refused to accept anything "so grotesque as adultery mentioned in the same breath with Mr. Muhammad's name."[3] Denial, in fact, was Malcolm's way of dealing with things that bothered him. It was the one trait, he said later, that "he didn't like about himself."[4]

On one occasion, in late 1962, during one of his visits to Chicago to deliver Mosque Number Seven's weekly donations, he saw three young women banging on the side door of Muhammad's house, shouting for him to open the door and give them money in order to buy food for their children. "He immediately felt," he said to his wife afterwards, "that he didn't belong there."[5]

In February 1963, after learning that the rumors of Elijah Muhammad's infidelities were spreading among non–Muslims too, Malcolm met with Wallace Muhammad, who confirmed for him the allegations of his father's infidelities. Throughout his life, said Wallace, he had seen his father, his various secretaries, and their children together. But practicing denial, like Malcolm, Wallace never let these events register in his mind.[6] Later, he could no longer deny them after one of Elijah's former secretaries told him that his father had seduced her and three others collaborated her story with similar ones of their own.[7]

Afterwards, Wallace said that his intention was never to separate or harm the relationship between Malcolm and his father. Yet, for Malcolm, who showed an exceptional closeness and trust with Wallace, his confirmation of his father's infidelities was "shattering."[8] If anyone other than Muhammad's son had told him that, he said later, he would have killed them himself.[9]

At any rate, for Malcolm, the realization of Muhammad's adulterous behavior precipitated an emotional crisis. "I discovered facts," said Malcolm later, "about a man who, up until that discovery, I would gladly have given my life for."[10] "It just took all the wind out of his sails," said his brother Wilfred.[11] "It was the hardest thing talking with him about," said close associate Charles Kenyatta.[12] To Paul Lee, while Muhammad's passive approach to the Stokes incident created a "small crack" in Malcolm's faith in him, the infidelity issue was "the major fissure."[13]

Since the rumors about Muhammad's infidelities had been going around for some time, that Malcolm should now become so upset by them surprised his closest associates. By 1963, however, his problems associated with the Chicago leadership and the developing tensions between Muhammad and himself had become unbearable. In this emotional climate, Muhammad's infidelities, formerly blotted out by Malcolm, now took on added importance.[14]

In 1963, Muhammad's bronchial asthma prevented him from attending the Nation's annual Saviour's Day Rally. Against the wishes of his family, he appointed Malcolm to give its keynote speech. Hence, on the afternoon of February 26, Malcolm addressed over four thousand people at the Chicago International Amphitheater on the Nation's familiar themes: berating the white race, calling for racial separation, and expounding on the glory of Islam. At one point, however, veering from the Nation's format, he called upon the audience to support black empowerment groups, including the NAACP and the Congress of Racial Equality (CORE).[15]

Following Malcolm's speech, others took the podium, including Ministers James Shabazz of Newark, Lonnie X Cross of Atlanta, John Ali and columnist Tynetta Deanar. Sitting in the front row, as usual, Clara Muhammad listened to these speakers frequently praising her absent husband in terms varying from "Lord of the World" to a "likeable black man who really knocks you out."[16] A second meeting convened that night both to attract those who worked in the day and to solicit more donations.

After the rally, making numerous appearances and speeches, Malcolm continued to remain in the Chicago area, further aggravating the tension between the Chicago leadership and himself. Finally, on March 10, Muhammad ordered Malcolm to return to New York City. Before leaving, Malcolm told the press that his wife had fallen and broken her leg, which was true, and he had to return home to assist her.[17]

In April 1963, Malcolm met with Muhammad at his Phoenix home. After alluding to the rumors of infidelity being spread about Muhammad, Malcolm said that Wallace and him had been studying the Koran and the Bible to support the argument that Muhammad's infidelities were the fulfillment of prophecy. Eluding to David's adultery, Lot's incest, and Noah's drunkenness, Malcolm said that their accomplishments outweighed their sins. Accordingly, since Muhammad was an incarnation of all three prophets, his sins, like theirs, was a fulfillment of prophecy.[18]

Before the meetings ended, according to Malcolm, he asked Muhammad for permission to tell other ministers about his fulfillment of prophecy. Then, if the truth came out, said Malcolm, they could better explain it to their members.[19] Although Malcolm said that Muhammad had agreed to this arrangement, he later denied it.[20] The latter was more likely since Muhammad no longer fully trusted Malcolm. In fact, that Muhammad even privately agreed with Malcolm's prophecy explanation was doubtful since that would have been a tacit admission of guilt.

Soon thereafter, Malcolm called together Captain Joseph, Maceo Owens, secretary of Mosque Number Seven, Ministers Lonnie X Cross of Atlanta, Isaiah Karriem of Baltimore, and Louis X of Boston. Malcolm, conceding that the rumors of Muhammad's infidelities were true, interpreted them as a fulfillment of prophecy.[21] Although he knew that they were probably familiar with the rumors, to his surprise, they seemed little concerned about the truth about them.[22]

That Malcolm included Captain Joseph and Louis X among the Nation's officials to inform of Muhammad's infidelities was difficult to understand.

By this time, he should have suspected, if not known before, that they were siding with the Chicago leadership against him. Predictably, "as a way to embarrass him," they told Muhammad that he was spreading rumors and "stirring things up."[23] They would "make it appear," said Malcolm later, that "instead of inoculating against an epidemic, I had started it."[24]

In May 1963, replacing Lucius X, who had failed to properly manage Washington's Mosque Number Four, Muhammad appointed Malcolm as its interim minister. While the FBI considered his transfer a "demotion," he told the press that he would continue as leader of the New York City movement, and that he would maintain residences in both cities.[25] At any rate, Muhammad, in less than a month, had chosen a new resident minister for Mosque Number Four. Still, the transfer, if only temporarily, may have been his way of warning Malcolm to behave himself.

Surveillance and Interference

Throughout the 1950s and 1960s, as a result of the national hysteria over Communism and the rise of the Civil Rights Movement, the FBI, under Director J. Edgar Hoover, who assumed that Communists were behind domestic social-protest movements, increased its surveillance and harassment of the Nation of Islam. Acting like "vacuum cleaners," by clipping news articles, recording radio and television broadcasts, transcribing speeches, taking photos, searching trash bins, opening mails, and conducting break-ins, FBI agents monitored the activities of the Nation's leading officials.[26]

Because Hoover's FBI was made up almost entirely of whites, in its surveillance of the Nation, it had few, if any, black agents trained for undercover work. Consequently, it had to rely on paid informants, which was a less reliable method of obtaining information. Also, it used information obtained from local and state police counterintelligence units, and FBI field offices sent headquarters regular reports on individual mosques and their activities.

Publicly, Muhammad said that he did not fear the FBI. Yet, as occurred in the World War II era, Muhammad sought to avoid a repeat situation when government repression almost destroyed the Nation. He made sure, for instance, that *Muhammad Speaks* regularly reminded its readers, which included the FBI, that Muslims were "law-abiding and unaggressive."[27]

Despite his concerns, however, Muhammad continued to engage in extramarital relations. Predictably, by early 1962, if not before, the FBI became aware of them.[28] Later that year, hoping to discredit him and in the process destabilize the Nation, its Chicago field office sent anonymous letters informing his wife Clara and "selected individuals" of his affairs. In a memorandum to headquarters, Chicago's Special Agent in charge (SAC) wrote that his agents took care "to prevent any possibility to tracing them back to the FBI," including writing them by hand and on "commercially purchased stationery without markings."[29]

Meanwhile, in another memorandum to FBI headquarters, Chicago's SAC proposed informing the Chicago Police Department's Security Unit of Muhammad's extramarital affairs. This would allow it, he wrote, "without embarrassment to the FBI," to conduct an independent police investigation of them, leading, hopefully, to a bastardy charge against him.[30] Nothing came of this, however.

The FBI kept particularly close watch on Malcolm X. Its agents tapped his telephones, bugged his office and meetings, followed him, taped and transcribed his speeches, used informants and questioned friends and neighbors.[31] On occasion, apparently, they even tried to "threaten and frighten" blacks from joining Mosque Number Seven.[32] And according to Malcolm, no fewer than twelve agents regularly watched it.[33]

Within the Nation, a favorite FBI tactic was to have its informants create divisiveness by spreading malicious gossip. As a result, the Nation forbid any gossiping among its members and Malcolm took violations of this rule seriously. In Mosque Number Seven, said Benjamin 2X, members gossiped at their own risk and embarrassment and Malcolm "saw to that."[34]

Along with intense FBI scrutiny, the Bureau of Special Services (BOSS), a branch of the New York City Police Department (NYPD), kept surveillance on Malcolm and his group. It used "all kinds of means to infiltrate the Muslims," said Deputy Commissioner Robert Mangum, including "people to get information."[35] Unlike the FBI, however, BOSS had access to black undercover operatives recruited from both within its own police force and outside ones. Gene Roberts, Malcolm's own bodyguard, in fact, was a BOSS undercover agent.[36]

"We knew," said Captain Joseph later, that Mosque Number Seven was "honeycombed with infiltrators and spies," but "you can't stop" just because of them.[37]

Birmingham and the March on Washington

In Birmingham, Alabama, throughout the spring of 1963, Dr. Martin Luther King's Southern Christian Leadership Conference led a campaign of protest marches to desegregate public facilities and end discriminatory hiring practices. The city's police, led by its commissioner, Eugene "Bull"

Connor, responded to the marches with nightsticks, fire hoses, and attack dogs.

But Bull Connor's tactics backfired. Not only did they not stop the marches, but they brought unfavorable attention to Birmingham. Consequently, on May 10, city officials agreed to desegregate lunch counters, restrooms, and drinking fountains, and end discriminatory hiring practices. "It was," said King afterward, "the most magnificent victory for justice we've ever seen in the deep south."[38]

On the following evening, however, white extremists set off bombs at King's motel headquarters and at the home of his younger brother, A. D. King. Although nobody was hurt, the bombing touched off a night of rioting in the city's black community. Pointing up the failure of King's "turn-the-other-cheek policy," it showed, said Malcolm, that if provoked, blacks would react violently.[39]

Malcolm, moreover, did not view the desegregation of Birmingham's public facilities as helpful to the city's black community. Now they can sit down "with some crackers" in a restaurant and drink coffee, he told reporters, but "they still don't have a job."[40] And as always, he was emphatic in his opposition to King's nonviolent strategy. "You need somebody who is going to fight," he said, not "any kneeling in or crawling in."[41]

In June, calling racial issue a moral issue, President John F. Kennedy sent to Congress the most comprehensive civil rights bill in American history. It included desegregating public accommodations, improving blacks' general economic status, providing federal registrars to enroll them to vote and withholding funds from federally financed facilities that discriminated against them.

With a vote scheduled for August 28, 1963, civil rights leaders, in support of Kennedy's civil rights bill, began preparing for a march on Washington. For many years they had considered the idea of a march on Washington under the slogan "Jobs and Freedom." At first, they wanted to emphasize jobs; but with Kennedy's call for civil rights legislation, they framed the slogan "Freedom Now," which became the main slogan of the civil rights movement.

Since the Nation of Islam was against integration, Elijah Muhammad instructed his followers not to attend the March on Washington. Malcolm threatened to impose a ninety-day suspension of any member of his mosque who attended it. If anyone belonged to a union which required him to participate in it, he said, they had better "get sick."[42] Yet, as an "uninvited observer," he would attend it. That he would have made this decision without Muhammad's permission was doubtful but, at that point, not inconceivable.

Upon arrival in Washington, Malcolm expected to see an angry crowd, made up mainly of young blacks, willing to "lie down in the streets, on airport runways [and] on government lawns" to demand immediate government action on civil rights.[43] Instead, to reporters outside the Statler Hilton Hotel, which served as march headquarters, he said that conservative civil rights leaders, along with white liberals, had converted the march from a militant endeavor to an "integrated, nonviolent and ineffective farce."[44]

Still, to the great surprise of the civil rights leaders, expecting a crowd of much less, 250,000 people, a third of them white, gathered at the Washington Monument. Then, wearing buttons that displayed a black hand clasping a white hand and singing "We Shall Overcome," they marched to the Lincoln Memorial, where Dr. King gave his powerful "I Have a Dream" speech.

Two weeks after the march on Washington, on Sunday morning, September 15, a bomb exploded in Birmingham's Sixteenth Street Baptist Church, which had been the staging point for King's desegregation marches,

On May 16, 1963, Malcolm X speaks to reporters in Washington, D.C. (AP/Wide World Photos).

injuring twenty and killing four black teenage girls. Among northern blacks, the bombing only increased their disillusionment with King's non-violent strategy. "Here you're talking about bombing a church and killing four little girls," said a resident of Harlem, summarizing the community's sentiment, and the "anger at not being able to do something was tremendous."[45]

Meanwhile, to many politicians, the March on Washington demonstrated widespread popular support for civil rights legislation. Eventually, under President Lyndon B. Johnson, Congress passed the Civil Rights Act of 1964 and the Voting Rights Act of 1965, which brought the federal government behind desegregation and for electoral franchisement for black Americans.

Drifting

In late September 1963, in an apparent effort to diminish the tension between them, Elijah Muhammad designated Malcolm X as the Nation of Islam's first national minister. Similarly, embracing him in front of thousands at a Philadelphia Rally, Muhammad praised him as his "most faithful, hardworking minister," who will "follow me until he dies."[46] Despite Muhammad's diplomatic moves, however, this would be their last public appearance together.

The following month, Wallace Muhammad informed Malcolm that his father was continuing to engage in extramarital affairs with young Muslim women. "This thing," said Wallace, "was as bad as it ever was."[47]

In early November, Malcolm defied the Nation's ban on political activism and endorsed a boycott in Queens of store owners who refused to hire blacks. To the Chicago leadership, this action by him was just another instance of his growing independence from their control.[48]

At the same time, on November 10, 1963, Malcolm, in an address to 2000 non–Muslims at the Northern Negro Grass Roots Leadership Conference in Detroit, signaled a major turning point in his orientation. His speech, entitled "A Message to the Grass Roots," was not only less religious and more political, but also implied a willingness to ally himself with non–Muslim militants.

In his speech, Malcolm discussed three basic themes: revolution, bloodshed, and black nationalism, which both Muhammad and the Chicago leadership either avoided discussing or disapproved of. It was, according to biographer James H. Cone, both Malcolm's answer to King's "I Have a Dream" speech and signaled his forthcoming break with Muhammad.[49] "God hardly came into his speech at all," said Peter Goldman, and "neither did Mr. Muhammad."[50]

In his address, unlike King's "Negro Revolution" marked by nonviolence, Malcolm equated revolution, a struggle over land, with bloodshed. Along with black nationalism in the United States, he identified the worldwide black revolutions with the Mau Mau in Kenya, the Algerian "bloody battle" with France, the Cuban Revolution, and the liberation struggles throughout the Asian continent.

Using slavery as an analogy, Malcolm made a distinction between house Negroes, the Uncle Toms, and the field Negroes, the masses. The modern Uncle Toms, the civil rights leaders, allowed white men to use them to restrain the masses from making a "real" revolution. To Malcolm, the March on Washington was an example of Uncle Toms allowing white men to take it over by both accepting their money and acquiescing to their demand on integrating it. Consequently, he said, it lost its militancy and became a "sell out."[51]

While Malcolm's "Message to the Grass Roots" expressed his disillusionment with the Nation's lack of political involvement in the black freedom struggles, he was also becoming disenchanted with its "cultic" religious beliefs and more interested in Orthodox Islam.[52] Since 1962, in fact, he had been discussing its tenets with a Sudanese Muslim, Ahmed Osman. Malcolm, according to biographer Louis DeCaro, found his appeals to Orthodox Islam irresistible since he could not ignore "reasonable, intelligent presentations."[53]

Along with Osman, Wallace Muhammad and his brother, Akbar, studying at Egypt's Al-Azhar University, had adopted many of the beliefs of Orthodox Islam and encouraged Malcolm, who admired both of them, to study it.

By the fall of 1963, Malcolm faced the dilemma of whether to remain in the Nation of Islam or to leave it. He no longer agreed with its nonengagement political stance and its view of Islam. The Nation had been his life for many years, and Elijah Muhammad had been like a father to him. Yet, the tensions within Malcolm had become too great for him to continue to slavishly follow Muhammad's policies. But the answer to his dilemma was still unclear to him.

CHAPTER 6

Disobedience and Suspension

On November 22, 1963, as President John F. Kennedy was riding in a motorcade parade in Dallas, Texas, shots rang out, killing him instantly. Along with whites, blacks, viewing him favorably because of his proposed civil rights legislation, grieved over his loss.

Within hours after the assassination, Elijah Muhammad ordered his ministers to make no public statements on it and to answer all queries with "no comment."[1] In this way, he hoped to prevent national grief, especially from blacks, to go against the Nation of Islam, whose officials had criticized Kennedy's belated civil rights efforts.

Disobedience

Malcolm X was particularly critical of Kennedy. At one point, he equated him with George C. Wallace, Alabama's segregationist governor. At Malcolm's first talk after the assassination, his followers, anxious to hear his views on it, packed Mosque Number Seven. Following Muhammad's orders, however, Malcolm refused to comment on it. Even so, he would not remain silent on it much longer.

Scheduled to speak at New York's Manhattan Center on December 1, 1963, Muhammad, to avoid giving in to the temptation of speaking out against Kennedy, canceled it. But since the Nation was unable to get back its rental money, according to Malcolm, he volunteered to take his place. Apparently, like Muhammad, nervous about what he might say, Malcolm discarded his usual method of using note cards and typed out his speech, entitled "God's Judgment on White America," a typical Nation of Islam theme. Then, he read it to a crowd of seven hundred people, including John Ali, who was there monitoring his talk for the Chicago leadership.[2]

In his address, Malcolm made no reference to Kennedy's assassination nine days earlier. But during the question and answer session, when asked by a woman to comment on it, Malcolm accused Kennedy of condoning the assassinations of Congo leader Patrice Lumumba and South Vietnamese leader Ngo Dinh Diem and Ngo Dinh Nhu. Kennedy, said Malcolm, "never foresaw that the chickens would come home to roost so soon." As the audience of Muslims laughed and applauded, he said that "being an old farm boy myself, chickens coming home to roost never did make me sad." As a huge grin spread across his face, he added, to the audience's glee, "they've always made me glad."

To more laughter and applause, Malcolm said that the white press had been baiting Muslim officials with questions about the assassination hoping to trap them into making a "fantastic inflexibly dogmatic statement," such as "Hooray, I'm glad he got it!"[3]

While the crowd laughed and applauded at Malcolm's remarks, John Ali sat unsmiling, and Captain Joseph appeared surprised. "I was really taken aback," he said later. "I couldn't understand that."[4] To them, Malcolm's remarks were more about "authority, rivalry, and betrayal" than about Kennedy's assassination, and they relayed them back to the Chicago leadership, who then informed Muhammad.[5]

Although making impolite comments to get media attention was part of Malcolm's strategy, not withstanding the fact that Kennedy's assassination was an extraordinary, traumatic national event, he disobeyed Muhammad's order to remain silent. As an act of rebellion, Malcolm was, in effect, both challenging Muhammad's power and daring him to do something about it.

Suspension

On December 2, the day after his Manhattan Center speech, Malcolm met with Muhammad at his Phoenix home for one of their regular monthly visits. After their customary embrace, Muhammad showed Malcolm newspaper headlines regarding his remarks on Kennedy's assassination. Since the whole country was in mourning, said Muhammad, making them was inimical to the Nation of Islam's interests. He then imposed on Malcolm a ninety-day suspension as the Nation's spokesman.[6]

In short, Malcolm had forced Muhammad's hand. He had to exert his authority both to impress upon the Nation's followers that the center of power resided in Chicago, not New York City, and that Muhammad, not Malcolm, headed the movement.

Malcolm assumed that his suspension as the Nation's spokesman was to remain, if possible, a private matter within it.[7] Upon returning to New York City, however, he learned that the Chicago leadership had announced his suspension to the news media and informed Mosque Number Seven's officials that he was no longer their minister. They told us, said Benjamin 2X, that if Malcolm came back to the mosque, "we should give him a job washing dishes in the restaurant."[8]

In a phone conversation to Muhammad on December 4, Malcolm sought clarification on his suspension status. As he understood it, he said, although he could neither make pubic speeches nor give press statements, he could continue his duties as minister of Mosque Number Seven, which included giving his weekly sermons. In reply, Muhammad said that while Malcolm could continue the mosque's administrative functions, the ban on public speaking also applied to his weekly sermons. Then, to Malcolm's surprise, Muhammad extended his suspension from ninety days to an indefinite period, whose end Muhammad would determine.[9]

By greatly diminishing Malcolm's authority at Mosque Number Seven, Muhammad's actions had enhanced the power of Captain Joseph, who now could select guest ministers to give the mosque's weekly sermons.[10]

During this time, Peter Goldman phoned Malcolm to express his sorrow over the way Muhammad had "set him down." By this time, because of Goldman's numerous *Newsweek* articles on Malcolm, which he approved of, a bond of sorts had developed between the two men. To Goldman, Malcolm, talking longer than usual, seemed worried, and Goldman sensed a vulnerability in him that he had never noticed before.[11]

Yet, that Malcolm would not have known that Muhammad would punish him for disobeying his orders to remain silent on Kennedy's assassination was doubtful. By his act of disobedience, in effect, Malcolm was declaring his independence from Muhammad's command. Acting swiftly, he, in turn, suspended Malcolm as a show of authority to the Nation's followers.[12] Still, Muhammad's action carried some risk. If he pushed Malcolm too far, he might go public over Muhammad's extramarital affairs as well as the Chicago leadership's financial abuses: either one of which would hurt the Nation.

To the press, Malcolm's suspension was Muhammad's way of ridding himself "of a dangerous rival."[13] Malcolm's "incautious remarks," editorialized the *New York Courier,* gave Muhammad the opportunity to cut him down to size, which he did "in a crude and abrupt manner."[14] "Insiders are predicting a split in the black Muslims," observed the *Chicago Sun Times*.[15] And according to the *New York Times*, Malcolm had become "so powerful" that he emerged as a "personality" rather than "as a spokesman for the movement."[16]

Malcolm's Weakening Position

On January 2, 1964, in an angry phone call to Malcolm, Muhammad ordered him to stop meddling in his private affairs and "to put out this fire." Malcolm was his "property," he said, and "could not prove any of this." He admitted, however, that competing factions and jealousies were a problem with the Nation, and that he was "just a man as the rest of them." Then, referring to Malcolm's friendship with Wallace, Muhammad criticized his son for taking family matters to outsiders.

Throughout the conversation, as usual, when speaking with Muhammad, Malcolm remained submissive, apologizing repeatedly for any mistakes that he may have made. But for Muhammad, whom Malcolm once considered like a father, to refer to him as an "outsider," despite the distance that had grown between them, must have deeply hurt him. Muhammad, on the other hand, was less concerned with Malcolm's feelings than how ungrateful he had been to the man who had helped him so much for the past twelve years. In the end, Muhammad repeated that Malcolm's suspension was for an indefinite period.[17]

Three days later, Muhammad, stripping Malcolm of all power, designated Minister James Shabazz of Newark's mosque to head Mosque Number Seven, the second most powerful base in the Nation of Islam.

The next day, January 6, in an unusual procedure, since the Nation's custom required the accused to have a hearing before members of his mosque, Muhammad, along with Raymond Sharrief and John Ali, ordered Malcolm to Phoenix for a closed hearing. This meeting, the last between the two men, was Muhammad's way of making his power play against Malcolm official. By and large, the meeting was similar to the telephone conversation between the two men four days earlier. Once again, Muhammad blamed Malcolm for instigating the rumors of his alleged infidelities, ordering him "to put out this fire."[18]

Back in New York City not long afterwards, while walking down Harlem's Amsterdam Avenue, Malcolm and his associate Charles Kenyatta, a well-muscled ex-convict, encountered a young Muslim brother standing nearby with "his fists clenched at his sides." Almost in tears, he said that one of Mosque Number Seven's officials, most likely Captain Joseph, told him that Malcolm was talking against Muhammad, and "if you knew what he said, you'd kill him yourself."[19]

The two men, shaking their heads, walked away while the young brother stared back at them.

Knowing how the Nation operated, Malcolm realized that any order to kill him would have had to first originate with Muhammad. He would have given it indirectly, said Malcolm later, as a veiled suggestion, not as an order, although others would take it as such.[20] The "death talk" concerned Malcolm less, however, than Muhammad's lack of appreciation for his twelve years of loyalty to him.[21] Likewise, Muhammad resented Malcolm's deviation from the Nation's nonpolitical stance and his loss of faith in its portrayal of Islam.

According to Malcolm, the reasons behind the conflict included both the Chicago leadership's jealousy over his media prominence and Muhammad's fear that he would go public with his extramarital affairs. While important, they expressed the symptoms, not the cause of the conflict, which had more to do with whether Chicago, directed by Muhammad, or New York, under Malcolm's leadership, would control the Nation's wealth and power.

By 1963, if not before, Muhammad feared that Malcolm, whose independence from him had become apparent, was challenging his leadership. Yet, Muhammad, by giving Malcolm an indefinite suspension and stripping his ministry, had inadvertently solved his dilemma of whether to remain in the Nation or leave it. "As a longtime hustler," he later told a reporter, "I sensed that once again, I had to leave town fast."[22]

Nevertheless, leaving the Nation of Islam left Malcolm in a "state of emotional shock." He felt "as though something in nature had failed," he said later, "too stupendous to conceive."[23] Complaining of splitting headaches, he went to his doctor, Leona A. Turner, who concluded that they were more psychological than physiological and that he "needed a rest."[24]

The Cassius Clay Interlude

Malcolm had first met Cassius Clay, a leading heavyweight boxer, at a Detroit rally in 1962. At that time, Malcolm had never heard of him. "He acted as if I was supposed to know who he was," recalled Malcolm, "so I acted as though I did."[25] Impressed by Clay's self-assuredness, however, he came to like him. In turn, hearing Malcolm speak, Clay considered him "so bold" that "God must be protecting him."[26] Soon, they became friends.

On January 15, 1964, to act as his spiritual advisor, Clay invited Malcolm and his family, with all expenses paid by him, down to Miami, Florida, where he was in training to challenge Sonny "the Bear" Liston for the heavy-weight championship. For Malcolm, Clay's invitation came at the right time, allowing him to fulfill his doctor's prescription for a needed rest. "I must always be grateful to him for that," said Malcolm later.[27]

Although Clay had completed the requirements for membership into the Nation of Islam, the Chicago leadership decided to hold up his registration and original name until after the fight. Officially, they could justify this by the fact that the Nation's rules forbid its members from either participating in or becoming a spectator of commercial sports, viewing them as useless diversions. Even so, the Nation discovered that it could not enforce these rules and overlooked violations of them by its members. In truth, the Chicago leadership did not think Clay had "a prayer of a chance to win," and if he lost, linking the Muslim image with him would embarrass the Nation.[28]

While Clay remained silent on any affiliation with the Nation of Islam, reporters automatically identified him as a Muslim. During his press conferences, they asked him less about the fight and more about his views on politics, race, and world affairs. At Liston's press conferences, on the other hand, their questions centered around the upcoming fight.[29]

When Malcolm walked into the Fifth Street Gym where Clay was working out, his trainers, fearing a white backlash against their man, panicked. At first, they demanded that Clay stay away from him. But for the fight of his life, Clay said that he needed Malcolm by his side for spiritual sustenance. They asked Clay, then, to keep his relationship with him discreet, but this too, proved impossible.[30]

Clay spent a lot of time with Malcolm and his family, who were staying at Miami's Hampton House Motel. While Malcolm, with a camera hanging around his neck, constantly took pictures, Clay, a natural born actor, joked with reporters, kissed babies, and played with Malcolm's three little girls.[31] To reporters, Malcolm praised Clay as a true champion who neither smoked, drank, nor chased women. "He is one of the few Negroes," he added, "we can look up to with adulation" and "who is also accepted by the white community."[32]

Malcolm and Betty, who was pregnant with their fourth child, also spent some time together. Nearly every night, they walked through Miami's black neighborhoods. But after only four days in the city, Betty and her children, for no discernible reason, flew back to New York City.

Before long, Malcolm recognized that Clay was not only a good boxer but also a master at psychological warfare. So that Liston would enter the ring overconfident, uncertain, and angry, Clay's goal was to convince him that he was both crazy and arrogant. With reporters, he clowned, read poetry, talked loud, brandished a cane, and slandered Liston, calling him "a big ugly bear." The press, according to observer George Plimpton, referred to Clay's antics as either an "act" or "born of terror or lunacy."[33]

Several weeks before the February 25 bout, the fight's promoter, Bill McDonald, discovered that his assistants had sold only enough tickets to fill half of the 15,744 seats at Miami's Convention Hall. He attributed the lack of sales to whites' concerns over rumors of Clay's affiliation with the Nation of Islam and his friendship with Malcolm. To resolve the problem, McDonald persuaded both Malcolm to leave town until the night of the fight and Clay to make no announcement of his Muslim affiliation until after the fight, which he had intended to do anyway.[34]

On February 4, while Malcolm was in New York City waiting to return for the Miami fight, two FBI agents appeared at his home. During their hour long interview of him, he would neither discuss his suspension with them nor furnish them with any information about the Nation of Islam except that which they would have known from public sources. Finally, frustrated by his obstinacy, they offered him money for information. In reply, he asked them "not to insult his intelligence" since the Nation's teachings were public and well known to the government.[35]

Two days before the February 25 fight, Malcolm returned to Miami to help Clay mentally prepare for it. Malcolm pictured the fight as a modern day crusade with a Muslim and a Christian facing each other and the whole world watching them. "Do you think," he said, "Allah has brought about all this intending for you to leave the ring as anything but the champion?"[36]

Only hours before the fight at Miami's Convention Hall, Clay threw a fit as Liston entered the room at the weigh-in ceremony. Pounding his cane on the floor, Clay shouted that he was ready to "rumble there and then." Visibly trembling, he lunged at Liston, but his aides restrained him. Afterwards, the fight doctor noted that Clay's pulse was beating at one-hundred twenty, twice its normal rate. To Malcolm, however, Clay's behavior was just another one of his "carefully planned provocations" to unnerve Liston.[37]

Clay continued his antics even in the ring. Just before the bell rang to start the fight, for instance, he leaned over the ropes to where the press sat and in the manner of a school teacher admonished them for predicting his defeat. "It's your last chance to get on the bandwagon," he said. "After the fight, you will be eating your words." Considering the circumstances, said George Plimpton, his speech was "wonderfully, preposterous," yet none of them even smiled.[38]

The fight was fast and furious. Liston carried the first two rounds. Clay bounced back in the third, leaving a gash under Liston's left eye. In the fourth, some kind of "chemical" got into Clay's eyes, but the bell saved him. Although he could barely see during the fifth, in the sixth, with his sight restored, he went on the offensive, pounding Liston with left-right combinations and uppercuts. As a result, Liston was unable to emerge from his corner in the seventh, and Clay, at twenty-two years old, was now the heavyweight champion of the world.[39]

On the following day, Clay informed reporters that he was a Muslim and a follower of Elijah Muhammad. In turn, on February 26, while speaking at the Nation's annual Saviour's Day rally, Muhammad ended his silence on Clay, welcoming him into the Nation. For Muhammad, Clay, as heavyweight champion, would bring to it national attention, money to its coffers, and replace Malcolm as a defiant symbol to attract young, disaffected blacks. Not long after, in appreciation, Muhammad bestowed upon Clay one of its highest honors: an Arabic holy name, Muhammad Ali.

With Clay, now Ali, in the Nation of Islam, Malcolm had lost not only a potential ally but also a good friend, and this deeply hurt him. In a voice betraying his hurt, he told Alex Haley that Ali had been "like a blood big-brother to him," but he had allowed Elijah Muhammad to use him, "to lead him astray."[40]

On March 1, 1964, after viewing the screening of a film about Ali's title fight with Sonny Liston, world heavyweight boxing champion Muhammad Ali (right) is shown with Malcolm X outside the Trans-Lux newsreel theater in New York (AP/Wide World Photos).

Malcolm's Decision

Back in New York City, Malcolm learned from Lukman X, a member of Mosque Number Seven, that Captain Joseph had ordered him to wire Malcolm's car with a bomb. He had picked Lukman X for the job, apparently, because he had acquired demolition training as one of Fidel Castro's freedom fighters during Cuba's 1959 revolution. But according to Lukman X, he had seen too much of Malcolm's "loyalty to the Nation" to participate in an assassination plot against him.[41] Malcolm, suspecting Lukman X of being a police agent, only half believed his assassination story.[42] Still, he gave it to the *Amsterdam News,* a black newspaper, to better prepare himself and his followers for an imminent break from the Nation.

Playing a role in Malcolm's strategy was Benjamin 2X. At a Mosque Number Seven meeting, holding up a copy of the *Amsterdam News,* he said that "Captain Joseph had sent Brother Lukman to plant a bomb in Brother Malcolm's car."[43] Then, in a dramatic gesture, he threw the newspaper down on the floor and walked out of the mosque. About a third of the audience, he said later, also disenchanted with the Nation, applauded and walked out with him.[44]

On March 2, 1964, Malcolm's ninety-day suspension had expired. Hearing nothing from Muhammad about it, he petitioned him by letter for a clarification of his status. In reply, Muhammad wrote that Malcolm had not remained silent since he had both talked to reporters in New York City and hobnobbed with others while in Miami for the Clay fight. Although technically correct, to Malcolm, these may have seemed like small errors of judgment, not gross violations. Nevertheless, Muhammad wrote that his suspension would continue indefinitely.[45] By this time, Malcolm may have reasoned that he could do nothing right by Muhammad's standards.

Muhammad's letter had convinced Malcolm that the time had come to publicly announce his break from the Nation of Islam. Although not an easy decision for him to make, it was long in the making. Before his suspension, in fact, he had realized that he could no longer slavishly abide by either the Nation's political or religious positions. In his speeches, moreover, he had been expressing his changing positions: talking more political than religious and urging social activism.

By 1963, if not before, the conflict between Malcolm and Muhammad, a struggle for control of the movement's direction, had become irreconcilable. To Paul Lee, Muhammad had to "force Malcolm out of the Nation of Islam since he would not have left it on his own initiative."[46] Yet, by discussing Muhammad's infidelities with other ministers and violating his orders to remain silent on Kennedy's assassination, Malcolm had forced Muhammad's hand. In that sense, then, the decision for Malcolm to leave the Nation was made by both men: himself and Muhammad.

CHAPTER 7

The Break

On March 8, 1964, at a press conference in Harlem's Theresa Hotel, Malcolm X announced a "declaration of independence" from the Nation of Islam. Blaming it on internal rivalry and personal jealousy, he said that he was not trying to split the Nation, urging its members to remain in it, but that he could better spread Muhammad's message by leaving it to work among America's twenty-two million blacks.

To the reporters, Malcolm criticized the Nation for being too narrowly sectarian and expressed his goals as forming a black nationalist party, engaging in social action against the oppressor, aligning with civil rights organizations, and persuading blacks to reject nonviolence for active self-defense against white supremacists. All of them, in fact, were inconsistent with the nation's program.

Elijah Muhammad had prevented him from participating in civil rights struggles, said Malcolm, but that he was going to join in the fight now "wherever Negroes ask for help." But to describe the nonviolent "Negro revolution" as a real revolution, he said, was nonsense. Using examples from the American, French, and Algerian revolutions, he added, he would tell blacks that revolution meant "shedding blood."[1]

Later that day, an angry Muhammad, learning that Malcolm was leaving the Nation, informed Captain Joseph that the former minister must give up his house and everything else that belonged to it. Two days later, Joseph led a delegation of Muslims to Malcolm's house in Elmhurst, handing him a notarized letter demanding that he surrender his house and all valuables belonging to the Nation. Although he gave them some things, such as papers of incorporation and securities from the Nation's national treasury, he refused to vacate the premises.[2]

Considering Malcolm's failure to vacate the house a "showdown," Muhammad began eviction proceedings against him.[3] To Malcolm, the brick bungalow, assessed at $16,200, was all he had to provide for his family.[4] If he vacated it, moreover, he would lose face to Muhammad, and that was something Malcolm's pride would not allow him to do.

Two days later, on March 12, to a jammed press conference at the Sheraton Hotel in midtown Manhattan, Malcolm announced the formation of the Muslim Mosque Inc. (MMI). For his followers, he said, it would provide both a spiritual and political base, welcome both nonbelievers and blacks of all faiths, and encompass the political philosophy of black nationalism, meaning blacks controlling their own communities. But whites could not join it, he said, because blacks cannot "think of being acceptable to others" until they have first proven acceptable to themselves.

Malcolm appeared ambivalent about working with civil rights leaders. He would, he said, forget everything bad that they had said about him, and he prayed that they could forget the many bad things he had said about them. As usual, however, he emphasized his adamant opposition to their commitment to nonviolence. They were acting "criminal," he said, to teach men not to defend themselves when they were "the constant victims of brutal attacks."

To defend their lives and property, Malcolm said that blacks should form rifle clubs. They should remain peaceful, he said, but if they are unjustly and unlawfully attacked, they should "fight back in self-defense." If the government considered him wrong for saying this, then it should start doing its job.

Recruiting youths "completely disenchanted with the old, adult established politicians," said Malcolm, would become one of MMI's most important goals. So as not to become the victim of another "political sellout," like the 1960 election where politicians promised much but delivered little, the MMI would keep its position on the 1964 presidential election secret until a later date.[5]

In the question and answer session, Malcolm said that he had made no effort to draw away any of Elijah Muhammad's followers, although some had come over to him. At any rate, he would neither reveal their numbers nor that of his supporters. As a member of the Nation of Islam, he said, he had learned "never to let your opponent know how strong you are," but "to keep him guessing." And "you will have him at a disadvantage."[6]

In his accustomed manner, Malcolm expertly handled difficult questions. Asked, for instance, if he would accept Communist support, he said that if he was trapped in a wolf's den, he would not care who opened the door and let him out. And when asked if he would garner widespread black support, he said that he would not have taken "extreme positions" unless he had "colored people" behind him. "You would not," he added, "get me to stick my neck out alone."[7]

Reaction

In response to Malcolm's declaration of independence and his formation of a separate organization, reporters twice converged on Muhammad's home in Phoenix. Each time, he expressed surprise at Malcolm's actions and emphasized that every member in the Nation of Islam had admired him. Now that he had left it, however, Muhammad referred to him as a "hypocrite," which to his followers meant someone who had rejected the guidance of "God's messenger."[8]

Malcolm's call for the formation of black rifle clubs concerned Muhammad. Fearful that the FBI would now intensify its surveillance of the Nation, he warned his followers that the devil was watching them and to keep their guns in their homes. Similarly, to the press, he stressed the Nation's peaceful nature, and that its members "do not carry guns or arms of any kind."[9]

Breaking from the Nation had made Malcolm an even more dangerous rival for Muhammad. It increased the rise in the possibility that Malcolm might go public with Muhammad's extramarital affairs, the Chicago leadership's corruption, or the Nation's dealings with the Ku Klux Klan and the Nazi party. Either one of the three could do incalculable damage to the Nation. Accordingly, Muhammad ordered Philbert X to warn Malcolm that "he was going to get himself in trouble at the rate he was going."[10]

In the escalating conflict, Muhammad had the advantage of a large organization, scores of FOI soldiers, and a newspaper whose subscribers numbered in the thousands. Malcolm, on the other hand, lacked supporters, money, and a power base. Yet, he still received widespread media attention and the support of young blacks disenchanted with King's nonviolent strategy.[11] Nevertheless, Malcolm did not have the resources to counter a carefully constructed Nation of Islam Jihad, a holy war, against him.

Soon, the Nation began an open campaign against Malcolm. While *Muhammad Speaks* began a series of weekly tirades against him, Muhammad openly denounced him as "doing more running off at the mouth than he can back up," and "whenever a brother walks away from us, all is gone."[12] In private, however, he was more direct, referring to Malcolm as the "chief hypocrite," "no good long-legged Malcolm," and "Judas." "The only way to stop him," said Muhammad, "was to get rid of him the way Moses and the others did with their bad ones."[13]

Malcolm's call for blacks to form rifle clubs got the most attention from the press. To the *New York Times*, "It was a call to arms against duly constituted police forces."[14] Baltimore's *The Evening Sun* said that it "damaged the cause of equal rights."[15] It mocks, said political observer Max Lerner, "the courage and devotion of millions of Negroes and whites working for a better America."[16] But to his colleague, Dick Schaap, Malcolm X was "too eloquent to be ignored."[17] And according to the *Washington Post*, Malcolm's assertion that "there can be no revolution without bloodshed" was real, forming "a cloud on the horizon" as the Senate debated the civil rights bill.[18]

Several top civil rights leaders also spoke out against Malcolm's call for black rifle clubs. He was "asking for a race war," said James Farmer, the director of the Congress of Racial Equality (CORE), "which can only end in anguish for the nation."[19] To Whitney M. Young, executive director of the National Urban League, America's blacks were under "no illusions" that they could "win a shooting war," hoping instead "to achieve victory through the power of right and justice."[20] By advocating rifle clubs, said Robert Long, president of Chicago's Urban League, Malcolm X was "really showing his colors."[21]

While referring to Malcolm's call for blacks to arm themselves as unfortunate, Dr. King recognized the value of using it as a means to frighten whites into passing the civil rights bill. If Congress watered it down, he warned, "responsible Negro leadership will find it much more difficult to keep the struggle disciplined and nonviolent."[22]

Not all blacks rejected the goals of Malcolm's new organization. Many blacks, said activist Bayard Rustin, lacking good jobs, decent housing, and adequate education, were beginning to lean towards "Malcolm's analysis."[23] "He can offer something that has not been offered before," said activist Gloria Richardson.[24] To Reverend Richard A. Hildebrand, "I welcome anybody who is going to help the civil rights struggle."[25] And James Forman, the Student Nonviolent Coordinating Committee's (SNCC) executive director, said that Malcolm's new position "opens up possibilities for non–Muslim blacks."[26]

Clarification

Functioning both as MMI's office and mosque, Suite 128, located on the Theresa Hotel's mezzanine floor, was Malcolm's main base. It consisted of one long room, crowded with folding chairs, and off to the side, he had made himself a semi-private office. Here, in his office suite, he would hold his frequent press conferences and talk with the many people, including reporters, photographers, camp followers, and United Nations delegates, who sought his time and attention.

Right off, Malcolm gathered with reporters to clarify his positions taken at his March 8 and 12 press conferences. With his statement on the need to form rifle clubs, he said, he did not, as reported by some, advocate armed rebellion. What he meant was that in cases where the federal government had "proved itself unable or unwilling" to protect blacks, they "have a right to defend themselves."[27] To make his point to reporters, he would often reach into his billfold and take out a small card, reading to them Article II of the United States Constitution, which gave the people the right "to keep and bear arms."[28]

To newsman Dick Schaap, however, Malcolm "wallowed in contradictions." He was, said Schaap, "not for violence" and operated "within the law," but on the other hand, chatting with a European reporter, who had covered revolutions in Africa and Southeast Asia, Malcolm was "speaking longingly of guerrilla warfare, of sniping and violence in the streets."[29]

On the need for blacks to arm themselves, in his speeches, Malcolm was unequivocal. The time to "fight back" was now, he said. Blacks need either a rifle or a shotgun in their homes; if attacked, they should "fight back like men" and "be ready to die like Patrick Henry." Those who followed him, he said, better be prepared to go either to jail, to the hospital, or to the cemetery, but "not without a fight" and "not without a reason."[30]

But blacks should not die alone. They can only die honorably, said Malcolm, by taking their enemies with them. When blacks die alone, moreover, whites do not look upon their deaths as bloodshed. Only when blacks shed white blood, he said, will whites consider the conflict "a bloody one." Therefore, he said, shedding blood should "be reciprocal."[31]

Despite Malcolm's violent rhetoric, his personal behavior was nonviolent. Benjamin 2X had never known him to commit a violent act.[32] Malcolm X had "never directly led an incident of violence," said newsman Dick Schaap. He preached it, but "no one ever saw him in a fight."[33] He "shrank from the fact of violence," said Peter Goldman.[34] "Behind his grim television image," said Bayard Rustin, "there was a compassionate and often gentle man with a sense of humor."[35]

Malcolm predicted that the summer of 1964 would become the "hottest" one in American history, since blacks were "awake" and would "explode."[36] He was only giving the warning, he said, not "trying to set the spark."[37] Whites, he added, "will be shocked when they discover that the passive little Negro they had known turns out to be a roaring lion."[38]

Maintaining that he was still a follower of Muhammad, Malcolm said that his "love and respect" for him was higher today than when he had joined the Nation twelve years ago.[39] But since he was given to making embarrassing statements, said Malcolm, he could better stay out of the Nation and work among blacks to make them aware that the only "real analysis" was Muhammad's "diagnosis and solution."[40]

Likewise, Malcolm blamed others, meaning the Chicago leadership, not Muhammad, for forcing him out of the Nation. Because some elements within the Nation thought that he was trying to take it over, said Malcolm, they used his assassination remarks as a pretext to banish him.[41] Thus, he broke from the Nation in order to both circumvent these elements and "expedite Muhammad's program as he understood it."[42]

With his break from the Nation, Malcolm's attitude towards whites did not appear to have changed much, if at all. While he told reporters that he was not "anti-white," only "anti-oppression," he would, at times, continue to refer to whites as devils. Asked if there were any good whites, he said that some of them might be sincere, although he had not met any of them.[43] He reserved his most severe criticism, however, for white liberals, charging them with attempting both to control the civil rights movement and to persuade its leaders to accept "crumbs."[44]

Yet, in his personal dealings with whites, Malcolm expressed neither animosity nor resentment of them; and although often accused of anti–Semitism, his blanket condemnation of whites did not appear to focus on any particular religious group. He was favorable, however, to college students, both white and black. While many black students were "eager to be part of a militant action group," he said, he also had faith in white students, whom he urged to "redirect their attention to the oppressed."[45]

Both on principle and fact, Malcolm said that he continued to oppose integration. "I couldn't integrate with my enemy," he said, and "I know who my enemy is."[46] He lambasted the 1954 Supreme Court decision calling for desegregation of America's public schools as being an impossible goal. "I'd rather you don't give me anything," he said, "than give me a check that I cannot cash."[47]

Still, Malcolm's position on civil rights struggles was not always entirely clear. In Harlem, he agreed to cooperate in two of them going on at the time, including one dealing with school integration. These included Milton Galamison's school boycott to end de facto racial segregation in New York City's public schools and Jesse Gray's rent strike for affordable housing. But except for verbal declarations of support for the school boycott and a speech at one of Gray's rallies, he did little else for them.

At subsequent press conferences, Malcolm clarified his definition of black nationalism. It was not, he said, as the Nation of Islam often defined it, neither repatriating to Africa nor partitioning off a separate state within America. It meant, he said, instead of whites controlling the black community, which was the case, blacks would exercise power over it. They would control its politics and schools, own its businesses, apartment buildings, and houses, and check its social problems, such as alcoholism and drug abuse. Once empowered, he added, they would no longer have to "beg some cracker for a job in his business."[48]

At times, Malcolm implied that black nationalism also meant that blacks would form both their own political party and army.[49] He often described it, too, as "a way of life," rejecting white symbols and culture and emphasizing, instead, "pride in being black."[50]

To advocate black nationalism, Malcolm told a group of Methodist ministers in New York City that he would adopt evangelist Billy Graham's method of preaching. But instead of preaching Christ's gospel to large audiences of people from different Christian denominations and telling them to go back to their churches and practice it, as he did, Malcolm would urge black audiences to join any group that was practicing black nationalism. But if its leaders were "pussyfooting or compromising" on black nationalism, he would tell blacks to "pull out of that group" and "find another one."[51]

At the same time, Malcolm began to internationalize America's race problems. Unlike civil rights leaders, who perceived it within the American context, he considered it a part of the African, Asian, and Latin American anti-imperialist "racial explosions." He proposed, moreover, presenting the case of American blacks to the United Nations (UN). In this way, they would both have the support of their Third World brothers and show the world the American government's hypocrisy.[52]

The Ballot or the Bullet

On April 3, 1964, at a CORE sponsored meeting in Cleveland, Malcolm summarized his evolving political views in a speech entitled the "Ballot or the Bullet," which he would thereafter give in various forms on different occasions. In some ways, his speech presented a counter-argument to Dr. King's August 1963 "I Have a Dream" speech.

In his speech, Malcolm said that he was not an American but a victim of "Americanism," and that democracy was "nothing but disguised hypocrisy." As a victim of this American system, he did not "see any American dream" but instead "an American nightmare." And in an election year, he said, that American system would force blacks to use either the "ballot or the bullet." The white politicians would come into the black communities with their trickery, treachery, and false promises, building up blacks' hopes, which would lead to one thing, an explosion.

In the close vote of the 1960 election, Malcolm said that the black vote put the Democrats in power. But although they passed "every kind of legislation imaginable," they saved blacks for the last. He was not trying to knock out the Democrats for the Republicans, he said, but when blacks put the Democrats first, Democrats put blacks last.

There existed a government conspiracy, said Malcolm, to deprive blacks of their voting rights, economic and educational opportunities, and decent housing. He held the government itself responsible "for the oppression and exploitation and degradation of black people in this country."

Calling President Lyndon B. Johnson, from Texas, a "Southern cracker," Malcolm said that the Dixiecrats, who came from states where blacks cannot vote, controlled the key congressional committees that ran the Congress. And the northern whites controlled black votes by gerrymandering — changing district lines to favor the white vote.

To Malcolm, America's twenty-two million blacks were waking up and becoming more politically mature. But if the government continued to deny them the vote, "it's going to end up in a situation where we're going to have to cast a bullet," he said. "It's either a ballot or a bullet."[53]

Back in New York City, Malcolm continued to repeat his "ballots or bullets" theme. Calling for a massive black voter registration drive, he said that those who did not register "should be run out of town." In some parts of the country, he added, "in order to start casting ballots, you have to have some bullets," so it's time to let the government know that "it's ballots or bullets."[54]

The Nation of Islam's Continuing Offensive

Flown into Chicago from Lansing on March 26, 1964, Philbert X, with John Ali by his side, read a prepared statement to a room crowded with reporters at the Nation of Islam's Shabazz Restaurant. Speaking in a monotonous tone, Philbert blamed Malcolm's break over his resentment of the suspension that Muhammad imposed upon him for violating his orders to remain silent on Kennedy's assassination. "Now," said Philbert, "Malcolm resorts to slander, slurs, and intimidation of Mr. Muhammad."

Calling Malcolm a hypocrite for betraying Muhammad, Philbert said that his brother was pursuing "a dangerous course," paralleling that of previous traitors, such as "Judas, Benedict Arnold, and Brutus." And those who followed Malcolm, he said, were themselves traitors and undesirables.

Then, calling Malcolm the victim of "a great mental illness," which beset his mother and one of his brothers, Philbert accused him of trying to smear Muhammad's name by using women "who have been dismissed from our group" because "they were weak and went contrary to Islam." Finally, he told reporters to warn "those who may be taken in by my brother's desire to promote his own selfish end."[55]

Later, Philbert said that he had brought his own statement to read at the press conference. Just as he was about to read it, however, John Ali placed a paper in front of him to read. "If I had looked at it," he said, "I wouldn't have read it." Afterwards, John Ali said, "The Messenger will be very pleased with the way you read it."[56]

Philbert's press conference had caught Malcolm on a bad day. At his office in the Theresa Hotel, he was suffering from a fierce headache, dosing himself with aspirins and drinking coffee. Soon, reporters began crowding around him, asking him to respond to his brother's statements.

At first, responding in mild tones, Malcolm said that Philbert's statements were said out of fear of losing his job. "We've been friends all our lives," said Malcolm. As the day dragged on, however, and reporters continued to dwell on Philbert's statements, Malcolm's tone became bitter and sarcastic. To his brother's charge, for instance, that he was a victim of "a great mental illness," he asked, how long had it existed? "Does he date it during the time I was organizing the people for Mr. Muhammad?" If so, "why didn't he tell me about it then?"[57]

Flying to Washington the next day, March 27, Malcolm sat in the Senate visitors gallery to observe the debate on the civil rights bill. To reporters, he described his visit as "a reconnaissance mission" and denounced the Senate proceedings as a "con game" in which the politicians "agree in advance what they are not going to do, then pretend they are doing something to get it."[58]

Even if Congress passed the civil rights bill, according to Malcolm, the politicians, fearful that it would bring about "a civil war to the south and a race war to the north," would never enforce it. Asked how he would obtain equal rights, he said that blacks were within their rights "to use any means to remove injustice," adding that he was not advocating violence, only self-defense.[59]

Meanwhile, in another section of the Senate gallery, Dr. Martin Luther King, Jr., was also watching the debate. Like Malcolm, King would periodically slip out to hold press conferences. At one of them, in a conference room just off the Senate chamber, Malcolm slipped into the back row. Afterwards, as King left by one door, Malcolm hurried out another one into his path.

As both men greeted each other with "grins and smiles," reporters gathered around them and photographers took pictures. Asked to comment on the civil rights bill, Malcolm said that if the white man rejected it, flashing a big grin, "I'm here to remind him of the alternative to Dr. King." If it failed to pass, added King, "our nation will be in for a dark night of social disruption." Still smiling, Malcolm, turning to King, said that he would now "get investigated."[60] Then they departed, ending the only face to face encounter between them.

Fearful that Malcolm's violent image would alienate white supporters, King continued both to avoid him and to publicly disavow him. To reporters, he acknowledged that Malcolm could articulate blacks' despair, but criticized him for his demagogic oratory, call for armed defense, and lack of any "positive creative alternative." Therefore, said King, "I feel that Malcolm has done himself and our people a great disservice."[61]

On April 8, the Nation of Islam officially filed eviction papers against Malcolm. They alleged that the Nation of Islam had purchased the house for Malcolm when he was minister of Mosque Number Seven; but since he broke from it on March 8, he was no longer entitled to live in the house. Malcolm's attorney, Percy Sutton, filed a countersuit, claiming that Malcolm's possession of it was not conditional on his continuing in the Nation of Islam.[62] While Muhammad and the Chicago leadership considered the eviction as a matter of equity, Malcolm looked upon it as an injustice for one who had served the Nation for twelve years.

Meanwhile, the Nation of Islam had escalated its attempts to create a climate of hate against Malcolm. The April 10 edition of *Muhammad Speaks* displayed a sketch titled "On My Own" which depicted Malcolm's severed head, prattling excuses for his break with the Nation, bouncing like a basketball toward a mount of skulls labeled "Judas, Brutus, Benedict Arnold, Malcolm, and Little Red."[63]

To Wallace Muhammad, the April 10 sketch meant that the Nation "wanted Malcolm dead."[64] Arriving at a similar conclusion, Malcolm decided that leaving the country for awhile was in his best interests. Consequently, in early April, he informed Alex Haley and Percy Sutton that he had decided to make a pilgrimage to Mecca, the Muslim holy city in Saudi Arabia.[65] As a result, Sutton got the Queen's Civil Court to postpone Malcolm's eviction proceedings until after he came back from Mecca, in May. "It was unclear," said Bayard Rustin, "whether Malcolm was running away from or toward something as he began another phase of his odyssey."[66]

CHAPTER 8

The Pilgrimage
and African Travels

Sometime in early March 1964, Malcolm X had decided to become an orthodox Muslim and to make the pilgrimage, the hajj, which Islam required a Muslim to undertake at least once in his lifetime, to Mecca, Saudi Arabia's holy city. His motives, however, were both spiritual and political. Now that he was out of the Nation of Islam, he needed to develop a different religious orientation to fit his changing political positions; otherwise, he might appear opportunistic and lose credibility.

Malcolm had other reason for traveling overseas, too. For one thing, he needed funds. Other than monies he received from lecture fees, magazine articles, and the tithes of his few followers, he was broke. Thus from Saudi Arabia's oil-rich rulers and sympathetic African governments, he hoped to establish some permanent sources of income. Furthermore, he sought to both create a link between the MMI and the 750 million orthodox Muslims of the world and obtain the support of their governments to bring the United States before the U.N. for violating the human rights of its black citizens.[1]

Before Malcolm could obtain a visa to travel to Mecca, he needed the permission of the Saudi Arabian government, which would not issue one to a non–bona fide Muslim. To become certified that he was, in fact, an orthodox Muslim, he needed a letter of recommendation from Dr. Mahmoud Youssef Shawarbi, the deputy director of the Islamic Center of New York and the director of the Islamic Federation of the United States and Canada.

On a number of occasions, Malcolm discussed Islam with Dr. Shawarbi at his office in New York City's Islamic Center. Right off, he told Malcolm that the Nation of Islam's white devil theory was an incorrect view of Islam, and that he would have to give it up before he could become an authentic Muslim. Later, he credited Dr. Shawarbi with being instrumental in helping him to understand orthodox Islam.[2] On the contrary, Malcolm was already familiar with it, having read about it while in prison and meeting orthodox Muslims during his 1959 Middle East visit.

At what point Malcolm had let Shawarbi know of his desire to visit Mecca was unclear. By early April, however, convinced of Malcolm's sincerity in converting to orthodox Islam, Shawarbi gave him a copy of the book *The Eternal Message of Muhammad* by Abd Ar-Kahman Azzam, a close advisor to Crown Prince Muhammad Al-Faisal, Saudi Arabia's ruler, and provided him a letter of recommendation so that he could obtain his visa. Likewise, Shawarbi gave Malcolm both the number of his son, Muhammad, a student at Egypt's Cairo University, and the number of Azzam's son, who lived in Jedda, Saudi Arabia, the last stop before Mecca.[3]

To make the trip, Malcolm obtained the funds from his half-sister Ella Collins, who thought that the hajj would "give him a walking stick so that he could better guide himself."[4] Embarrassed to admit where he got the funds, however, he told the *Amsterdam News* that because he had converted to Islam, the airfare to Egypt had been provided for free, and the MMI members had helped finance the rest of the trip.[5]

Without fanfare, on April 13, Malcolm took a flight to Frankfurt, Germany, and then boarded a plane to Cairo. During the flight, he noticed that most of the passengers were Muslims from different ethnic and racial backgrounds, but there "wasn't any color problem" among them. The effect on him, he said later, was "like stepping out of prison."[6]

After spending two days sightseeing in Cairo, including a visit with Shawarbi's son, Muhammad, Malcolm flew to Jedda.

At Jedda's airport, despite Shawarbi's letter, custom inspectors refused to believe that Malcolm was a bona fide Muslim since few Americans practiced Islam. Before he could continue his journey, then, they told him that he would have to first appear before an Islamic court to prove his credentials.

Because of the late afternoon hour, customs inspectors escorted Malcolm to a huge dormitory and placed him in a room filled with Muslims in the act of doing their daily prayer rituals. Making matters worse, he did not know how to do them properly. He said later that he had never "felt more alone and helpless."[7]

After about sixteen hours in this predicament, Malcolm remembered that in the book which Shawarbi had given him was the telephone number of the author's son, Omar Azzam, an engineer whose sister was Prince Faisal's wife. Malcolm rushed downstairs, found an official who spoke English, and got him to place a call to Azzam. When he learned that Malcolm was stuck at the airport, he immediately offered to help him.

When the light skinned Azzam arrived at the airport, Malcolm realized that in America Azzam would have been considered a white man. But Malcolm had "no feeling" of him being one.[8] In less than thirty minutes Azzam got Malcolm released and retained his suitcase and passport from customs.

After acquiring a hotel room for Malcolm, Omar took him to his father's home for dinner. The elder Azzam embraced Malcolm as if he were "a long-lost child." In turn, he looked upon the elder Azzam with awe for his knowledge and wisdom. What's more, that these two white men, whom Malcolm had never seen before, treated him so good was amazing since he could see no "selfish motive for their kindness."[9]

Granted, the Azzams, along with other distinguished elites of Saudi Arabia, were kind to Malcolm, but that they had no unselfish motives for it was doubtful. While he possessed neither money nor an organizational base, he did have personal charisma, attention from the news media, and widespread sympathy from disaffected blacks. Thus, through him, they perceived an opportunity for Muslims to gain a foothold in the American community.[10]

Meanwhile, Malcolm learned that Prince Faisal had made him a state guest. The Saudi government would now pay all of Malcolm's expenses, provide him with a chauffeur driven car, a guide, servants, and air-conditioned lodgings. Before the hajj court, moreover, Faisal's deputy chief of protocol intervened on Malcolm's behalf, prompting it to immediately issue him certification to make the hajj."[11]

For a Muslim, the hajj, which included a one-hundred twenty mile six-day trip from Jedda to the holy sites and back again, was a profound statement of his devotion to Allah, rejection of sin, and a celebration of unity with all Muslims.[12]

Taking place between April 17 and April 23, Malcolm began the hajj at the Great Mosque, housing the Ka'ba, a cube-like stone edifice that orthodox Muslims regarded as the House of God. Encased in silver, the Black Stone was embedded in its wall. According to tradition, it was the surviving shrine that Abraham and his son Ishmael had erected to honor Allah.

After walking around the Ka'ba seven times, Malcolm prostrated himself in prayer and then drank from the 140-foot deep well of Zamzam. At its site, according to tradition, as Hadjar, Abraham's concubine, ran back and forth between two large hills searching for water for herself and son Ismail, Gabriel, the archangel, revealed himself to her. As ritual dictated,

Malcolm walked the path she took seven times. Also, Malcolm performed the other rituals at Mecca, including the journey to Mina and Mount Ararat; the night at Muzdalifah; and the final sacrificial ceremony where he cast the traditional seven stones at the devil.[13]

After Malcolm's completion of the hajj, Prince Faisal requested that he meet with him at Riyadh, the capital of Saudi Arabia. Aware of the media attention that Malcolm would receive in the U.S. and his potential to influence American blacks, Faisal needed to know that the former member of the Nation of Islam understood his responsibility to promote the true meaning of Islam.

Being his first meeting with a head of state made Malcolm both nervous and unusually quiet. To Faisal, who was expecting to meet a "fire breather," Malcolm appeared "timid and shy." Pressing him, however, Faisal wanted to know, now that Malcolm had fulfilled all the rituals and requirements of the hajj, if he understood true Islam. Answering affirmatively, he said that to obtain a true understanding of it was why he had come to Saudi Arabia.[14]

Malcolm's response left Faisal somewhat skeptical. Ignorance was no excuse, he said, since there was an abundance of written material in English about Islam. But now, he added, Malcolm had no excuse to mislead people into believing "the wrong Islam."[15] In line with that, Faisal arranged to have a religious leader sent to New York City to teach his followers the Islamic rituals and gave Malcolm twenty scholarships to distribute among American blacks interested in studying Islam in Saudi Arabia and awarded him a paid religious position.[16]

Malcolm's Open Letter

Dated April 20, 1964, Malcolm sent his associates an open letter to distribute to the press. He wrote that the hajj had forced him to "toss aside" some of his previous assumptions about the white man. He had shared food and drink with fellow Muslims whose skin was the "whitest of white," eyes the "bluest of blues," and hair the "blondest of the blond," and yet, for the first time in his life, he "didn't see them as white men."

Malcolm credited the Muslims' belief in the oneness of God, Allah, as responsible for their non-racial attitudes. He then raised the possibility of reconciliation between the races in America. "If white Americans," he wrote, "would accept the religion of Islam, they would cease to measure others always in terms of their differences in color." But he did not seem to have much hope that this would occur.

Ending his letter on a dire note, Malcolm wrote that America was on a "self-destructive path," and only Islam could remove the "cancer of racism" from "the heart of white Americans" and save the country "from imminent racial disaster." It was the same destruction, he added, that Hitler's racism had brought upon the Germans.[17]

Malcolm's letter appeared to have worked to the Chicago leadership's advantage. His new attitude on the white man, they said, was "a complete about face," and only proved that he was "a thousand percent hypocrite."[18] By pointing to Malcolm's letter as proof of his betrayal to them, said his associate Charles Kenyatta, it provided the Chicago leadership "with more ammunition against him."[19]

To civil rights activist Bayard Rustin, Malcolm's letter "signaled an official announcement in support of integration."[20] In disagreement, Betty X said that it was only her husband's observations that white Muslims were gracious and friendly to him, not an endorsement of integration.[21]

To some, Malcolm's letter did not mean that he had changed his view of American racism. Political observers had misinterpreted his letter, said John Henrik Clarke. He understood that blacks' condition in America had "not changed one iota."[22] Although Mecca gave Malcolm hope that whites were "not necessarily racist," said Yuri Kochiyama, one of his followers, changing those whites "imbued with the American way of thinking" would remain difficult.[23] Malcolm still considered America, said Peter Goldman, a culture where "racism was so deeply ingrained that the great majority of whites couldn't escape it."[24]

Malcolm was not as naive about orthodox Islam's non-racist philosophy as he portrayed in his letter. During his 1959 Middle East visit, as mentioned earlier, he would have met white Muslims who treated him with kindness and respect; from his man U.N. visits, too, he had associated with numerous white Muslims; and as far back as his prison years, a member of Boston's orthodox Muslim movement, Abdul Hameed, had explained to him how Islam's principle of "brotherhood" contradicted Muhammad's teachings about whites.[25]

Before his visit abroad, in fact, Malcolm had decided to drop the Nation's white devil theory, since it hindered his attempts to broaden his movement. To offset the charge of political expediency, however, he pointed to his experiences on the hajj as the reason for dropping it.

Lebanon and Nigeria

At the end of April, Malcolm left Saudi Arabia for a speaking engagement at the University of Beirut, in Lebanon. To a large audience of students, faculty, and observers, he discussed how American blacks were "living in modern slavery," and that moderate leaders, such as Dr. King, had "made no political gains toward achieving civil rights."[26] When he finished, the students surrounded him; some hugged him while others asked for autographs. Their reactions, he said later, were typical of the "less inhibited more down-to-earth" Middle Eastern and African student audiences.[27]

Malcolm still had "eyes for pretty women." During his walks throughout Beirut, he noticed the bold dress and libertine mannerisms of the younger Lebanese women, but his prudery, apparently, would not allow him to give in to temptation.[28] Instead, he blamed their "moral weakness" on the European influence on material things, which undermined their spiritual values.[29]

On May 6, Malcolm embarked on a three week tour of Africa. His first stop was at Ibadan, Nigeria, for a speaking engagement, sponsored by the National Union of Nigerian Students, at the University of Ibadan. To a standing room audience at Trenchard Hall, he denounced Washington's claims of civil rights progress. Then, he spoke on the need for African nations to bring the U.S. before the U.N. for human rights violations; to link up American blacks and Africans in their respective struggles; and to expose the U.S. Peace Corps as "espionage agents" for neo-colonialism.[30] He would repeat the same themes, in fact, throughout his African travels.

The students responded to Malcolm's speech with rousing cheers. Afterwards, in the question and answer session, when a West Indies professor took the stage and called Malcolm "fundamentally dishonest," a dozen students rushed towards him. The professor barely escaped ahead of them.[31] "Never let anyone say that our African brothers aren't in complete sympathy with our plight," said Malcolm of the incident. "They understood the true picture of it."[32]

After the question and answer session, student members of the Nigerian Muslim Students' Society held a reception for Malcolm at the University's Union Hall. While he was there, they made him an honorary member of their society and endowed him with the name "Omowale." He told them that he had never received a more "treasured honor."[33]

Ghana

Officially Malcolm came to Accra, Ghana's capital, at the invitation of the University of Ghana's Marxist Forum, a student group. He knew, however, that Ghana had been the center for pan–Africanism, and that a small but vocal colony of American black expatriates, led by Julian Mayfield and his wife, Ana Livia, lived in Accra.

Upon Malcolm's arrival, the Mayfields drove him from the airport to the writer Maya Angelou's house, where they assembled with the other members of the Malcolm X Committee. A mix of left-leaning business and professional people, they included Alice Windom, Victoria Garvin, Sylvia Boone, Lesley Lacy, Ted Pointiflet, Jim and Annette Lacy, and Frank Robinson.

After dinner, the expatriates, sitting on chairs, stools, tables, and on the floor, crowded around Malcolm, who seemed unusually quiet. Finally, rubbing his newly-grown beard, he said that the hajj had changed many things about him. When he returned to America, he would make statements that would "shock everybody." Then, recalled Angelou, "the golden man laughed," and all of us "were surprised at Malcolm's lightheartedness."[34]

Reiterating common themes, Malcolm told the expatriates that while he still considered the United States a racist country, he no longer regarded whites as devils, and that the race issue was a human rights problem that the U.N. needed to address. Also, he talked about issues other than politics, including family, love, food, religion, and fashion, which showed, according to Angelou, that he was "not a man without eyes."[35]

For the next week, the Malcolm X Committee escorted Malcolm through days filled with visits, lectures, and press conferences. Most of the time, said Alice Windom, "we were all nearly crazy with fatigue," except Malcolm, who was always "strong, alert, and responsive." He attributed his stamina, he said, in part "to the discipline of his religion," which included neither drinking nor smoking and watching his diet.[36] The expatriates, recalled Lesley Lacy, had "to cease and desist all those activities which we considered offensive to our puritan leader."[37]

Ghana's independent newspapers not only gave Malcolm extensive coverage but also paid his hotel expenses. The government controlled papers, on the other hand, the *Ghanian Times* and the *Evening News,* treated his visit in "a moderate and subdued manner." To some observers, this indicated that American officials had convinced President Kwame Nkrumah to downplay Malcolm's visit.[38]

During his speaking tour in Ghana, Malcolm continued to repeat a number of basic themes. These included establishing ties between American blacks and Africans (pan–Africanism), taking the United States to the U.N. for violating the human rights of its black citizens, and counteracting the distorted version of treating its racial situation as "a minor problem rapidly on its way to a solution."[39]

While in Accra, Algeria's Ambassador Taker Raid, a white Muslim revolutionary, told Malcolm that his racially motivated black nationalist philosophy was too narrow because it alienated white Muslims, such as himself, not only in Algeria but also in places like Morocco, Egypt, Iraq, and Mauritania.[40]

Raid's criticism floored Malcolm. That white Muslims might view black nationalism, whose analysis he understood to be better apply to the American situation than to Africa or the Middle East, contradicted his thinking on the need for International Islamic solidarity was not good. While he continued to use the term black nationalism, he said it less often, which probably expressed his rising ambivalence in regards to it, too.

Talking with the Ghanian press, Malcolm would often refer to blacks as "Negroes," the standard American usage of the time. One day, however, a reporter informed him that "Negroes" was not a word favored by Africans; instead, they preferred the term African Americans as expressing "greater meaning and dignity."[41] Thus, for the rest of the trip, he used African Americans or blacks, avoiding the term "Negroes."

At the Kwame Nkrumah Ideological Institute, Malcolm spoke to its two-hundred elite students on their "own high level of awareness." Afterwards, similar to the occurrence at Nigeria's University of Ibadan, a lone dissenter in the audience, which had responded enthusiastically to Malcolm's talk, said that he was not qualified to judge the American race situation. Immediately, to calls of "stooge" and "CIA agent," the students shouted him down.[42] But whether the American government, as they assumed, was planting dissenters in the audience in an attempt to discredit Malcolm was unclear.

Next, Malcolm spoke to a packed audience of both students and non-students at the University of Ghana's Great Hall in Legion. Throughout his speech, he played off the whites in the audience. Talking directly to them, he said that he had never seen so many whites so nice to blacks. In America, African Americans were trying to integrate, but they should come here to see whites integrating with Africans. "What they want to integrate with," he added, "was the mineral wealth of Africa."[43]

When Malcolm, whose eyes were "rimming with tears," finished, the students rose in "a wail of cheering" and chanting their football song, "Asante Koloko," referred to as "the Ghanian violent elation."[44] They fell in love with him, said Alice Windom. "The chemistry was perfect."[45] They talked about Malcolm "for days after he left," said Leslie Lacy, creating a song in his honor called "Malcolm Man" and forming the Malcolm X Society.[46]

In the question and answer session, a student asked Malcolm that since he looked like a white man, why did he call himself black? At first, he appeared taken aback; then, throwing his head back, he laughed "loud and long." Before now, he said, nobody had ever called him a white man. But he blamed white slave-holders, who raped their slave women, for the fact that African Americans were less black than Africans.[47]

When a faculty member accused him of inciting people to violence, Malcolm, knowing that Africans liked his use of analogies, said that if he warned his neighbor that his house was on fire, would he accuse him of it or thank him for his concern?[48]

Later, in Accra, at one of the numerous parties given in Malcolm's honor, he met the leader of Ghana's National Assembly, Kofi Buako. Impressed by Malcolm's personality, he invited him to address its members, an honor usually reserved for visiting heads of state. In his address to them on May 14, Malcolm congratulated them for their continued criticism of South Africa's apartheid but scolded them for remaining silent on American racism. They should not allow American propaganda agencies to mislead them into believing that Washington was doing all it could to improve race relations.[49]

On the following day, in another unprecedented move for a non-head of state, President Kwame Nkrumah granted Malcolm an audience. After a thorough search on the capital grounds, he entered Nkrumah's long office. Wearing ordinary dress, Nkrumah stood up, walked from behind his desk, extended his hand, and smiled. The two men sat on a couch and talked.

Malcolm and Nkrumah agreed on the importance of African unity for the continent and pan–Africanism as a key policy for those Americans of African descent. Yet, there was a distance between the two men. Although sympathetic with Malcolm's positions, Nkrumah was not entirely free to act on them. A poor country, Ghana was dependent on foreign aid from the superpowers, so he could not afford to offend either the United States or the Soviet Union.[50] Nevertheless, "moved and gratified" by the visit, Malcolm promised him that he would relay to African Americans his personal regards.[51]

On May 16, Al Haji Isa Wali, Nigeria's high commissioner, gave a luncheon in Malcolm's honor, presenting him with an African robe and turban worn by Muslims in his country. Afterwards, he visited at the home of Shirley Graham Du Bois, the widow of W.E.B. Du Bois, the famous American black writer and activist. That evening, Cuba's Ambassador Armando Entralgo Gonzalez gave a farewell party on Malcolm's behalf. Asked to say something, he found himself uncharacteristically speechless, touched by the warm response of his entire visit.[52]

Like Malcolm, Muhammad Ali (formerly Cassius Clay), who hoped to avoid him, was also touring Africa. Yet in Accra, Ali and his entourage had inadvertently registered at the same hotel where Malcolm was staying. Learning of Ali's presence, Malcolm, not wishing to embarrass him, sought to stay out of his way.

But on May 17, Malcolm's last morning in Accra, as he was chatting outside his hotel with the Mayfields and other expatriates, Ali and his entourage accidentally came upon them. The moment "froze," said Angelou, and then "very courteously" Ali greeted them, except for Malcolm, whom he ignored. But as Ali turned to walk away, Malcolm, stepping in front of him, said that he still "loved him" and considered him "the greatest."[53]

Shaking his head, Ali said, "You left the Honorable Elijah Muhammad," and "that was the wrong thing to do, Brother Malcolm." Leaving him standing there with his shoulders sagging, Ali then walked away. Shortly thereafter, turning to his companions, he said, Malcolm's "gone so far out" that "he's out completely" and "nobody listens to him anymore."[54]

On the ride to the airport, Julian Mayfield asked Malcolm if Ali's actions came as a surprise to him. Avoiding the question, he said, somewhat reflectively, that Ali was young and "to be kind to him" for "his sake and mine" since "he has a place in my heart."[55]

Shortly after Malcolm's departure, officials in the American Embassy in Accra reported to Washington that his visit was neither damaging to American interests nor his views shocking to Ghanaians since they have heard others express them on America's racial situation, "though less eloquently." Embassy officials added that Ghanaians tended to discount such views as too extremist. The officials concluded that Malcolm X created "less of a stir than the American Embassy had feared."[56]

At the same time, Nkrumah allowed one of his aides, M.M. Dasner, a white South African expatriate, to publish a highly critical Marxist interpretation of Malcolm's views in the government controlled *Ghanaian Times.* To American Embassy officials, although Dasner was a Marxist, his article was Nkrumah's way of distancing himself from Malcolm, endeavoring, perhaps, to win U.S. favor and aid for his seven year economic development plan.[57]

Back Home

After stopovers in Monrovia, Liberia, Dakar, Senegal, Casablanca and Morocco, Malcolm, on his thirty-ninth birthday, arrived in Algiers on May 19. After visiting its Casbah, which reminded him of Harlem, he booked a flight back to New York City.

On May 21, Malcolm landed at New York City's John F. Kennedy Airport. As he came into the terminal, observers noticed his new look: a reddish goatee and an African walking stick, giving him "an exotic cast." Waiting for him there were his family, a sizeable force of his followers, and fifty reporters, which pleased him since his letter writing campaign from

Africa not only kept his name alive, but also generated even more interest in him.

Although Malcolm's associates had arranged an official press conference for him that evening, he stopped for a moment to answer some of the reporters' questions. Mainly, they wanted to know, as he stated in his letter, if his attitude towards whites had really changed. During the hajj, he said, he had met white Muslims who practiced "true brotherhood," and that led him to reject the Nation of Islam's white devil theory. Then, to emphasize one of the reasons for his trip, he said that he hoped it had established the MMI's "authentic religious affiliation with the 750 million Muslims of the orthodox Islamic world."[58]

Similarly, Malcolm told reporters that he had added to his official name, which the Nation had given him, from Malik El-Shabazz to El-Hajj Malik El-Shabazz, but that he would continue to use Malcolm X as long as the racist situation that led to his adoption of it continued to exist. However, his wife would drop her X and became known as Betty Shabazz.

Before departing in a motorcade of six cars, Malcolm and his family posed for photographers. To his family, in fact, he appeared like a new man. His old zest had returned and his daughter Attallah recalled that he "looked brand new."[59]

That evening at the Theresa Hotel's Skyline Room, packed with reporters, television cameramen, followers, and well-wishers, Malcolm, accompanied by his wife and Alex Haley, sat down at a two-chair table while everyone gathered around them in a semicircle.

Pressed again by the news media to discuss his racial views, Malcolm admitted that they had changed but only to the degree that with Muslims "the notion of skin color vanishes." In the United States, however, unless whites adopted Islam as their religion, he said, brotherhood between the races was remote. Likewise, in an attempt to dispel fears that he had mellowed, he added that no matter how much respect or recognition whites showed him, if they do not do the same for all blacks, "it doesn't exist for me."[60]

Malcolm criticized State Department people for doing a good job "making Africans believe that America is doing everything for the American Negro." He referred to himself, on the other hand, as their "traveling antidote," knocking down the "good image" of America fostered by them. The United States, he added, had colonized American blacks just as Europeans had colonized Asians and Africans. Then, he hinted that he had promises of support from African leaders to bring America's race problem before the U.N.[61]

Malcolm said that blacks could learn from the example of the Jews. They raised their status in America, he said, "through their philosophical identification with Israel." In the same way, blacks can raise their status by becoming "deeply involved philosophically, culturally, and psychologically with the new African nations." Thus, he concluded, the Jewish experience in achieving status in American life can provide valuable lessons for blacks struggling for equal justice.[62]

Summing up one view, Helen Dudar, a *New York Post* reporter, said, "The lyrics are slightly altered, but the melody is unchanged."[63] To civil rights activist Dick Gregory, Malcolm used to give the impression that "his message was just to black folks," but now, "it was for everybody."[64]

CHAPTER 9

By Any Means Necessary

Home from his trip abroad, Malcolm X faced the same problems that he had left behind in April. *Muhammad Speaks* continued its biweekly attacks against him, making the fact clear to him that his life was still in danger and he had no source of income other than what he could get from speaking engagements, pieces sold in newspapers, and a few dues paying members.

Without an insurance policy, investments, or savings, the only thing Malcolm had to give his family was his house, which technically belonged to the Nation of Islam. From his point of view, however, since he had given so much to the Nation and received so little financially from it, the least Elijah Muhammad could do was to let him keep the house.[1]

At this point, facing physical danger and homelessness for his family, Malcolm decided "to sling some mud" and go public with Muhammad's infidelities. In this way, too, Malcolm might lure disaffected Muslims into his own organization. Having to withstand a three month "public humiliation" for violating Muhammad's orders, he would now turn Muslims' attention into judging Muhammad, the "man most at fault."[2]

Although Malcolm realized that going public with Muhammad's infidelities was playing with fire, he felt that under the circumstances, the best defense was a hard hitting offense.[3] He was basically a fighter, said Herman Ferguson. He had stayed back in the corner, "ducking and dodging," but he realized now that unless he started fighting back, he would be knocked out.[4] Yet to DeCaro, he was "stooping kind of low."[5]

For Malcolm, going public meant that the rise in the possibility for reconciliation with Elijah Muhammad would no longer remain. Infidelity was a serious offense to charge his father with, said Wallace Muhammad. "It would really mean that somebody in the Nation might kill you."[6] Going public, said Goldman, "was cashing in his life insurance," and "he knew it."[7]

Before Malcolm went public, he tried to persuade two of Elijah Muhammad's former secretaries, Evelyn Williams and Lucille Rosary, both living in Los Angeles, to file paternity suits against him. If they came out first, they could both serve as collaborating evidence and diminish the revenge factor of his announcement. As things turned out, however, their paternity suits came after Malcolm went public.[8]

Beginning on June 4, 1964, Malcolm broke the story of Muhammad's infidelities. In an interview over Philadelphia's WDAS radio station, Malcolm accused him of engaging in extramarital relations with his personal secretaries and fathering from them six illegitimate children.[9] Three days later, after repeating the charge to an audience at Harlem's Audubon Ballroom, he said that "the Nation would even commit murder to keep this secret quiet."[10]

On the following day, June 8, Malcolm told newsman Mike Wallace that he had previously seen indications of Muhammad's infidelity, but "my religious sincerity had made me block it out of mind." Asked if he was not afraid of what would happen to him in making this charge, he said that he was "probably a dead man already."[11] Meanwhile, his wife received a call from an unknown man who told her that Malcolm was "as good as dead."[12]

In Boston four days later, just before Malcolm was to appear on Paul Benzaquin's WEEI radio talk show, the police received an anonymous phone call from a man who said that "Malcolm X was going to be bumped off."[13] As a result, a heavy police guard accompanied him to the radio station.

To Benzaquin, Malcolm said that he broke from the Nation because Elijah Muhammad had fathered six illegitimate children, and that the mothers were "teenage sisters" working for him as secretaries. Since no one stood with the girls when they were brought before the Chicago mosque to stand trial for their actions, said Malcolm, its members assumed that non–Muslim males were responsible for their pregnancies. In 1963, however, he learned from Wallace Muhammad that his father was responsible for them, and that he was still continuing his adulterous behavior. At that point, said Malcolm, he could no longer represent him.[14]

Malcolm re-echoed the same theme that evening on Jerry Williams' WMEX radio talk show. On June 13, the next night, however, Williams' guest was Louis X, who denied all of Malcolm's accusations made the previous evening. Within moments, Williams received a call on the air from Malcolm, challenging Louis X to meet him at the station on the following week. Then, said Malcolm, he would repeat the charges of Muhammad's infidelities to Louis X's face. Naturally, he declined Malcolm's challenge since Muhammad would never agree to having him involved in a face-to-face encounter with the Nation's former champion debater.[15]

Although Malcolm had publicly announced that he would assemble with local civil rights activists and disaffected Muslims from Louis X's Mosque Number Twelve at Ella Collins' house on June 14, his followers convinced him that staying in Boston any longer was too dangerous.[16] Consequently, he asked Benjamin 2X to take his place.

The next afternoon Benjamin 2X assembled with about one-hundred twenty people at Collins' house. He was hoping that those in attendance would become the nucleus of an MMI chapter. Still, because of Malcolm's absence, which Elijah Muhammad's followers were unaware of, Benjamin 2X could not accomplish much at this meeting.

At the end of the two hour meeting, Rodnell Collins, Malcolm's cousin, offered to drive Benjamin 2X back to Boston's Logan Airport so that he could catch his flight back to New York City. Just then, several of those present said that they saw a group of Muhammad's Boston followers, led by Captain Clarence X Gill, in the area earlier that day; but since Malcolm had left town, they assumed that there was little cause for concern. Nonetheless, several brothers, including Benjamin 2X's old army buddy, Goulbourne Busby, insisted that they ride along with him and Rodnell to provide protection.

As Rodnell Collins' four-door, 1959 Cadillac pulled away from his house, a white 1962 Lincoln accelerated down the street after it. Just as the Cadillac was reaching the Callahan Tunnel at the Southeast Expressway which headed north to the airport, the Lincoln passed it, pulled out in front of it, and slowed to make it stop. But Collins swerved the Cadillac to the left, passing the Lincoln. At the same time, however, a 1955 Chevrolet pulled up in front of the Cadillac, forcing Collins to stop.

Without delay, Collins hollered to Busby that there was a shotgun and a bag of shells wrapped up in a rug on the floor of the back seat. Just then, two men got out of the Lincoln and another two from the Chevrolet. "You're not leaving here," said one of the men, holding a nickel-plated revolver. "You're going to get killed."[17]

Similarly, Busby rolled down the back window and pointed the shotgun at the four men, who then retreated. At the same time, Collins, shifting gears and gunning the Cadillac forward, slammed into the Chevrolet's fender, swung by it, and sped through the tunnel.

In order to attract the police's attention, Collins drove the Cadillac into the airport at 90 miles an hour, stopped it in the middle of the road, and its occupants, with Busby carrying the shotgun, raced into the terminal. The police immediately arrested them for disturbing the peace and carrying a loaded shotgun. While Ella Collins posted bail, Malcolm, over the phone, told Benjamin 2X to inform the press that the incident was an attempt by the Nation to kill him for going public with Muhammad's infidelities.[18]

The following day, June 15, in discussing the Callahan Tunnel incident and recent death threats, Malcolm told reporters that he was sure that they had been made by the followers of Elijah Muhammad since there were no people in the United States better able to carry out this threat than them. "I know," he added, "I taught them."[19]

Eviction Hearing

In connection with the eviction case filed against him by Mosque Number Seven, Queens County Civil Court scheduled Malcolm to appear before it on June 15. As the day of his hearing approached, an anonymous caller phoned his wife that someone would kill her husband on the courthouse steps. The police, the MMI, and the *New York Times* received similar phone calls warning of Malcolm's imminent death.[20]

Consequently, on the day of Malcolm's hearing, eight of his men brought him to court, and thirty-two uniformed policemen and twelve plainclothes detectives escorted him inside. Court officials chose the smallest courtroom in the building and kept the shades down to hinder potential snipers. As Malcolm sat nervously at the defense table, glancing around the room at sudden noises, his people sat on one side of the aisle while the Nation's representatives sat on the other, glaring at each other.[21]

In front of Judge Maurice Wahl, Captain Joseph, speaking on behalf of the Nation of Islam, and Percy Sutton, Malcolm's lawyer, presented their cases. According to Joseph, Mosque Number Seven was paying the mortgage and taxes on the house, and the agreement was to allow Malcolm to use it only as long as he was a member of the Nation, which was no longer true. But even if the deed, said Sutton, read that the house belonged to Mosque Number Seven, the Nation had not properly fired Malcolm as its minister; therefore, he was entitled to remain in the house.[22]

Taking the stand on the second day of the hearing, Malcolm told Sutton, somewhat dubiously, that he had never quit the Nation, that he was still under suspension and that he was waiting for a hearing yet to take place. Then, to Sutton's chagrin, Malcolm said that his remark about Kennedy's death was not the real reason behind his suspension; instead, it came about because he had "found out" that Elijah Muhammad had fathered nine children (Malcolm had previously said six) from six different girls.[23]

For Malcolm, as he sat through the last routine testimony, the rest of the day was anticlimactic. Afterwards, escorted by the police and his followers, a five-car caravan brought him back to Harlem. That day, said one of his followers later, Malcolm had "crossed the Rubicon."[24]

Three months later, Judge Wahl announced his decision. Since Malcolm had not put the house's title in his name, enabling him to avoid paying property taxes on it, the Nation had legal rights to it. Even so, the judge would allow Malcolm and his family to live there for five more months: enough time to find another place to live.

Mounting Tension

To Malcolm's disappointment, the press, fearing libel suits for printing unsubstantiated innuendos, generally ignored his allegations of Muhammad's infidelities, concentrating instead on reporting political schisms between the black nationalists. Nonetheless, the Nation of Islam took Malcolm's allegations against its leader seriously. While the Chicago leadership publicly called Malcolm "a liar" and "a low base, vile man," Muhammad privately told an associate that he would never forgive nor forget him.[25]

On June 16, the last day of Malcolm's court hearing, a woman, calling herself Mrs. Small, phoned the telephone company and requested that it disconnect Malcolm's phone because his family was going on vacation. When Malcolm's brothers (his followers) tried to call him that evening, they received a recorded "disconnect message." Alarmed by it, a half-dozen armed brothers hurried to Malcolm's house. But he and his family were safe.

Calling the phone company, Malcolm learned that a Mrs. Small had disconnected his phone. Since her name was a play on his slave name, Little, which the Nation had been calling him after his break, he guessed that she was one of the Nation's sisters.[26]

After reassuring themselves that Malcolm and his family were safe, the brothers drove to Mosque Number Seven's restaurant. About ten Muslims were standing in front of it, talking. William George, one of Malcolm's men, got out of the car and held a rifle to the group, ordering them into the restaurant. When none of them moved, he cursed and walked back to the car. At that point, the police converged on the scene and arrested Malcolm's men on weapons and felonious assault charges.[27]

Not long after, similar confrontations took place between Malcolm's and Elijah Muhammad's followers in Los Angeles, Chicago, Detroit, Boston, and New York. The *Amsterdam News* captioned "Muslim Factions at War" and *The New York World Telegram and Sun* headlined "Malcolm X: Man Marked for Death," reporting that he went nowhere "without police shadows and his own core of rifle-bearing bodyguards."[28] His people were not after him, said Muhammad: "Allah was after him."[29]

Published in the *New York Post* on June 26, Malcolm wrote an open letter to Muhammad in an attempt to diminish the escalating violence. In it, Malcolm urged him "to call off this unnecessary bloodshed," and, instead, to work together in "unity and harmony" to help solve the problems of black people. If Muhammad, however, continued "to stir others up" to do his "murderous dirty work," wrote Malcolm, historians would declare him "guilty not only of adultery and deceit but also of murder."[30]

The Organization of Afro-American Unity

After Malcolm came back from his overseas travels, he learned that the MMI's membership was not expanding. Part of the reason was Malcolm's extended absence overseas. Yet even after his return, the average attendance of the three MMI meetings held weekly was only twelve to fourteen persons per meeting.[31] From this, he concluded that he needed another organization, separate from the MMI, to attract non–Muslims. That Malcolm did not have "a single approach" to confronting the racist system, said Herman Ferguson later, was what "made him such a remarkable person."[32]

At first, Malcolm had decided to model his new organization after Algeria's and Kenya's independence movements and to call it the Afro-American Freedom Fighters. Upon reflection, however, he realized that the Organization of African Unity (OAU) was a better model because it advocated a pan–African philosophy and included all of Africa's independence movements. Consequently, he named his new organization the Organization of Afro-American Unity (OAAU). While its base would remain in New York City, he would eventually set up chapters in Africa and Europe.

Malcolm scheduled the OAAU's opening rally at Harlem's Audubon Ballroom on Sunday, June 28, 1964. Either coincidentally or on purpose Elijah Muhammad had scheduled a "Monster Muslim Rally" on the same day at New York City's 369th Armory. Each man, then, would be competing to see who could get the biggest crowd out for their event.

Shortly before the June 28 rally, Malcolm publicly announced the formation of the OAAU, patterning it after "the letter and spirit" of the OAU. Similarly, he sent letters to various civil rights organizations, human rights groups, and African delegations to the U.N. inviting them to send representatives to the OAAU's opening rally.[33]

At a press conference at the Nation's New York City restaurant, James X said that he had received a tip from one of Malcolm's followers that his group was planning to assassinate Elijah Muhammad when he arrived at Kennedy International Airport on Sunday morning, June 28. Asked about the allegation, Malcolm said that no follower of his would think of assassinating Muhammad. "We don't have to kill him," he added. "What he has done will bring him to his grave."[34]

On the day of the rally, Muhammad arrived in New York City without incident. To reporters, he said that his goal was "to bring peace to Harlem," calling the situation there "very dangerous." Asked about Malcolm, he said that "defectors from our organization are dead," therefore, "they do not concern us."[35]

That afternoon Muhammad's followers lined up in the street outside New York City's 369th Infantry Armory. While the police were there in force, the FOI, wearing plastic armbands that read "We Are with Muhammad," outnumbered them. In fact, every available FOI member throughout the East Coast was there, for as FOI's Assistant Supreme Captain Elijah Muhammad Jr. said, "There was no telling what might occur."[36]

The FOI searched everybody attending the rally. At one point, its members yanked a man from the crowd when somebody yelled that he was one of "Malcolm's men." While some FOI men locked arms, forming cordons to keep back the police, the others began beating the man as the crowd chanted "Kill him! Kill him!" After beating him senseless and throwing his body against a fence, FOI men next turned their anger against a black man who was handing out leaflets calling Muhammad a mixed-bred phony. They broke the man's nose and knocked two of his teeth loose.[37]

About 6,000 people filled the 9,000 seat armory to hear Muhammad's seventy-five minute talk on the need for "peace through separation." Yet, with a phalanx of FOI men surrounding him and plagued by bad acoustics, the audience could barely see or hear him. The armory, moreover, was "unbearably hot," which added to the distress of his bronchial asthmatic condition, forcing him at times to interrupt his talk with gasping, coughing, and wheezing. Finally, his asthma forced him to sit down without finishing his address.

In his talk, although Muhammad made no direct reference to Malcolm, he said that "some person wants to be what I am, but to be what I am because he has not been revealed what has been told me."[38]

By and large, Muhammad had succeeded in his goal of upstaging Malcolm's OAAU kickoff scheduled for that evening. Although many of those in Muhammad's audience came to New York City in buses from distant places, he would, nevertheless, pack into his rally ninety percent more people than Malcolm did at his rally that evening. Thus, Muhammad had made his point: he not only commanded a substantial number of followers, but also was still a force in Malcolm's New York City stronghold.

Afterwards, Muhammad, recognizing the danger of remaining in New York City, immediately left under heavy escort of FOI men and law enforcement officers for the airport and the flight back to Chicago.

To over a thousand people at Harlem's Audubon Ballroom that evening, Malcolm announced the formation of the OAAU. Its goal, he said, was to win freedom, justice, equality, and dignity for Americans of African descent "by any means necessary," which became its motto. Its program, moreover, would encompass the whole gamut of problems facing American blacks. But its immediate objective, he said, since Washington was unwilling to solve its race problem, was to take the United States to the U.N. for human rights violations.

Anybody of African descent could join the OAAU, said Malcolm. Its members would fight anybody who got in their way "in seeking complete independence of people of African descent," and they would fight "by any means necessary." They want freedom now, added Malcolm, or else they "don't think anybody should have it."[39]

About ninety people at the rally joined the OAAU, and Malcolm collected a little less than two hundred dollars in donations. To reporters, he said that there was "no way of knowing how many supporters he now had," but that more would have joined if they had the two dollar initiation fee. Asked about financial support, he said, "We are scratching," but "I don't have any expensive habits," and "I have never met a true revolutionary who worried about money."[40]

While the press reported that Malcolm had over a thousand followers, Muhammad placed the figure at only two hundred, and most of them, he added, were Greenwich Village's "fishes and freaks" who joined the OAAU "for sport and play."[41] Malcolm now "stood alone," said Captain Joseph, who predicted that he would soon fall because his success had depended on the Nation of Islam, which enabled him to speak with authority.[42]

Clifton DeBerry, black presidential candidate for the Socialist Workers Party (SWP), welcomed Malcolm X's OAAU "as a giant step towards the real black revolution in America."[43] FBI Director J. Edgar Hoover, who regarded the SWP a Trotskyist Communist group and as a subversive organization, ordered his New York City agents to prepare news releases stating that Malcolm X was accepting support from subversives.[44]

Shortly thereafter, newsmen began writing that Malcolm X was attracting "the FBI's scrutiny."[45] At one point, asked by a reporter if he would accept Communist support, Malcolm, reverting to his genius for analogy and metaphor, said that if a wolf held him prisoner, he "would accept release from any source." When the reporter asked him if that meant "yes," he said, "I only told you a story about a wolf."[46]

By Any Means Necessary

For Malcolm, the slogan "by any means necessary" became a working definition of where his movement was heading as well as opening up avenues that had not previously existed for the Nation of Islam, which included rent strikes, ghetto uprisings, electoral campaigns, and guerrilla warfare. Sometimes, he qualified "by any means necessary" with as long as it was "intelligent, just, and legal."[47] Yet he said that blacks "would never get results" playing by "the power structure's ground rules" since they were "unjust, illegal, and criminal."[48]

In subsequent interviews, referring to the U.S. Constitution's "right of every American citizen to bear arms," Malcolm said that blacks had the right to armed self-defense. He would not, he said, "call on anybody to be violent without a cause," but when white people attacked, sicked dogs, or used fire hoses on them, they were within their rights to protect themselves by "whatever means necessary."[49]

Malcolm often compared America's race problem to a battlefield where blacks faced a vicious enemy. When Bayard Rustin accused him of resorting to "emotionalism," Malcolm said that when a man was sitting on a hot stove, he does not cry out "unemotionally," but jumps off it: "violently or nonviolently doesn't even enter the picture."[50] To Malcolm, in fact, for someone to tell blacks to remain nonviolent in the face of injustice was criminal.[51]

Stressing reciprocal retaliation, Malcolm urged blacks to even the score with whites. If a black man died, he said, a white man should die too.[52] The Ku Klux Klan should know, he said, that the OAAU will give Klansmen "tit for tat, tit for tat," and that the OAAU has members who are "able, equipped, and ready to do that."[53]

To Malcolm, reciprocal violence was the only language racists understood. "How," he asked, "are you going to fight a violent man nonviolently?"[54] Once blacks learn the language the Klan speaks, he said dialogue and understanding would result.[55]

While Malcolm would work with civil rights leaders on issues, he would never teach nonviolence. The OAAU, he said, would recruit and train blacks to protect southern voter registration workers.[56] Again, whenever the black man works on behalf of his people, he could die. But dying "must be reciprocal," he said, and if "it's not worth that, stay home."[57]

Quoting Patrick Henry, the American revolutionary, Malcolm refused to accept the fact that "give me liberty or give me death" was exclusive to the white man, who now expected blacks to remain nonviolent in their fight for freedom. But they are not going to change the white system, he said, by getting on their knees and singing "We Shall Overcome."[58] When the white man becomes nonviolent, he added, the black man can become nonviolent too.[59]

Counteracting Malcolm, Roy Wilkins, the National Association for the Advancement of Colored People's (NAACP) executive secretary, said that historically black Americans as a group "have never committed to retaliatory violence as a policy." If they did not reach "for shotguns and rifles," he said, when lynchings were at a "twice a week average" and segregation and discrimination were at their peak, they are not about to "immolate themselves now" just when things were improving and when whites outnumbered them nine to one.[60]

Yet, by spring and summer of 1964, Malcolm's call for armed defense was gaining sympathy with young disaffected blacks. Talking more of revolution than integration, Student Non-Violent Coordinating Committee's (SNCC) John Lewis started advocating the need for force if nonviolent methods proved inadequate to bring about social change, and the NAACP's branch president in Monroe, North Carolina, Robert F. Williams, was arguing for "effective self-defense" of black communities against "racist terrorists."[61]

In the northern ghettoes, Malcolm best articulated the rising anger and frustration of younger blacks who had grown impatient with the nonviolent assimilationist philosophy of the civil rights movement. While they did not understand the issues "intellectually," he said, they felt the problems "so acutely that no form of self-expression other than violence was possible for them."[62] This generation was coming up, he said, and letting the world know that "they're going to be men, or they just won't be a human being anywhere else."[63]

In articulating the anger of northern black youth, Malcolm was challenging whites to "take the warning," for they could still "save themselves." But if they continued to deny blacks their freedom, he said, they were ready to fight for it, and he did not mean any "turn the other cheek fight" because "those days were over."[64]

To Malcolm, the willingness of blacks to use retaliatory violence was an expression of rising black manhood. To him, King's nonviolent strategy was perpetuating the historical legacy of black men who were too passive to fight back against white oppression, which had robbed them of their pride and dignity. Likewise, Malcolm scolded his black audiences for being "afraid to bleed," for he had no use for nonviolent blacks. "If you show me a non-violent Negro," he said, "I'll show you a Negro whose reflexes don't work, one who needs psychiatric care."[65]

While political observers described Malcolm as the "angriest Negro in America," in his personal behavior, he conveyed the impression of "a soft-spoken, non-smoking, non-drinking gentle Muslim."[66] He was "extremely cordial in private," said Peter Goldman. "If you were friendly to him and treated him with respect, he would reciprocate."[67] Yet, for Malcolm, 1964 was "a time for anger."[68]

With time, in fact, Malcolm began advocating both offensive and defensive violence to counter white oppression. He told reporters, for instance, that he regarded Kenya's Mau Mau, who overturned British colonial rule in the 1950s, as Africa's greatest guerrilla fighters. Admiring their "bold use of violence" and referring to them as liberators of their people, he said that black America needed a similar group to win freedom and equality.[69]

According to Malcolm's critics, however, Kenya's Mau Mau guerrillas did not fit the black situation in the United States since they operated in a country that was majority black while American blacks only made up a small minority among the majority whites. To this, Malcolm said that although blacks were a minority in America, in the context of Africa, Asia, and Latin America, they were part of the worldwide black majority. He referred to American blacks as the "wick" in the powder keg of the worldwide black revolution against white colonialism. "You can touch the powder all day long and nothing happens," he said. "It's the wick that you touch that sets the powder off."[70]

On July 4, Malcolm told newspersons that blacks must "fight fire with fire" in Mississippi and use guerrilla tactics, the only way open to the under-dog to equalize the situation in fighting bigots who seek to murder them. Asked by reporters if he was serious about this, he replied, "dead serious." The OAAU, he said, had trained volunteers from "coast to coast" who were ready to go "anywhere south of the Canadian border" to fight racists who threatened blacks' lives.[71] Advocating the use of guerrilla tactics, said news-woman Marlene Nadle, was the exception to Malcolm's "defensive strategy."[72]

Shortly thereafter, Malcolm sent a telegram to Dr. King, who was then engaged in a desegregation campaign in Saint Augustine, Florida. "If the Federal Government will not send troops to your aid," wrote Malcolm, "just say the word and we will immediately dispatch some of our brothers there to organize our people into self-defense units, and the Ku Klux Klan will receive a taste of its own medicine."[73]

Because King would not compromise on his strategy of nonviolent direct action, he rejected Malcolm's offer of assistance. Yet, Malcolm would have known that King would never accept any offer of help of a violent nature. That Malcolm sent the telegram in the first place was difficult to understand, unless he wanted to make a statement about his willingness to go on the offensive against the Klan.

Civil Rights

Although Malcolm sought to work with civil rights leaders, they were not sympathetic to him. They both disagreed with his stand against nonviolence and feared losing white support if they aligned with him. Nevertheless, he never gave up trying to find some common ground with them. To reporters, he said that for black leaders to fight among themselves "needlessly" served no useful purpose, and that they accomplished more when they sat down in private and ironed out their differences.[74] He concluded that he would have "to go to the people first" and "let the leaders fall in behind them."[75]

Malcolm's willingness to work with civil rights leaders generated some controversy over his stand on integration. He saw his role, according to James Farmer, "as an extremist frightening white people into acceptance of the comparatively moderate civil rights organizations."[76] In that sense, said activist Bayard Rustin, Malcolm was moving in the direction of the civil rights movement.[77] To Herman Ferguson, however, at no time did Malcolm ever talk about "integration as the solution to the problem"; instead, he advocated "fighting for human rights."[78]

By this time, although Malcolm remained flexible, he was neither for integration nor separation. To him, people were naturally drawn to those whom they had most in common with, and he concluded from this that a combination of racial solidarity with interracial cooperation and understanding seemed the most workable state of affairs to help secure full human rights for black Americans.[79]

For one thing, Malcolm had little faith in the 1964 Civil Rights Act which Congress had passed earlier that year. While it proposed to desegregate public facilities in the south, he said, it would do nothing to help the general economic and political conditions of American blacks. In New York City, for instance, he said that there was nothing in the Civil Rights Act to prevent police brutality or to stop discrimination in jobs, housing, and education.[80]

The U.N. Card

Rather than advocating a physical return to Africa, Malcolm sought to raise black awareness of their cultural and spiritual links to it. He felt that the solution for American blacks and Africans were "one in the same," said Herman Ferguson. "Until Africa was free and independent, the black man in America would never be free and independent."[81]

For Malcolm, furthermore, America's black freedom struggle was about human rights, not civil rights, and that went beyond Washington's jurisdiction. His goal was to internationalize America's race problem by first linking it to the worldwide struggle against colonialism and second, so that the entire world could have a voice in it, to present it to the U.N. as a human rights issue.[82]

Most blacks, however, did not respond favorably to Malcolm's call to internationalize the race problem. To explain this, he blamed the white man, who had "thoroughly brainwashed the black man to see himself as only a domestic civil rights problem."[83] But that the black masses did not support his proposed alliance with Africans and Arabs was not surprising to Rustin. "For what," he said, "did a Harlem Negro, let alone an Arab Bedouin, have in common with a feudal prince like Faisal?"[84]

By midsummer 1964, Malcolm had undergone so many changes that to describe his ideology was difficult to do. According to one of his followers, Yuri Kochiyama, he went from "black nationalism to pan–Africanism to internationalism and finally to revolutionary internationalism."[85] Rather than moving closer to the mainstream civil rights movement, as Rustin had maintained, he was becoming more radical.

To the news media, Malcolm said that he was no longer a racist nor did he subscribe to any of the tenets of racism. During his pilgrimage to Mecca, Malcolm said, he had seen that all white people were not bad. Experiencing a "spiritual rebirth," he now neither regarded them as devils nor did he hate them. "I have done a complete about face," he said, and "I'm man enough to admit it even if it makes me look ridiculous in the eyes of the world."[86]

Yet Malcolm still distrusted whites. They were human beings, he said, as long as this was "borne out by their humane attitude towards Negroes."[87] While he could admit the rise in the possibility that some white people were sincere, they would first have to prove it to him.[88] According to Peter Goldman, he never retreated from his "first premise" that American whites were "deeply and perhaps irretrievably racist."[89]

When blacks questioned Malcolm's changed attitude towards whites, he would answer that he had not changed but only saw things on a broader scale. A white man cannot help being white, he said. "We've got to give the man a chance, but he probably won't take it, the snake."[90] Nevertheless, he would remain flexible: "My mind is wide open to anybody who will help get the ape off our backs."[91]

While the MMI would accept white members, only blacks could join the OAAU. They must "take the lead in their own fight," said Malcolm. Sincere whites, on the other hand, could best help by organizing among themselves to develop strategies to combat racism in their communities.[92] They have got to do their "proving of themselves," he said, "not among the black victims, but out on the battle lines of where America's racism is — among their own fellow whites."[93]

In the 1964 presidential race, Malcolm favored Republican Senator Barry Goldwater of Arizona over Democrat President Lyndon B. Johnson of Texas. Calling Goldwater a "wolf" and Johnson a "fox," Malcolm said that they were about the same since both "would eat the black man." Nonetheless, favoring the former, he said that with Goldwater blacks would "know they were fighting an honestly growling wolf rather than a fox who could have them in his stomach and have digested them before they even knew what was happening."[94]

Malcolm took some heat for favoring Goldwater over Johnson. "Why, should any Negro in his right mind vote for Goldwater?" said New York City's black councilman Irvine I. Turner. Instead, "Malcolm X should be praising President Johnson for at least trying to pave the way for freedom by fighting vigorously for civil rights."[95] "As every opinion poll has shown," said the *New York Post,* "the vast majority of Negroes does not share his pro–Goldwater neutralism."[96]

To Malcolm, however, the leading racists were not Goldwater Republicans but Johnson Democrats, whom he called Dixiecrats since southern congressmen dominated most of the congressional committees. "If you check," said Malcolm, "whenever any kind of legislation is suggested to mitigate the injustices that Negroes suffer in this country, you will find that the people who line up against it are members of Lyndon B. Johnson's party."[97]

Still, on a practical level, Malcolm's aim was to get blacks to register as independent voters. By registering Republican or Democrat they would automatically align themselves with a candidate and thus lose their bargaining power. To keep that power and use it to their advantage, they needed to register as independents. In that way, he said, they would gain the political leverage to bargain with the politicians.[98]

CHAPTER 10

Back Overseas

Indirectly, by a signal and suggestion, Elijah Muhammad ordered Malcolm X killed. To his followers, Muhammad said, "The brother's eyes need to be closed," and he encouraged them to say and to write threatening statements about him.[1] This helped create an atmosphere, said Herman Ferguson, "in which it would be possible to take Malcolm out."[2]

In public, although Muhammad said that he would "rather Malcolm live and suffer his treachery," he kept referring to him as the Nation of Islam's "chief hypocrite." In the Nation, said Benjamin 2X, the word hypocrite had a different meaning than in Christianity, where it meant one who posed as a friend. When a member of the Nation accused another of being a hypocrite, he said, his life was "on the line."[3]

The Chicago leadership, including Raymond Sharrieff, Elijah Muhammad, Jr., John Ali, and Herbert Muhammad, was at the forefront of the campaign against Malcolm. Wallace Muhammad blamed them for creating a "fiery" and "volatile" climate in which "offhand threats could become self-fulfilling prophesy and Malcolm's murder a holy obligation."[4]

Malcolm appeared to have accepted the reality of an early death. He told political observer Charles Wiley that he was "certain" that the Nation of Islam would eventually kill him.[5] And to newsman Theodore Jones, Malcolm said that he knew brothers in the movement "who were given orders to kill him."[6] As a result, he never made appointments too far in advance because he "didn't want to stand anybody up."[7] Likewise, he told Alex Haley that he did not expect to live long enough to read his autobiography in finished form.[8] "Malcolm knew what the circumstances were," said Captain Joseph.[9]

In late June 1964, Malcolm persuaded Evelyn Williams and Lucille

Rosary to file paternity suits in a Los Angeles court against Elijah Muhammad and retained a prominent attorney, Gladys Towles Root, to take their case. With their paternity suits filed, Malcolm was hoping that the press would no longer fear libel suits and print the story of Muhammad's extramarital affairs.[10]

On July 2, in Los Angeles Superior Court, Root filed paternity suits on behalf of Rosary and Williams, charging Elijah Muhammad with fathering their five children. Along with the paternity suits, Root submitted affidavits alleging that Muhammad's "fanatical followers" might try to kill the two women for going public with his infidelities."[11]

Some of the newspapers printing the story included *The Los Angeles Sentinel, The Chicago Tribune, The Herald Examiner* (Los Angeles), and *The Chicago American*. Giving it the most coverage, however, was *The Amsterdam News,* New York City's black weekly. Its storyline noted that the paternity suits charged Elijah Muhammad with fathering Williams' two children and Rosary's three children, including a recently born baby girl, and the newspaper included a picture of the two women with their children showing Rosary still bloated from the effects of just giving birth to her third child.[12]

Speaking for the Nation of Islam, Raymond Sharrieff and John Ali disputed Rosary's and Williams' accusations that Muhammad had fathered their children. Malcolm had "put them up to it," said the two men, because of his "evil, jealous, and malicious intentions." Nevertheless, Mosque Number Two's poor treasury would continue to provide them with food, clothing, and shelter. As to who was the father of the children, Sharrieff and Ali said that "only Allah knows."[13]

Shortly after Root filed the two women's paternity suits, however, to Malcolm's chagrin, she became distracted by her own legal problems from a previous case and did not pursue them, which nullified their impact.[14]

The paternity suits only generated more danger for Malcolm. On July 3, as he got into his car, two black men suddenly came out of the shadows towards it. Reacting quickly, he locked the doors, sped away and circled the block. Back at his house, the two men nowhere in sight, he rushed into it and grabbed his rifle just in case they returned. "I have weapons, and I would use them without hesitation," he later told reporters. "But I would hate to use them against Muslim brothers who are just dupes of Elijah Muhammad."[15]

Two days later, an unknown caller warned Malcolm that orders had gone out in Chicago to kill him in New York City. Later that day, an almost exact repeat of the July 2 incident occurred. As he was getting into his car, four black men with knives came at him. Again, he sped off, circled the block, came back home and got his rifle, but the men were gone.[16]

Meanwhile, Hassan Sharrieff, Elijah Muhammad's grandson, informed *The Chicago Daily Defender* that he had defected from the Nation of Islam. He accused both his grandfather and the Chicago leadership of misuse of money and improprieties with various women. Sharrieff said, in effect, that "corruption ran rampant through the Nation of Islam." His uncle, Wallace Muhammad, had convinced him, moreover, that his grandfather's teachings were incorrect, leading Sharrieff to become an orthodox Muslim and severing all ties with the Nation.[17]

Shortly thereafter, Sharrieff informed the FBI that he feared for his life and considered getting a gun for protection. Although there were no specific threats made against him, he said, he was still "in danger of bodily harm" because those who deviate from the Nation got a "whuppin" or worse.[18]

Back Overseas

Only seven weeks after Malcolm's return from abroad, he decided to go back for another tour of the Middle East and Africa. Part of his reason for returning abroad was to escape the escalating level of violence being directed by the Nation against him, but he also hoped to generate financial and political support for the OAAU among the various heads of state in the two regions.

Another reason for going abroad just then was to attend the second OAU Summit Conference, being held in Cairo, Egypt, from July 17 to July 22. While there, he intended to inform its representatives of "the true plight of America's Negroes" and to persuade them that Washington's handling of its race problem was as much a violation of the U.N.'s human rights charter as South Africa's Apartheid policy, which sanctioned its white minority to rule over the black majority.[19]

From July 9 to November 24, 1964, Malcolm traveled throughout the Middle East and Africa. His first stop was Cairo, where the OAU, attended by nearly all of its thirty-four member states, granted him observer status, permitting him easy access to its representatives. Its officials even allowed him to stay on the *Isis*, the yacht housing both Africa's leading freedom fighters and heads of state.

Malcolm, in fact, was the only American to have full observer status at the OAU conference. To cover it, the U.S. State Department had assigned two of its foreign service officers, a senior Africanist and an OAU specialist, but OAU officials would not let them past the lobby of either the Shepeard or the Nile Hilton hotels. To the State Department's embarrassment, while its two men had difficulty getting the ear of the African heads of state, Malcolm seemed "free to go everywhere."[20]

Although Malcolm was not permitted to address the conference, the OAU allowed him to circulate an eight page memorandum among the delegates. Endeavoring to link America's race problem to Africa's situation, he wrote that whites would never recognize Africans as free human beings until blacks received their proper due. Racism, he wrote, was not just a "Negro problem," not one of civil rights, but a problem for humanity and human rights. He prayed that Africans had not freed themselves from European colonialism "only to be overcome and held in check now by American dollarism."

Blaming Washington for preaching integration "while deceitfully practicing segregation" was a major theme of Malcolm's memorandum. The passage of the 1964 Civil Rights Act, he wrote, was not a sincere effort by Washington to correct racial injustice but a part of its "deceit and trickery" to keep the African nations from condemning America's racist policies before the U.N. as the OAU was doing regarding South Africa's apartheid.

Getting to his main point, Malcolm wrote that the OAU needs to bring America's race problem before the U.N. on the grounds that Washington was "morally incapable" of protecting the lives and property of twenty-two million African Americans, and that their "deteriorating plight was definitely becoming a threat to world peace."

Passages in Malcolm's memorandum, however, indicated that he had encountered some resistance by African leaders to his ideas. Some of them, apparently, had implied that they had enough problems in Africa without adding the African American problem. To this, he gave them an analogy: a good shepherd who had left ninety-nine sheep at home to go to the aid of one who had fallen into the hands of an "imperialist wolf."[21]

Although considerably more moderate in tone than Malcolm had desired, the OAU passed a resolution condemning racism in the United States. While it noted with satisfaction Washington's recent enactment of the 1964 Civil Rights Act, it was "deeply disturbed" by the continuing racial bigotry and oppression by white Americans against its Negro citizens. The resolution urged Washington to intensify its efforts to eradicate all forms of discrimination based on "race, color, or ethnic origin."[22]

The OAU resolution was "tame stuff" for Malcolm, but it was an important gesture to what he hoped would become a link between Africa and black America. For Washington, however, it represented an embarrassment that Malcolm, whom it openly disavowed, was both the only American welcomed to the OAU conference and that he had persuaded its members to pass, at least in part, his resolution.[23]

Unfortunately for Malcolm, because of pressure from Washington, the U.N. failed to act on the OAU resolution.

The Home Front

On July 16, while Malcolm was in Cairo, a white Harlem policeman, Thomas Gilligan, shot and killed James Powell, a black teenager, for allegedly resisting arrest as a robbery suspect. Soon thereafter, an angry crowd formed outside the 123rd Street Police Station, the same one where the police had held Hinton Johnson seven years before, demanding Gilligan's arrest for murder. When the police began making arrests, the crowd dispersed into small clusters and began spreading out over Harlem, smashing store windows, taking its goods, and setting fire to buildings.

Harlem's riot lasted five days, spreading unrest into New York City's black community in Brooklyn and black neighborhoods in Buffalo and Rochester, New York. The state's racial upheavals forced Governor Nelson Rockefeller to call out the National Guard to maintain order and safeguard property.

To foreign observers in Cairo, Malcolm, rejecting American newspapers' depiction of the rioters as hoodlums and thieves, described the Harlem riot in political terms. The whites, he said, who lived elsewhere, owned Harlem, forcing blacks to pay the "highest rent for the lowest type boarding place" and the "highest prices for the lowest grade of food." Frustrated by their condition, then, the only way for blacks to get at whites was to destroy their property.[24]

More and worse riots would "erupt," added Malcolm, and "outright police scare tactics" would no longer work because the Harlem riot had shown blacks, who were "not afraid," the whites' "underbelly of guilty fear."[25]

Before leaving the United States, Malcolm had failed to delegate proper authority among his followers within the OAAU and MMI. The difficulty lay with both his underestimation of their abilities and his tendency towards perfectionism, which made him impatient when they did not carry out his orders with "military-like dispatch."[26] As a result, serious conflict developed among them. Some wrote him to express their dislike of his giving women positions of power while others conveyed their fears that non–Muslims had gained too much control. Most agreed, however, that he should come home as soon as possible to give them direction and help build the movement.[27]

In a letter to his followers, dated August 29, 1964, Malcolm wrote that dissatisfaction with him and disunity within the movement "doesn't excite or worry" him. Of those among them who wanted to "walk away," he wrote, they have both the right to do so and to establish other organizations. But he asked those followers who wanted to remain in the OAAU and MMI to stop fighting each other. They could either make both organizations a success or they could destroy them. Regardless, with the strength that Allah gave him, if necessary, he would start over from scratch. After stating his love for all of his followers, he ended his letter with the words "Salaam Alaikum" (peace be with you).[28]

Overseas Monitoring

Since Malcolm was using his overseas visits as an opportunity to influence foreign nations to oppose both the United States' racial policies at home and its military and economic policies abroad, a number of government agencies were keeping their eye on him. Among them were the FBI, the Central Intelligence Agency (CIA), the U.S. State Department, and the U.S. Information Agency (USIA). They, in turn, shared their information with the U.S. Secret Service, the U.S. Army, Navy, and Air Force intelligence agencies, and the assistant attorney general, J. Walter Yeagley.[29]

Described by some as one of the FBI's "certified friends," newsman Victor Reisel, writing in the *New York Journal American* on July 23, the day after the OAU conference closed, called Malcolm X's efforts there "a propaganda operation." And when he wanted to meet with his pro–Communist friends, wrote Reisel, he went to the headquarters of Ghana's pro–Communist delegation at the Omar Khayan Hotel. Likewise, added Reisel, now that Elijah Muhammad's Muslims had declared war on Malcolm X, of "considerable interest" to the intelligence agencies of several countries was the source of his funds.[30]

At the same time, another anti–Malcolm newsman, Samuel Schreig, writing in the *Chicago Sentinel*, accused him of obtaining his money from President Gamal Abdel Nasser of Egypt, and promoting his interests in the United States. According to law, then, wrote Schreig, Malcolm X should register "as a foreign agent."[31]

Accordingly, on September 2, Assistant Attorney General Yeagley asked FBI Director Hoover to investigate whether Malcolm X had violated either the Logan Act or the U.S. Foreign Agents Registration Act. While the former forbade American citizens from private correspondence with foreign nations to the detriment of the United States, the latter required registration of any United States organization receiving funds from or serving as an agent for a foreign government.[32]

Nevertheless, except for Nasser's government paying Malcolm's motel expenses in Cairo and Egypt's Supreme Council on Islamic Affairs paying his plane fare, the FBI found no evidence that he had violated either the Logan Act or the Foreign Agents Registration Act.[33] For his second trip, in fact, most of his money came from a forthcoming magazine article in the *Saturday Evening Post* and from Doubleday and Company for Alex Haley's work in progress on Malcolm's autobiography.[34]

Throughout his travels, although Malcolm knew that he was under constant surveillance by American agents, he usually ignored them. One morning, however, while eating his breakfast at a Cairo restaurant, he became annoyed with this one agent who kept staring at him. Walking over to the agent, Malcolm challenged his manner of spying on him. When the agent denied being a spy, Malcolm called him a "fool" for belying his intelligence. Unnerved, the agent referred to Malcolm as "anti–American" "seditious," "subversive," and probably "Communist." His tirade, said Malcolm later, only proved how little the intelligence agencies knew about him.[35]

On July 23, while dining at Cairo's Nile Hilton Hotel with Milton Henry, an attorney friend, Malcolm began experiencing intense abdominal pain. As a result, an ambulance took him to the hospital where doctors pumped his stomach. One of them, according to Henry, said that someone had placed a "toxic substance" in Malcolm's food. Although the other doctors present did not collaborate the evidence of food poisoning, Malcolm suspected that American intelligence agencies had tried to poison him.[36] Yet, they did not view Malcolm as a policy problem until after the OAU had passed its resolution; even then, they were slow to react.

Other Countries

During his second trip, besides Egypt, Malcolm visited thirteen countries. They included Saudi Arabia, Kuwait, Lebanon, Sudan, Ethiopia, Kenya, Tanganyika, Zanzibar (New Tanzania), Nigeria, Ghana, Liberia, Guinea, and Algeria. Unlike his first trip, however, which was impromptu and informal and where he often got stuck waiting at airports, his second was more formal and public and foreign leaders treated him like a head of state.

Malcolm had audiences with seven heads of state and, in some instances, even addressed their parliaments. He spent an hour and a half with President Nasser of Egypt; three hours with President Jomo Kenyatta of Kenya; talked with President Azikwe of Nigeria and again with President Nkrumah of Ghana; and lived for three days in the home of President Sekou Toure of Guinea.

In the religious sphere, Malcolm achieved considerable success. Before he left Cairo in September 1964, the Supreme Council on Islamic Affairs offered him twenty scholarships for black Americans who wished to study at the city's Al-Azar University. In Mecca, he received from the World Muslim Council, the supreme religious body in the Muslim world, official certification to spread Islam in America; fifteen scholarships for black Americans who wished to study at the University of Medina in Saudi Arabia; and a spiritual advisor and teacher, Sheik Ahmed Hassourn, to help Malcolm in his efforts to correct the "distorted image" of Islam that American "hate groups" have given it.[37]

In late September, while in Mecca, Malcolm learned that Judge Wahl had ruled against him on the eviction proceedings brought by the Nation in April and gave him until January 31, 1965, enough time to file an appeal, to vacate his residence.[38]

Partly out of anger over losing his home, Malcolm, in what was probably the most pronounced religious attacks against Elijah Muhammad up to that time, sent an open letter, dated September 22, to *New York Times* reporter M. S. Handler. Calling Muhammad a "religious faker" who had "fooled and misused" unsuspecting blacks, he promised never to rest until he had "undone the harm" that he had done to so many "well-meaning innocent Negroes" because of his "evangelistic zeal" as one of the Nation's ministers.

For twelve years, wrote Malcolm, he had lived within the confines of the Nation's "strait-jacket world" because of his belief that Muhammad was a messenger from God. Proclaiming his faith in orthodox Islam, which accepted all human beings as equals before God, Malcolm regarded Muhammad's "Islam" as "a racist philosophy," deceitfully labeled "Islam" only "to fool and misuse gullible people." On the other hand, Malcolm, in ending his letter, emphasized that he was trying to remain open-minded, to "weigh everything objectively," and to include among his friends people of all religious and political persuasions, including "Uncle Toms."[39]

From Mecca, Malcolm flew to Kuwait and then by way of Beirut, Lebanon, and Khartoum, Sudan, to Addis Ababa, Ethiopia, where he spoke to over five-hundred students at the city's University College. In his address, he concentrated on his familiar theme of bringing the United States before the U.N. for violating the human rights of its black citizens. Though he was "less emotional" than usual, the audience was enthusiastic, periodically interrupting him with applause.[40]

From Ethiopia, Malcolm traveled to Nairobi, Kenya, where he spoke with a number of sympathetic government officials. Noticing, however, that American visitors were avoiding him, he complained to Ambassador William Attwood about "an alleged effort" by the American Embassy to discourage them from meeting with him. Denying this, he asked Malcolm "not to speak out so strongly against the conditions of Southern Negroes because it hurt our image among Africans." But instead of attempting to quiet him, replied Malcolm, Attwood should "tell the U.S. government to put an end to oppressions of black people both here and abroad."[41]

At the Nairobi Hotel, where Malcolm was staying, he crossed paths with two of SNCC's prominent leaders, John Lewis and Donald Harris, who were touring Africa. From their discussions, said Lewis, he got the feeling that Malcolm was "in the process of becoming a changed man" since he kept repeating that "he really wanted to be helpful and supportive of the civil rights movement."[42] Harris, too, who had spoken with Malcolm the year before, noticed a change in his "overall perspective." He talked about bringing together all of the civil rights factions so they could "speak with greater effectiveness," and he had changed his manner of speaking to people, making "a conscious effort not to frighten them off."[43]

From Kenya, Malcolm returned to Addis Ababa, hoping to meet with Ethiopia's Emperor Haile Selassie. He refused to meet with Malcolm, however, because Selassie feared losing United States aid, which he was dependent on. "There were governments," said American expatriate Alice Windom, "that weren't about to exercise any manhood that would make them do something that the American government didn't want."[44]

Leaving Addis Ababa and after a short stop in Ibadan, Nigeria, Malcolm journeyed to Accra, Ghana. But unlike his first visit, where he was in continual motion giving speeches and addresses, he spent most of his time quietly visiting with his black expatriate friends. He was more pensive and searching, said Lesley Lacy, and he looked very tired and fearful. Although he had been preoccupied with the thought of death and assassination on his first visit, she said, as he talked, "sometimes coherently," she felt "a strange feeling of finality."[45]

During Malcolm's visit, several Chinese reporters interviewed him. Mainly, they wanted him to comment on China's successful test explosion of its first nuclear bomb earlier that year. Calling its nuclear test the "greatest thing that had happened in the twentieth century," he said that it was not only good for black people, but also "for all people in the world fighting against imperialists." Yet he praised, on the other hand, China's call for a world summit conference to discuss "the complete prohibition and thorough destruction of nuclear weapons."[46]

Just as Malcolm was preparing to leave Accra, his expatriate friends, realizing that his life was more in danger than ever if he returned to the United States, tried to persuade him to stay with them and to later send for his wife and children. Earlier, Presidents Nasser of Egypt and Nkrumah of Ghana offered him employment. While the former wanted to appoint him head of Cairo's foreign ministry, Nkrumah was willing to create a position for him as an anti–American speech writer and policy advisor on East-West relations.[47]

Why then, despite numerous offers of accommodations did Malcolm decide to return to the United States? To his expatriate friends, he said that they had taught him "the true meaning and strength of unity," and if he could pass this on to American blacks, his life would "be a small price to pay for such a vision."[48]

According to his OAAU followers, Malcolm returned home because helping America's blacks to achieve equality and freedom was too important a task for him to allow "fear to sidetrack him."[49] He thought, said Herman Ferguson, that "the black man had run too often and that now was the time to stand up and fight."[50] To Malcolm, said Yuri Kochiyama, America was the "black man's battlefield."[51] Since he could not deliver what people demanded of him, said Charles Kenyatta, "he decided to sacrifice himself for us."[52]

From Accra, Malcolm journeyed to Monrovia, Liberia, and next to Conakay, Guinea, spending three days as a guest of President Sekou Toure; and from there, he flew to Kakar, Senegal, and then to Casablanca, Morocco. Finally, he flew to Algiers, Algeria, and from there by way of Bern, Switzerland, to Paris, France, where Presence Africaine, an African cultural organization, had invited him to speak.

Back Home and Then to London

Returning home on November 24, 1964, Malcolm had spent a total of twenty-five weeks abroad. Yet he would remain in the United States only six days before embarking for London, England. Like his last homecoming, he was met at New York's Kennedy Airport by his family and supporters holding placards that read "Welcome Back Brother Malcolm."

After greeting his family and supporters, Malcolm talked briefly with reporters who had assembled at the airport. Throughout his travels in Africa, he said, the people and their leaders greeted him with "open minds, open hearts, and open doors." Now that he was back home, he said, he was willing to meet with any sincere group, whether white or black to find "a solution to the racial problem." Asked if that applied to Elijah Muhammad, whom he had called a "religious faker" in his September 22 open letter sent from Africa, Malcolm replied that he would "seek a spirit and atmosphere of unity" with him.[53]

In response, Captain Joseph and Henry X told reporters that Malcolm was a "self-serving hypocrite consumed by a passion for personal power." Rejecting, at the same time, reports that he won the official support of the World Muslim Council, they warned him to stop attacking Elijah Muhammad or his followers would fight Malcolm as hard as he fought them.[54]

Before leaving for London to participate in Oxford Union Society's annual debate at Oxford University, Malcolm flew to the home of his estranged brother, Philbert X, in Lansing, Michigan. Days earlier, he had arranged the release of their mother from Kalamazoo State Hospital, where she had been a patient since 1939. Although she had only improved slightly since he had last seen her shortly after his release from prison in 1952, he rejoiced quietly over her freedom.[55]

Televised throughout England on December 3, the Oxford Union Society's topic was "Extremism in the Defense of Liberty is No Vice, Moderation in the Pursuit of Justice is No Virtue." Although there were other speakers, Malcolm was both the main attraction and the one the British upper class students were most wary of.

Rejecting unjustified extremism, Malcolm said that exercising extremism in defense of liberty was "no vice" and that moderation in pursuit of justice was a sin. Extremism, he said, would prove more effective in the struggle for civil rights than all the "little wish-washy love-thy-enemy approaches" currently espoused by American civil rights leaders.

Extremism, said Malcolm, lay at the "very heart of the American struggle for human liberty." Calling Patrick Henry an extremist, Malcolm quoted Henry's famous statement: "Give me liberty or give me death." Then, Malcolm quoted Shakespeare: "To be or not to be." He was in doubt, said Malcolm, about "whether it was nobler in the mind of man to suffer the slings and arrows of outrageous fortune in moderation or to take up arms against the sea of troubles and by opposing end them."

Agreeing with Shakespeare, Malcolm said, "If you take up arms, you'll end it." But if you wait for the one who's in power to make up his mind that he should end it, you'll be waiting a long time.

For Malcolm, then, the present was a time for extremism, "a time for revolution." Ending his address, he asked the students to join with people of all races to "wrest power from those who have misused it and to change this miserable condition that exists on this earth." The students, no longer wary of him, gave him a standing ovation.[56]

After giving talks in Manchester and Sheffield, Malcolm returned to the United States on December 6. His short visit, about a week, made a positive impression on the British, who liked his "careful manner of speech and decorum."[57]

Wallace's and Akbar's Defections

In a letter to his father in late June 1964, Wallace Muhammad, who had earlier embraced orthodox Islam, announced his withdrawal from the Nation of Islam. His father's followers, he wrote, and the family were "withering like dying flowers," lacking the righteousness that they had exhibited at an earlier time. He could no longer excuse his father from the "explosive situation" that his infidelities had created or the corruption by the Chicago leadership in gaining wealth from "excessive contributions" and underpaying Muslims who worked in the Nation's various enterprises.[58]

Shortly thereafter, Wallace began receiving death threats. Fearful that "punch-your-teeth-out" FOI squads, as he called them, were targeting him, he went to the police. At the same time, he told the Chicago leadership that he had gone to the authorities. As a result, the threats stopped.[59]

In September, Wallace announced the formation of the Afro-Descendants Upliftment Society, whose platform called for both black voter registration drives and education programs. Its members, he said, would obey the law, and they would remain apart from Malcolm because of his "violent image." Hassan Sharrieff, who had deviated earlier from his grandfather's teachings, would become Wallace's aide, but he had no plans for other officers.[60]

Short on funds and supporters, however, Wallace's new organization would never get off the ground. To support himself, he worked as a painter and welder. For him, since he had never before been outside the Nation of Islam, leaving it meant "isolation and hardship."[61]

For some time, Wallace had been corresponding with his brother Akbar, who was then living in Cairo, attending the University of Al-Azbar, and working as a correspondent for *Muhammad Speaks*. While studying for his Ph.D. in Islamic Jurisprudence, he realized that his father's teachings did not conform to Orthodox Islam. And from Wallace, Akbar learned of both his father's infidelities and the Chicago leadership's corruption. Upset by these facts, Akbar decided to return to the United States and discuss the situation with his father.[62]

But when Akbar arrived in Chicago in late 1964, Elijah Muhammad, dismissing Wallace's allegations against him and the Chicago leadership, would only discuss his problems with Malcolm. During their five hour talk, Muhammad insisted that his son visit the various mosques throughout the country and denounce Malcolm as "an ingrate and a hypocrite." Before he would do that, said Akbar, his father would have to prove to him that Malcolm was "unworthy" on the basis of the Islamic theology and the Muslim holy book, the Koran. Frustrated and angered by his son's reply, Muhammad told Akbar to get out of the Nation of Islam.[63]

Although Akbar quit the Nation on December 5, he waited until January 14, 1965, to make it official. At that time, he told reporters that he could neither agree with his father's "concocted religious teachings," which were in most cases "diametrically opposed to Islam," nor adhere to his "politically sterile philosophy of the Afro-American struggle." While Akbar would not join another movement, he sympathized with Malcolm X and others in their efforts to establish an orthodox Muslim movement among American blacks.

Despite the fact that neither Akbar nor Wallace joined with Malcolm, the Nation blamed him for their defections, creating another mark against his name.[64]

CHAPTER 11

Under the Wire

Back from England on December 6, 1964, Malcolm X appeared demoralized. At times, his friends and associates described him as "tense," "frustrated," "irritable," "unsure of himself," "tired," "worn," "exhausted," and "used up."[1] He gave the appearance, moreover, of a man without a set identity, fluctuating between teacher, minister, Muslim, African, internationalist, and revolutionary. "I won't deny I don't know where I'm at," he told the press. "But by the same token how many of us can put the finger down on one point and say I'm here."[2]

Malcolm's goal was to achieve freedom for blacks "by any means necessary." Still, if he was to get anywhere, he needed to build his movement. Yet he was lacking money and followers and trying to stay alive. To his attorney friend, Milton Henry, Malcolm said that people were looking to him to organize the entire black nationalist movement, but for one man, that was "a task of frightening dimensions" and "an awful responsibility."[3] Despite such pressure, however, said Alex Haley, "his image demanded that he be stoic and move on."[4]

During this time, Malcolm's relationship with Betty was unclear. She was pregnant again, raising their four children, and he was traveling a lot, said Herman Ferguson. These things "would have had to affect their relationship."[5] Malcolm and his wife were "having problems," said Charles Kenyatta, since she wanted that American lifestyle, and there was talk of divorce.[6] Malcolm, said Yuri Kochiyama, was about "being constant in principles but never about money."[7]

Nevertheless, Malcolm, knowing that time was running out for him, wanted to provide for his family. Without money or anything useable to sell, he tried to obtain a life insurance policy. While walking the streets of Harlem on a cold wintry December day, he told Benjamin 2X that the insurance company denied him one without bothering with the "formality of a physical," and "that tells you how much my life is worth."[8]

Despite problems at home, Malcolm did not appear to have ever engaged in extramarital relations. According to Kenyatta, the Nation of Islam was trying to entrap Malcolm by "sending women his way," but he refused to take the bait.[9] Calling him a "straight arrow," Kochiyama said that he "would not do the things other men did."[10] Opportunities were there, said biographer Louis DeCaro, but Malcolm probably backed away from them because he felt the "burden of living a clean lifestyle" in order to present Islam "in the most pure form."[11]

Even before Malcolm had come back from England, the Nation had intensified its campaign against him. In the December 4 *Muhammad Speaks,* referring to Malcolm as that "cowardly hypocritical dog," Louis X wrote that such a man as him, "especially after such evil, foolish talk about his benefactor," was "worthy of death."[12] On December 12, Chicago's weekly *The Crusader* published a similar message by Raymond Sharrieff, warning him that the Nation "shall no longer tolerate" further "scandalizing" of its leader.[13]

Throughout the winter, said Benjamin 2X, Malcolm received death threats by mail and over the phone, and rumors of assassination plots were frequent.[14]

By this time, although Malcolm did not like being escorted around by bodyguards, which reminded him of Elijah Muhammad and the Nation, his followers insisted that at least a dozen of them accompany him whenever he gave talks in New York City and, if possible, outside of it, too. They further insisted on screening all of his visitors at the Theresa Hotel, checking buildings before he entered them and following his car in their own cars.[15]

While Malcolm never sanctioned a shooting war with the Nation, he kept both a pistol and an automatic carbine rifle in his home and carried with him two tear gas fountain pens at the ready position.[16] Also, the NYPD, beginning in 1964, began assigning security guards at Malcolm's public meetings. At the same time, BOSS increased its surveillance of him, including undercover agents, bugging the OAAU's phone, and checking the trash which Malcolm and his family took out at their Queens home.[17]

As mentioned earlier, during Malcolm's second extended trip abroad, his lieutenants wrote him of bickering, jealousy, and defections among the members of the OAAU and MMI. Consequently, when he came home, he found that the combined membership of both organizations had declined from four hundred to forty "hard core" members and two hundred "hangers-on."[18] Yet, fearing for his life and lacking money, he neither had the time nor the energy to keep his movement together.

The Socialist Workers Party

A splinter group from the American Communist Party, the Socialist Workers Party (SWP), looked upon Malcolm X as a means to attract blacks to its movement. On several occasions, it invited him to speak at its Militant Labor Forum, and its newspaper, *The Militant,* gave him heavy coverage. The SWP "really jumped on Malcolm's bandwagon," said a radical black journalist to Peter Goldman. It had "never made any real inroads with the brothers before."[19]

Malcolm was grateful to the SWP for offering him both a platform to speak and extensive coverage in its newspaper. Indeed, he said to reporters, it was the only one that told the complete truth about him.[20] In return, he used his influence in Harlem to get speaking engagements for the SWP's presidential candidate, Clifton DeBarry, a fair-skinned black who had publicly welcomed the formation of the OAAU.

That the SWP would exert undue influence over Malcolm was a concern of OAAU members. "Every time you went to an OAAU rally," said Charles Kenyatta, "you saw a lot of SWP people there."[21] "Malcolm was a beautiful tool to be used unwittingly," said Charles Morris, an OAAU lieutenant.[22] Yet, according to an FBI report, the SWP neither dominated nor unduly influenced him.[23]

By late 1964, some argued that Malcolm was drifting in the direction of socialism. He was pro-socialist, said SWP writer George Breitman, although he was not yet a Marxist.[24] "He liked the SWP," said Kochiyama, "not just because it gave him a platform, but he liked its thinking."[25] That he would have become a socialist was inevitable, said Herman Ferguson, but he would "never have joined the SWP."[26] Becoming a member of the SWP would "never have worked for Malcolm," said Charles Kenyatta, because he was "too deeply committed to blacks."[27] Since he had a "race first view," said Paul Lee, "it would have been correct to say that he was a pro–African Socialist."[28] Because he "distrusted most whites," said biographer James Cone, he would not have joined any "Marxist groups in the United States."[29]

Since leaving the Nation of Islam, Malcolm was leery of any group, such as the SWP, with too structured a system of thought. "I'm not going to be in anybody's straitjacket," he told reporters. "Now I think with my own mind."[30]

Lacking any set views, Malcolm, in fact, was in a period of transition.

To some extent, he tailored his speeches to different audiences. He talked to blacks one way and to whites and mixed groups another; in churches, he spoke in religious terms, and at colleges and universities, he became professorial. He would take a stance in support of the SWP at one point and a statesman-like pose for African leaders at another. But at the same time, he was always simplifying, making understandable the conditions and problems that blacks faced living in a racist society.

The Los Angeles Skirmish

On January 22, 1965, according to Malcolm, three of Elijah Muhammad's followers jumped him as he came out of his house. After a brief scuffle, however, they ran away. Policemen searched the neighborhood but found no trace of them.[31]

Six days later, Malcolm flew to Los Angeles to meet with Lucille Rosary and Evelyn Williams and their lawyer, Gladys Towles Root, about their paternity suit. Waiting for him at the airport were Allen Jamal, a Nation of Islam defector, and Edward Bradley, publisher of the *Roll Call,* a small newspaper. Before Malcolm's plane landed, however, they spotted John Ali sitting inside the terminal. Fearing a stakeout by Muhammad's followers, they notified airport officials. In turn, they radioed the pilots of Malcolm's plane to divert their landing to a gate on the opposite side of the airport.[32]

After Malcolm got off the plane, Jamal and Bradley immediately hustled him off to the Statler Hilton Hotel. While Malcolm checked in and went up to his room with Jamal to drop off his suitcase, Bradley waited for them in the lobby. To his astonishment, six of Muhammad's followers, including John Ali, walked through the hotel's front entrance. As Bradley leaned later, however, none of them were aware that Malcolm was in town. Ali, in fact, was in Los Angeles on business and his flight had just landed within minutes of Malcolm's plane, and both men happened to have registered at the same hotel.

As the six Muslims walked across the lobby to check in, the hotel's elevator doors opened and out stepped Malcolm and Jamal. They were not more than ten feet from the Muslims. According to Bradley, the Muslims were "stunned" and Malcolm's and Jamal's faces "froze." After only a moment's hesitation, they quickly walked out of the hotel, assembled with Bradley, and left in his car.[33]

Driving to the home of Rosary and Williams, Bradley noticed that the encounter with Muhammad's followers had made Malcolm nervous. Fearing that they were watching the women's home, he asked Bradley not to stop in front of it, but he was to send Jamal on foot to tell them that he would pick them up several blocks away.

Soon thereafter, Malcolm, the two women, and Root assembled in her office. He informed them that Muhammad was both immoral and corrupt since he had not only engaged in extramarital affairs but also pocketed large sums of money collected from his followers to build schools and other benefits promised to them. While intending to tell all of this in court when the women's cases came to trial, Malcolm said that if Root did not hurry them, he would "never be alive" to attend it.[34]

Driving back to the hotel, Bradley and Malcolm spotted groups of Muslims milling about. As a result, he ran from the car into the lobby and took the elevator up to his room. Almost immediately, the phone rang. "Nigger, you are dead," said the caller, and then hung up. The call unnerved Malcolm, who covered his face with his hands for a moment of silent thought. He decided, then, that further visits were too dangerous; instead, he spent the next two hours talking on the phone to wavering members of the Nation's Los Angeles Mosque Number Twenty-Seven.[35]

Before taking Malcolm to the airport the next day, Bradley phoned LAPD's intelligence department, asking for police protection at the terminal. But why he did not ask for a police escort to the airport, too, was a mystery.

While driving Malcolm to the airport, Bradley noticed two cars filled with Muslims following them. By zigzagging and executing several U-turns, he was able to elude one of the cars, but the other one managed to catch up and pull alongside of him. At that point, Malcolm picked up a walking cane, which Bradley used because of a bad back, from the floor of the car, lowered the back door window, and pointed it at the Muslim driver as if it was a rifle. When he slowed, Bradley swerved across the freeway heading for the nearest exit. At that point, the Muslim driver got tangled in traffic and was unable to follow him up the exit ramp.[36]

When Malcolm and Bradley arrived at the airport, eight policemen escorted them to the ticket counter. While Malcolm was buying his ticket to Chicago, where he would assemble with representatives from the Illinois Attorney General's office who were investigating the Nation of Islam, the police spotted two Muslims walking into the terminal. Forming a protective cover around Malcolm and Bradley, the police rushed them into a small office and then to the runway through an underground chute.

Meanwhile, the plane's pilots, fearing that Malcolm's enemies may have placed a bomb aboard, refused to take off until the police thoroughly searched the plane and its baggage.[37] Once done, Malcolm thanked Bradley for all that he had done for him and boarded the plane, which soon departed for Chicago. "We missed death by inches," said Bradley later, and "we knew it."[38]

The Chicago Encounter

On the plane flight to Chicago, the FBI had placed an informant in the seat next to Malcolm. But when the informant inadvertently admitted to being a former police officer, Malcolm suspected him of still being one. Nevertheless, talking freely, Malcolm said that the Nation of Islam had turned into a "hate organization" and its members were out to kill him. Because of their devotion to Elijah Muhammad, he added, "they would jump into fire if he ordered it." To the informant, Malcolm seemed "very frightened" and "appreciative of any protection given him."[39]

Before landing in Chicago, where Malcolm would spend three days, from January 29 to January 31, the LAPD had informed the Chicago police about the assassination attempts against him. Consequently, when his plane landed at Chicago's O'Hare Airport, six police officers, headed by Edward McClellan, met him at the terminal and escorted him to his suite at the downtown Sherman House Hotel. While suspicious of their motives, Malcolm welcomed their protection. He told McClellan that although "nothing will stop my mission," Muhammad's followers were "tracking my presence for the purpose of killing me."[40]

As stated, the purpose of Malcolm's visit was to meet with representatives of the attorney general's office. Because of his bitter dispute with the Nation of Islam, they hoped to persuade him to testify on their behalf against Muslim inmates at Statesville Penitentiary who were suing Illinois for denying them permission to hold religious services and access to both a Muslim chaplain and Islamic reading material.

At the time of Malcolm's visit, the state's case against the Muslim inmates was temporarily deadlocked. The U.S. District Court for the Northern District of Illinois had dismissed their petition for redress, and the U.S. Court of Appeals affirmed it, arguing that the Nation of Islam constituted a threat to the prison's racial peace, and that its followers might not obey non–Muslim authority. The U.S. Supreme Court, however, reversed the appeals court, remanding the case back to the district court for trial on March 22, 1965.

Ironically, Statesville's Muslims were demanding the same religious privileges that Malcolm had fought so hard for when he was an inmate at Charleston Prison. Also, while in the Nation of Islam, he had urged Muhammad to fund litigation to compel New York State to permit Islamic services at its Attica Prison. Now, the State of Illinois was asking him to testify against the movement that he was once so much a part of.

While testifying on behalf of Illinois against the Muslim inmates was a way to hurt the Nation, which was out to get him, Malcolm appeared ambivalent about it and whether he actually agreed to it was unclear.[41] In another matter, however, on whether the State of Illinois should award the Nation tax exemptions normally given to religious organizations, he apparently gave "secret testimony" to the attorney general's office about its finances.[42]

On January 30, in a television interview with Chicago columnist Irv Kupcinet, Malcolm seemed particularly bitter in his denunciations of Elijah Muhammad. He was critical not only of Muhammad's infidelities but also of his treatment of the women who engaged in them with him. To have "gotten weak" for a woman was one thing, said Malcolm, but after "completely destroying her reputation," for Muhammad "to do nothing whatsoever to protect her as a woman" made him less than a man. Attacking his religious credentials, too, Malcolm called Muhammad a "phony" and a "faker" whose religion was "a concocted, distorted product of his own making."

In addition, Malcolm discussed the attempts on his life. He was so certain of being killed, he said, that he had "a letter on his desk naming the persons assigned to kill him."[43] If true, however, it remained a mystery since he never showed it to anyone.

Afterwards, as Malcolm left the television studio in an unmarked police car with two detectives and a trail car filled with policemen, a Volkswagen truck pulled out in front of them. At the same time, from the sidewalks, a dozen Muslims converged on the lead car. But before they could get to Malcolm, the police in the trail car jumped out with drawn revolvers and dispersed them. Then, to everybody's astonishment, the Muslims regrouped and continued to follow the official convoy back to Malcolm's hotel.[44]

At the hotel, Malcolm spotted about fifteen Muslims loitering nearby. Turning to the detectives, he said that "Elijah seems to know every move I make." Later, in his hotel room, he told McClelland that "it was only a matter of time" before the Muslims caught up with him since he knew too much about them.[45] The next morning, the police escorted Malcolm to O'Hare Airport, where he caught his plane back home.

The Alabama Visit

Four days later Malcolm flew to Tuskegee, Alabama, where over three thousand students at the predominantly black Tuskegee Institute heard him predict that "extreme racial unrest and violence" would take place in the United States that year. Elijah Muhammad, he said, was willing "to sit and wait on God to come," but "if he doesn't come soon, it would be too late." Malcolm said that his religion would have to include political, economic, and social action "designed to eliminate injustice" and "make a paradise here on earth while we're waiting for the other."[46]

Although Malcolm had planned to fly back to New York City the next morning, Tuskegee students persuaded him to speak to civil rights workers at a local church in Selma, Alabama. In Dallas County, where Selma was located, although blacks outnumbered whites, the white ruling structure used intimidation and archaic laws to prevent all but one percent of its black population from registering to vote.

Consequently, SNCC and King's Southern Christian Leadership Conference (SCLC) had organized marches of young people to the voter registration offices at the county building to sign up to vote. City and county police greeted them with billy clubs and arrests, which by February 3 totaled 3,400 people, including Dr. King, who was then in his fourth day in jail.[47]

In Selma, SNCC had scheduled Malcolm to speak to three-hundred voter registration workers at Brown Chapel. When he arrived, he found that while SNCC's activists welcomed him, SCLC officials, fearful that he would inflame the situation with his militant style, tried to coach him into what to say at the chapel. He told them, however, that nobody puts words into his mouth.[48] Determined, nonetheless, to neutralize him, they "sandwiched" his speech between SCLC staffers James Bevel and Fred Shuttlesworth.

In his address, Malcolm told the voter registration workers that black people had the right to vote, and that he was one hundred percent behind their effort to get it "by any means necessary." The white man, he said, should "thank God that Dr. King has held his people in check" because there were others "ready to lead a different kind of movement." Calling Klansmen cowards, Malcolm said that the time would come when their "sheets will be ripped off." But "if the federal government doesn't take them off," he added, "we'll take them off."[49]

Afterwards, the audience gave Malcolm a rousing cheer and applauded furiously. Anxious that the fired up civil rights workers might not remain non-violent in the face of police harassment, SCLC officials canceled that day's voting rights march. After Shuttlesworth spoke, moreover, they persuaded Dr. King's wife, Corretta Scott King, to say "a few inspirational words" to quiet the audience down.[50]

Just before giving his speech, Malcolm had told Mrs. King that he had not come to Selma to make her husband's job more difficult. "If the white people realize what the alternative is," said Malcolm, "perhaps they will be more willing to hear Dr. King."[51] Later that day when she told her husband what Malcolm had said, she recalled that he did not "react too much one way or the other."[52] "I would never have invited Malcolm X to come to Selma when we were in the midst of a non-violent demonstration," said King later, but "this says nothing about the personal respect I had for him."[53]

Malcolm wanted to visit Dr. King in jail, but he had to catch a plane in Montgomery to return to New York City and then prepare for a flight to London to attend the Congress of Council of African Organizations.

Although Malcolm addressed the voter registration workers in Selma and, apparently, was willing to work with civil rights activists on specific actions, that he was moving in the direction of the Civil Rights Movement, as some later claimed, was doubtful. To do that, said Peter Goldman, "would have meant compromises on his part that he was not prepared to make."[54] Most important, he could never have accepted the commitment to non-violence that civil rights leaders would have demanded of him. It neither fit his personality nor would he have kept his credibility among his northern ghetto followers if he had gone along with it.

On February 4, 1965, Malcolm X talks at a Selma, Alabama, church to young blacks taking part in voter registration protests. "There should be more militancy in the demonstrations," said Malcolm (AP/Wide World Photos).

Overseas Respite

Of the eleven months since he had left the Nation of Islam, Malcolm had been abroad about half of it. During his second trip overseas, however, his followers wanted him to come back to the United States and help build their movement. Yet going abroad for him, despite his stated intentions, meant postponing what he now regarded as his imminent assassination. Still, before he left for London, on February 5, 1965, he told his supporters that he would announce a militant action program at the next OAAU rally, scheduled for February 15.

In London on February 8, at a meeting of the first Congress of the Council of African Organizations, Malcolm addressed over one hundred delegates from African student groups throughout Europe. Calling the Western press "the strongest weapon of imperialism," he said that over the years its editors had developed "a science of imagery" by which through skillful maneuvering they were able to isolate Africans from their brothers in America and elsewhere. Equally important, he said, they made the "African freedom fighter" appear like "a criminal."

Ending his speech, Malcolm urged African journalists to project Africa's image in a positive light and to "stop following blindly" what Western newsmen wrote since their sole aim was to "project Africa negatively."[55]

The next day, Malcolm flew to Paris, where members of the Federation of African students in France and the Committee of the Afro-American Community in Paris had scheduled him to speak that night. But when he landed at Paris' Orly International Airport, the French police handed him a government order stating that his presence might "trouble the public order" and escorted him from the aircraft to a transit lounge where he would remain in their custody while waiting for his flight back to London.

When the police refused his request to phone the American Embassy, Malcolm became enraged and sat there glowing for a long moment. Then, he told them that this must be "Johannesburg" (South Africa), not Paris. Reaching into his pocket, he took out a penny. "Here," he said. "Give that to De Gaulle [president of France] because the French Government is worth less than a penny." They would not take it, however, so he flung it on the floor.[56] Moments later, they escorted him to a London bound Air France Caravelle.

The reason behind France's decision to bar Malcolm from entering the country was unclear. To some observers, the pro–Western Ivory Coast and Senegal Republics — fearing that he might have been given both encouragement and material help from anti–Western African governments, such as

Egypt and Ghana, to incite France's African community against them — had pressured the French not to let him into their country.[57] Others suggested that the French banned him because they had discovered a CIA plot to murder him on French soil, so that the Communist trade unions, alarmed at the threat of racial divisions between French Africans and Arabs within their ranks, successfully pressured De Gaulle to keep him out of France.[58]

Keeping Malcolm out of France may have had more to do with maintaining public order than anything else. Because she had a sizeable combined African and Arab population, her politicians, many of whom considered Malcolm's speech given during his November 1964 visit as "too violent," were afraid that another one by him might "provoke demonstrations that would trouble the public order."[59]

Back at London's airport, as Malcolm disembarked from his plane, about twenty delegates from different African organizations gathered around him. If British authorities had tried to stop him from re-entering the country, the delegates told him that they were there "to raise hell."[60] To reporters nearby, he expressed shock at his treatment in France. "The authorities would not even let me contact the American Embassy," he said. "I thought I was in South Africa."[61]

Shortly thereafter, Malcolm gave part of his address, calling for unity between blacks in the Western Hemisphere and those in Africa, by phone to Carlos Moore, a French supporter, who recorded, transcribed, and then read it that night at Paris' Mutualite to over three hundred people.[62]

Two days later, delivering a lecture to a packed hall at the London School of Economics, Malcolm condemned American involvement in Vietnam. The Americans, he said, would fare no better than the French, whose highly mechanized army lost to guerrilla fighters with nothing but sneakers on and carrying only rifles and bowls of rice. Also, dismissing the accusation that he was "a hate teacher," he said that white Americans had taught blacks to hate themselves. "Why," he said, "Uncle Sam is a master hate teacher, so much so that he makes somebody think he's teaching love when he's teaching hate." To this, the students, who were somewhat conservative, responded with guffaws, cat calls, and laughter.[63]

On February 12, Malcolm, accompanied by a British Broadcasting Corporation (BBC) television crew, made a three hour visit to Smethwick, a city on the outskirts of Birmingham which had gained notoriety as a symbol of racism. To counter an influx of immigrants, city officials were buying up all available houses and apartments and renting them only to whites. Commenting on the city's actions, Malcolm compared the treatment of Smethwick's non-white immigrants with Hitler's treatment of the Jews. If this continued, he said, "a bloody battle" would result, but he "would not wait for the fascist element in Smethwick to erect gas ovens."[64]

Malcolm's comments generated a storm of criticism. To Mayor Clarence V. Williams, he was endeavoring to turn his city "into a kind of Birmingham, Alabama." While Smethwick's leading Tory politician, Peter Griffiths, called on London to ban Malcolm from future visits to Britain, officials from the standing conference on West Indian Organizations for Birmingham said that his remarks about gas ovens were "the worst thing anybody could say."[65]

But Malcolm did not appear bothered by the controversy. Pictures showed him walking the streets of Smethwick in his topcoat, Astrakhan fur hat, and a wide grin. He liked being a celebrity, said Peter Goldman, and an "object of high debate in the press and commons."[66]

Later that afternoon, Malcolm held a press conference in nearby Birmingham. To questions that his remarks in Smethwick might provoke racial violence, he said that he had "avoided anything that could create an incident." Asked about the city council's plans to buy up houses to prevent blacks from moving in, he said that colored people must organize "against any color resistance" and that "the worst form of human being is one who judges another human being by the color of his skin."[67]

To the Birmingham University's Islamic Student Organization that evening, Malcolm essentially repeated the same theme that he had given to reporters that afternoon. He added, however, that he was advocating "intelligent self-defense." Since racists spoke with "brute force," he said, blacks must reply with the same language and then "more communications and understanding would result."[68]

On the following morning, February 13, after being interviewed by Alan Scholefield for the *Sunday Express* of Johannesburg, Malcolm flew home. Although he had spent less than a week overseas, he obviously enjoyed himself, playing his roles as both statesman and militant agitator. Yet, this was his last trip abroad and the last time in his life that he would feel safe.

CHAPTER 12

The Last Days

Returning from London on February 13, 1965, Malcolm X, looking tired and nervous, got off the airplane at New York's John F. Kennedy Airport. Meeting him there were radical lawyer William Kunstler and SNCC staffer Mike Thelwell. Malcolm kept repeating, said Kunstler, that "the situation was desperate"; he felt threatened by the FBI and the Nation of Islam, and that he was "going to be dead." Somewhat naively, Kunstler said that "nobody can do anything to you."[1]

The next morning, however, at around 2:45 A.M., the fire department received two calls stating that Malcolm's East Elmhurst home was on fire. While a neighbor woman made the first call after being awakened by the sound of broken glass and seeing flames in his living room, a cab driver made the second call after noticing a bush burning in front of Malcolm's home and heard glass breaking. Later, the two callers told the NYPD that they neither saw nor heard any person or vehicle leaving the area.[2]

According to Malcolm, at about 2:35 A.M., after waking up to a smoke-filled house, he rushed his wife, who was pregnant again, and their four daughters through the rear door to the back yard, where the temperature outside was only twenty degrees. As his family shivered in their nightclothes, he ran back inside to get warm clothes and whatever belongings he could grab. While inside, although he did not see anybody, he felt that "someone strange was in the house."[3]

In Betty's version, Malcolm and she woke up "to a conglomeration of strange sounds." Smelling smoke, they raced from their bedroom to an adjoining one occupied by the three older children and then into a small bedroom where their seven month old baby girl was sleeping and hurried them all out the back door.[4] At a time of terror and shock, she said later, she was almost frightened by her husband's "courage and efficiency."[5]

At about 2:50 A.M., when fire and police vehicles arrived on the scene, Malcolm was standing on the front sidewalk holding a twenty-five caliber pistol. He told police that after hearing a commotion inside his house, he tried to fire into it, but a broken firing pin prevented the gun from going off. Since he did not have a permit for it, the police wanted to arrest him, but their superiors vetoed it, fearing that it might provoke another Harlem riot.[6]

The blaze, which gutted Malcolm's house, took about an hour for firemen to extinguish. They surmised that arsonists had thrown four Molotov cocktails, gasoline filled bottles with rags attached, at strategic areas around his home. One of them, thrown at the back door, grazed a windowpane and exploded harmlessly on the lawn, allowing Malcolm and his family to escape.[7]

Afterwards, Malcolm and Betty went back inside to get whatever salvageable clothes they could find. In the rear bedroom on top of their youngest daughter's dresser, Betty noticed an unbroken and upright whiskey bottle without a rag attached to it and pointed it out to the firemen. When they gave it to the police, they accused Malcolm of burning down his own house. Enraged at this accusation, he said that it sounded like a Ku Klux Klan tactic: bombing someone's home and then blaming it on the victim.[8]

To reporters, the police said that they had offered Malcolm police protection on five separate occasions, but he refused it each time. After the firebombing of his home, they again offered it to him, but he said that he could "take care of this" himself.[9] "We told him that he was a marked man," said a police spokesman, but "he didn't trust us anymore than he trusted the Black Muslims."[10]

Malcolm told reporters that the firebombing "doesn't frighten me," and "it doesn't quiet me down in any way or shut me up."[11] According to Alex Haley, however, Malcolm was really upset because "underneath the fearsome image" this "got to the father."[12]

To reporters, Malcolm blamed the Nation of Islam for firebombing his house. Its members were not only out to get him, he said, but the Nation held title to the house, and it would collect the insurance money.[13] In turn, to gain publicity and sympathy for himself, the Nation blamed him for the firebombing. Calling him obsessed with the notion that the Nation was after him, James X said, "We had no need to burn the property we gained in court."[14]

Later that Sunday morning, February 14, with his family safe at a friend's home, Malcolm's followers drove him to the John F. Kennedy Airport to catch a flight to Detroit, where the Afro-American broadcasting and Recording Company had scheduled him to speak that evening at the Ford Auditorium. On the drive to the airport, he told them that he would continue to wear his scorched overcoat so that blacks could better understand "the high cost of freedom." Although his followers wanted him to take a bodyguard with him, none of them had any funds for it.[15]

Wearing his smoke-damaged clothes and looking tired and haggard, Malcolm arrived in Detroit that afternoon. Concerned by his appearance, his hosts procured a doctor to give him a sedative so that he could sleep the rest of the afternoon and collected two hundred dollars to help replace his clothes.[16]

At the Ford Auditorium that evening, Malcolm apologized to an audience of about four-hundred blacks for wearing a rumpled suit and an open-necked sweater. Then, he told them about the firebombing of his home and the sedative that the doctor had given him because of lack of sleep and over-exposure to the cold in the early morning hours.

Apparently, the sedative was still having its effect on Malcolm. Unlike his usual dynamic self, he tended to ramble throughout his talk, going back and forth between the African anti-colonial struggles and American race relations, and his attacks against Elijah Muhammad were particularly scathing. Malcolm berated him for allegedly sanctioning murder, maiming people and misusing the Nation's finances.[17]

On Monday morning, back in New York City, Malcolm learned that Civil Court Judge Maurice Wahl denied any further stays and ordered the family from the house "forthwith."[18]

At an OAAU rally in the Audubon Ballroom that evening, Malcolm, unnerved by the firebombing and losing his home, discarded his usual cool and steely demeanor and shouted to an audience of over seven-hundred people that he had no mercy or forgiveness for anyone who attacks sleeping babies. Hurling invectives at Elijah Muhammad, he accused him of firebombing his home, of impregnating nine teenage girls, and of "using Ku Klux Klan" tactics. Then, hinting at revenge, he said that there were hunters and those that hunt them. By his statements, he said, he was well aware of what he was setting in motion. But "let the chips fall where they may."[19]

At one point during Malcolm's address, quarreling among a couple of spectators from the audience drew some of his lieutenants away from their posts and distracted the crowd. But when he asked the audience to "cool it," the uproar died down.[20]

While the commotion was occurring, one of Malcolm's bodyguards,

Gene Roberts, an undercover Bureau of Special Services (BOSS) agent, saw a young man wearing the Nation of Islam's uniform, a blue suit, white shirt, and red bow tie, come down the middle aisle and take a seat at about the second or third row. Also, he noticed several people there that he had never seen before at the Audubon rallies. Afterwards, he informed his superiors that he had "just seen a dry run on Malcolm's life." While they assured him that they "would take care of it," that was the last he heard from them.[21]

Down to the Wire

After the firebombing, Malcolm began to unravel under the pressure. His friends and supporters described him as tense, jittery, and nervous.[22] To newsman Theodore Jones, Malcolm said, "I live like a man who's already dead."[23] He knew, said Benjamin 2X, that "time for him that winter was fast running out."[24] Betty, too, was aware of the inevitable, and her husband tried to prepare her for it, but she was "never totally prepared."[25]

Yet, Malcolm would not allow his psychological deterioration to slow him down. On Tuesday, February 16, he flew to Rochester, New York, for lectures at Colgate-Rochester Divinity School and Corn Hill Methodist Church. To both audiences, he repeated his familiar themes that the race problem was a human rights, not a civil rights, issue and that blacks were "within their rights" to fight those whites who exploited them "by any means necessary."[26]

On February 18, early Thursday morning, Malcolm, along with several of his followers, arrived at his vacated house, out-maneuvering the city marshal, who was to arrive there later that day with a court eviction order to board it up. Within four hours, they had loaded all of his family's salvageable possessions into two station wagons and a small van.[27]

In an interview with *New York Times* reporter Theodore Jones later that morning, Malcolm said that he lived like a man who was already dead. "It doesn't frighten me for myself," he said, "as long as I felt they would not hurt my family." Asked about "they," he referred to his former associates in the Nation of Islam and "that man in Chicago," Elijah Muhammad. The press, he continued, gave the impression that he was "jiving about this thing," but it ignored the evidence and the actual attempts on his life.[28]

Afterwards, Malcolm received a phone call from Eric Lincoln, who wrote the first major work on the Nation of Islam, asking him to speak to Brown University's undergraduates at Providence, Rhode Island, on the following Tuesday. When Malcolm said that he might "be dead on Tuesday," a skeptical Lincoln told him to "cut the bullshit" and come on up. Soon, however, realizing that Malcolm was serious, Lincoln asked him why he did not go to the police. "They already know it," said Malcolm, who agreed to come up if he was still alive.[29]

At a press conference in the Theresa Hotel that afternoon, Malcolm charged New York City's police and fire departments with a conspiracy against him. He demanded an immediate FBI investigation into the firebombing of his home and announced that he had applied for a pistol permit at the Twenty-Eighth Police Precinct. But since he had a police record, he said, the police would probably not grant him one. Still, he added, he had reached the end of his rope and needed to carry a pistol to protect himself and his family.[30]

On New York City's WINS radio that evening, Malcolm continued his merciless attack against Elijah Muhammad and the Nation of Islam. To radio announcer Stan Bernard, Malcolm said that it was not even an Islamic movement, and that Muhammad was probably more anti–Arab than the Israelis. His infidelities, moreover, had caused moral deterioration within the Nation, which accounted for the fact that Muslims were fighting each other.[31]

In an interview with *Life* reporter Gordon Parks on Friday, Malcolm referred to his days in the Nation of Islam as a time of "sickness and madness," and said that he was "glad to be free of them." But now, "it's a time for martyrs," and "if I'm to be one, it will be in the cause of brotherhood."

Then, Malcolm reminisced about the time a white college student had come into the Nation's New York City restaurant asking if there was anything that she could do to help, and he told her that "there wasn't a ghost of a chance," and she went away crying. After a moment of silence, he said that he had not only regretted that incident but also many others while a member of the Nation. But a man's "entitled to make a fool of himself," he said, "if he's ready to pay the cost," and "it cost me twelve years."

As they parted, Malcolm, placing his hands on Parks' shoulders, said "Asalaam Alaikum, brother."[32]

"And may peace be with you, brother," said Parks.

On Saturday morning, February 20, Malcolm and Betty discussed buying a house with a real estate man. He showed them one in a predominantly Jewish neighborhood on Long Island which they both liked, but it required a three-thousand dollar down payment and another thousand dollars for moving expenses. If they could find the money, they agreed to buy it.

Shortly thereafter, phoning Alex Haley, Malcolm asked if his publisher, Doubleday and Company, would advance him four thousand dollars against the profits from his autobiography. Haley said that he would find out for him on Monday. Then, changing the subject, Malcolm said that he kept thinking about what happened to him in France, and that he was going to stop blaming the Nation alone as the only group seeking his death. He did not, he added, "expect to live to read the book in its finished form."[33]

At a friend's home later that day, Malcolm assembled with about a dozen OAAU members. Noticing that he was tired and restless, they asked him if he wanted to postpone the meeting, but he insisted that it was too important to delay. Basically, it was a brainstorming session on how best to reorganize the OAAU so that women would have more clearly defined roles. Nothing was decided upon, however.

Afterwards, Earl Grant, an OAAU lieutenant, asked Malcolm to spend the night with him and his family. Declining his offer because he did not want to endanger them, Malcolm reminded him that they had discussed his death before, and that he did not want an organization that depended on the life of one man.[34]

On Saturday evening, Malcolm checked into an eighteen dollar room on the twelfth floor of New York City's Hilton Hotel, leaving it only to have dinner at the hotel's lobby restaurant. At 10:00 P.M., three black men asked the front desk clerk for Malcolm's room number. Refusing to give it to them, he alerted the hotel's security men. Yet, despite their obvious presence, the three men continued to hang around the lobby for about an hour before leaving the hotel.[35]

Meanwhile, twice that night, detectives visited Malcolm's room to ask if he wanted police protection. Refusing both times, he said that he could take care of himself. "He didn't trust us anymore than he trusted the Black Muslims," said one detective.[36]

Sunday

Early Sunday morning, Malcolm picked up the phone to hear a man tell him to "wake up, brother." Immediately calling Betty, he said that unlike other phone threats that he had received since leaving the Nation, this caller's voice was white — which remained a mystery. Then, while he had previously told her not to attend his 2:00 P.M. Audubon Rally that day, he now asked her to attend it and bring their children, too. "It was out of the ordinary," recalled his oldest daughter Attallah. "That was a rhythm change with all the things that were going on."[37]

Next, phoning Earl Grant, Malcolm said that he got a room at the Hilton to avoid endangering his family. He told him about the white man's voice on the phone and that he needed four thousand dollars to buy and move into a new house. That he was discussing these matters over the phone, however, surprised Grant since Malcolm's policy, fearing FBI phone taps, was neither to discuss personal information nor talk business over it. For safety's sake, although Grant wanted to accompany him to the Audubon that afternoon, Malcolm said that he would meet him there instead.[38]

Malcolm made two more phone calls. First, he called his half-sister in Boston. He told her that "they" would not rest until "they" got him.[39] He was so sure, she said later, "that this was it."[40] Then, he called his friend, Dick Gregory in Chicago. To him, Malcolm's voice sounded frightened and sad, as if he knew that "something was going to happen." Although Gregory wanted to tell him that he would see him soon, he knew better and said instead that he loved him.[41]

At 1:00 P.M., Malcolm checked out of the Hilton and got into his blue Oldsmobile. Although the weather was warm for February, he had put on long johns, wore a dark brown suit, and buttoned his black cardigan coat to the top. Rather than finding a parking place near the Audubon Ballroom, he parked his car about twenty blocks away, fearing perhaps that it would make him too visible if assassins were waiting for him there.

As Malcolm waited for a bus to take him to the Audubon, a car bearing New Jersey license plates pulled over and the driver, a young black man named Fred Williams, waved him over. Wary at first, because Malcolm did not know him, he soon relaxed when he noticed an OAAU member, Charles X Blackwell, sitting in the back seat. Since both men were on their way to the Audubon, Malcolm accepted their offer of a ride.[42]

Apparently, while in the car, Malcolm mentioned to Williams and Blackwell that earlier in the week someone had given him a list of five Muslims who the Chicago leadership would dispatch to New York City to kill him. At the Audubon that afternoon, said Malcolm, he was going to reveal their names.[43]

Located between Broadway and St. Nicolas Avenue, Harlem's Audubon Ballroom was an old two-story building which the OAAU had frequently rented for public meetings. On this day, Malcolm's assistants, arriving early, had set up four-hundred wooden chairs with aisles on either side of them and placed a speaker's stand and arranged eight chairs in a row on the stage. The backdrop, a painted mural, showed a restful country scene.

Because Malcolm's speech was going to outline the OAAU's strategy and tactics, his lieutenants expected a good sized crowd that afternoon. By 1:30 P.M., however, they noticed that several people had already seated themselves up front. Although they attributed little significance to this, since people often came early to the Audubon rallies, Benjamin 2X said later that he was suspicious of three men sitting there with folded overcoats over their laps in "dead silence" as if something was "going on inside of them."[44]

When Gene Roberts, BOSS' undercover agent within Malcolm's close circle, arrived at the Audubon, he was also suspicious of the same three men. But he remained silent, he said later, because they were there before he had arrived, and he figured that they had "already been checked out."[45] Malcolm, however, had given his lieutenants a "no frisk order," refusing to adopt the tactics practiced at Elijah Muhammad's rallies where the FOI searched everybody at the door.[46]

Also, Malcolm informed the Thirty-Fourth Street Precinct's duty captain that he did not want a large police presence at the Audubon since it made people "feel uncomfortable." Consequently, the precinct's duty captain assigned only one man, Thomas Hoy, from his twenty man police contingent to guard the front entrance and placed two others, Gilbert Henry and John Carroll, unobtrusively in the Rose Ballroom, which adjoined the main hall. The duty captain then stationed the other seventeen men out of sight in the Columbia Presbyterian Medical Center across the street.[47]

Gene Roberts recalled that he had "never seen so few officers" attend one of Malcolm's OAAU meetings.[48] To Charles Kenyatta, the "whole situation was not right."[49] And Charles 37X, another lieutenant, "sensed something was wrong."[50]

Waiting for the 2:00 P.M. rally to begin, Malcolm was backstage slouched in a chair. Occasionally, he got up and paced the floor, staring out to see how many people were coming in and then slumped back into his chair. To those present, he seemed ragged, moved clumsily, and appeared preoccupied.[51] Upset by his behavior, Earl Grant asked him to "leave the building right away," but Malcolm said that he would be all right.[52] Then, Malcolm asked Grant to telephone his family to see if they were coming, which he did, and learning that they had left for the Audubon, he informed him of that fact.

To open up the rally, the OAAU had booked the Reverend Milton Galamison, a Presbyterian minister who had organized boycotts in Brooklyn's schools to protect the city's de facto segregation of them, and Ralph Cooper, a popular disc jockey and well known talent scout with ties to Harlem's famous Apollo Theater. Just before 2:00 P.M., however, representatives of both men informed Malcolm's assistants that extenuating circumstances would prevent them from speaking that day.

At the same time that Malcolm's assistants informed him of the two speakers' cancellations, they said that his drafting committee had failed to complete the OAAU's charter on tactics and strategy for his presentation that day. Uncharacteristically, Malcolm shouted at them to get out of the room and leave him alone. At this outburst, Benjamin 2X sensed that a "metaphysical weight" had fallen on Malcolm's shoulders, and that there was no way that his followers could lighten the burden for him.[53]

Waving his assistants back into the backstage room, Malcolm told them that he had been too hasty in accusing Muhammad's followers for the firebombing of his home. "Things have happened that are bigger than what they can do," he said. "Things have gone beyond that."[54]

At 2:00 P.M., Malcolm told a woman assistant that he needed a preliminary speaker to both warm up the audience and introduce him. She suggested Benjamin 2X, who was standing nearby. Malcolm said, "You know you shouldn't ask me right in front of him!" After collecting himself, he asked Benjamin to "make it plain," which meant to bring him forward quickly. Feeling the heaviness in Malcolm's soul, Benjamin began to perspire profusely as he made his way dazed and unsteady to the podium.[55]

By this time, Betty and the children had arrived and taken their seats in the audience. Yet, Malcolm probably failed to notice them since he was trying to concentrate on Benjamin's rambling, which took an interminable twenty-five minutes before he introduced him as "a man who would give his life for you." As the applause rose from the audience, Malcolm turned to his woman assistant and apologized for raising his voice to her; then, he walked onto the stage and took his place behind the lectern.[56]

The Assassination

After four-hundred people stood and clapped for forty-five seconds, Malcolm said, "A Salaam Alaiken," and the audience responded with "peace be with you also." At that instant, a man in the audience started shouting at the person next to him to get his hand out of his pocket. In a tense voice, Malcolm said, "cool it brothers," and asked the audience not to get excited. Meanwhile, his bodyguards left the stage and began moving towards the commotion, leaving him open and unguarded.[57]

Almost immediately, while a smoke bomb exploded near a window facing the right side of the stage, a gunman, pulling out a sawed-off twelve gauge double-barreled shotgun, rushed the stage and fired his first load directly at Malcolm's chest. With the blast, his hands flew up, eyes rolled inside his head, and he toppled backwards, crashing into two empty chairs. As the shotgun wielding gunman fired his second load, two other gunmen, one armed with a luger and the other with a forty-five automatic, ran out onto the stage and squeezed off several rounds into Malcolm's body.[58]

In the flurry of shots, two spectators were hit. William Harris got struck with a random thirty-two bullet in the stomach while William Parker got a shotgun pellet in the foot.

As the people in the audience started screaming and running for the doors, Benjamin 2X sat frozen in his chair backstage, knowing that Malcolm was gone and feeling relief for him.[59] Betty, on the other hand, reacted to the shots by shoving her children to the floor and covering them with folding chairs. Then, she ran to the stage and bent over Malcolm, who seemed to her to be gasping and not dead yet.[60]

Concealed in the Rose Ballroom when the shots rang out, Gilbert Henry, a black policeman, and his white partner radioed for help. Receiving no answer, they took out their thirty-eights and ran into the main ballroom.[61]

After the shooting, as the gunmen and their accomplices were running for the exits, Gene Roberts tripped one of them. The gunman, waving his forty-five, immediately got up and started running again. At that moment, Reuben Francis, an OAAU member, shot him in the leg. Despite the gunman's wound, he got up again and half-limped to the stairway where Malcolm's followers wrestled him to the floor. In the process, his forty-five fell to the floor; someone picked it up and squeezed the trigger, but it jammed.[62]

While Thomas Hoy, the police guard at the front entrance, tried to pull gunman Talmadge Hayer from the mob, police officers Alvin Aronoff and Louis Angelos, cruising by in their patrol car when they heard gunfire, came to Hoy's aid. To scatter the crowd, Aronoff fired a shot in the air. Then, the three officers dragged Hayer to their patrol car. As the crowd rushed it and began beating on its doors and windows, the three officers slowly inched it into the thoroughfare and drove to Harlem's Thirty-Fourth Precinct.[63]

On the ride to the precinct, the three policemen frisked the suspect. In his pocket, they found a forty-five automatic clip, four rounds of ammunition, and thirty dollars. Although he gave his name as Talmadge Hayer, they heard it as Thomas Hagan, but he failed to correct them. Consequently, they booked him as Hagan at the station house.[64]

At the Audubon, meanwhile, while Malcolm's lieutenants were pacing the stage floor in anger and grief, Gene Roberts tried mouth-to-mouth resuscitation on him, but after five minutes, he gave up. Taking over, Betty began pumping her husband's arms, giving him the old arm-lift method. Realizing that this technique was futile, she said, "Oh no, he's gone, and I'm pregnant."[65]

About fifteen minutes after the shooting, a number of OAAU men ran across the street to the Columbia Presbyterian Medical Center to get a stretcher. Similarly, the seventeen policemen who had been stationed there sauntered into the Audubon. "They were strolling at about the pace one would expect of them if they were patrolling a quiet park," said Earl Grant later, and "not one of them had his gun out."[66]

After commandeering a stretcher, Malcolm's men ran back into the Audubon and placed him across it. Laying there with his head tilted back and his teeth exposed in a twisted snarl made obvious the intense agony he felt during his final moments.[67] While four policemen rushed Malcolm's stretcher across Broadway to the medical center, his lieutenants ran beside them shouting to bystanders to "get out of the way or we will kill you."[68]

Back in the ballroom, about one-hundred and fifty people wandered about as though in a daze, muttering to each other or to themselves. Some of the women began to wail. "Lord, I don't think he is going to make it," said one woman. One man said, "What are we supposed to do now?"[69]

At the hospital, interns grabbed the stretcher from the police and ran with it onto an elevator to the third floor emergency operating room where a team of doctors and nurses cut his chest open and started massaging his heart. Saving his life was hopeless, however, and they soon gave up. As one doctor said later, he was dead when he entered the hospital.[70]

On Sunday night, city officials moved Malcolm's body to the medical examiner's office and Dr. Milton Helpern, the chief medical examiner, finished his autopsy at 2:00 A.M. the next morning. Counting twenty-one wounds in all, his report confirmed that the shotgun wielding gunman's blasts to Malcolm's chest had killed him, and that the other two gunman's shots had penetrated his thighs and legs after he had fallen to the floor.[71] Later that morning, Betty, accompanied by Percy Sutton, Ella Collins, and Joseph E. Hall, manager of Harlem's Unity Funeral Home, made the official identification of her husband's body at the medical examiner's office.

Earlier, at the station house late Sunday afternoon, the police were trying to interrogate their suspect, but he was so obviously hurt from his gunshot wound that they soon transferred him to the Jewish Memorial Hospital, the closest one nearby. After an initial checkup, the doctors reported that a bullet had shattered his thigh bone, and that they would have to place his leg in traction for two weeks until it healed enough to permit an operation to take the bullet out. Accordingly, the police transferred him to Bellevue Hospital's prison ward, a more secure facility.[72]

Meanwhile, the police charged Reuben Francis, Malcolm's bodyguard, with felonious assault in the shooting of Hayer and violation of the Sullivan Law, possessing a gun without a permit.[73]

Reaction

To the press and political observers, Malcolm's stress on violence brought on his own death. According to the *New York Times,* his ruthless and fanatical belief in violence marked him "for a violent end."[74] The hatred and violence that he had preached had "overwhelmed him," said the *New York Tribune.* He died, said Sam Crowther, "by the violent creed that had shaped his life."[75] "Violent words, violent emotions, and a violent death," said Robert Laird. "This was Malcolm X."[76]

To some political observers, the fact that blacks had killed Malcolm was the ultimate incongruity. Despite his "hatred for the white man," said Dick Schaap, "Malcolm X died at the hands of blacks," and "he might have smiled at the irony."[77] He was "a victim of his own exaggeration," said Walter Winchell, and he "never reconciled the truth with his private delusions."[78] But to James A. Wechsler, "Malcolm X was a complicated introspective man" undergoing a "personal transition when he was struck down."[79] And to Jim Powell, as long as America produced "bigoted sects," she needed "Malcolm X to meet it on its own terms."[80]

For many Africans, Malcolm's assassination made him a martyr. They called him an "American Lumumba" after the Congo's Premier Patrice Lumumba, whose 1961 murder they blamed on the West.[81] In a number of African capitals, Africans held marches and rallies, blaming "Yankee imperialism" for Malcolm's assassination.[82] He "fought and died," said Lagos Nigeria's *Daily Times,* "for what he believed to be right."[83] Accura's *Ghanaian Times* eulogized him as "the militant and most popular of the Afro-American anti-segregationist leaders."[84]

Carl Rowan, on the other hand, the U.S. Information Agency's black director, criticized African newspapers for portraying Malcolm X as "a martyred hero" instead of "an ex-convict, ex-dope peddler, who became a racial fanatic."[85]

To Western Europeans, Malcolm's assassination was big news, stirring among them more interest and controversy than when he was alive.[86] Peking's *The People's Daily,* mainland China's Communist newspaper, said that "U.S. Rulers had killed Malcolm X because he had become a thorn in their side."[87] But Moscow's Communist *Pravda* only briefly mentioned Malcolm's assassination and gave it no editorial comment.[88]

Expressing sorrow at Malcolm's death, civil rights leaders and activists blamed the racist society that bred him. Despite their disagreements, said Dr. King, Malcolm X's assassination "saddened" and "appalled" him.[89] Edwin Berry, head of Chicago's Urban League, said Malcolm X should have used his great mind to serve the civil rights movement, not black nationalism, but "such is the tragedy of a sick society."[90] According to Bayard Rustin, Malcolm X "articulated angry subterranean moods more widespread than any of us like to admit."[91] "No matter who had pulled the trigger," said activist and writer James Baldwin, "the white community would have to share the blame."[92]

While denying that the Nation of Islam was behind Malcolm's assassination, James Farmer, CORE's director, was somewhat vague as to who did it. At first, he called it "a political killing with international implications." Then, he said that drug dealers may have been behind it since Malcolm had been "fighting the Harlem drug traffic."[93] But to Roy Wilkins, the NAACP's executive director, talk of "international conspiracy" had "a dark and rolling sound," nobody had any proof.[94]

Under police protection at the home of friends, Betty told reporters that she knew her husband would "be killed some day." When asked who killed him, however, she just shook her head and stared blankly.[95] Percy Sutton said that Malcolm had intended to name "the picked assassins" at Sunday's Audubon rally, and that he had given their names to the police beforehand, which they neither confirmed nor denied.[96]

The Nation of Islam denied any involvement in Malcolm's assassination. "We knew nothing about it," said Captain Joseph.[97] While Wallace Muhammad said that neither his father nor any Muslim official had "anything to do with it," he admitted that "some individuals in the organization were capable of it."[98] According to Los Angeles' Minister John Shabazz, none of Elijah Muhammad's followers could have been responsible for it because the Nation's rules forbid them from "carrying weapons or initiating violence."[99] Visibly shaken upon hearing of his brother's death, Wilfred refused to comment on the Nation's involvement; instead, he said, "This is the kind of times we are living in."[100]

On Sunday, FBI agents had monitored a call from someone in New York City warning the Chicago leadership that six of Malcolm's followers were on their way there to kill Elijah Muhammad.[101] The FBI passed this information on to the Chicago police, who set up a twelve man task force to mount a round-the-clock vigil at Muhammad's three story mansion on the city's south side. Along with the task force, the police assigned unmarked police cars to cruise the immediate area and placed guards at Mosque Number Two and the University of Islam, both of which were within a mile of Muhammad's home. In all three places, moreover, FOI men maintained a heavy presence.[102]

On Monday afternoon, the day after the assassination, Elijah Muhammad held a press conference in his home. After walking through two multiple-locked doors and submitting to a thorough body search by FOI men as well as being photographed by them for future reference, over thirty reporters assembled in his living room, a big chamber with bay windows and white silk on the walls and see through plastic covers on the furniture. Sitting in a big chair, Muhammad, flanked by his son Herbert, John Ali, and Minister James Shabazz, greeted them.[103]

Denying that Talmadge Hayer's name was in the Nation of Islam's records, Muhammad said that his people were making their own investigation "to find where the assassin came from." Malcolm left on his own terms, said Muhammad, because he disagreed with the Nation's rule forbidding members to carry firearms. He died according to his preaching, which was "war," while the Nation preached "peace." Weapons, added Muhammad, had become "Malcolm's God."[104]

That evening, Muhammad appeared on Wesley Smith's WVON radio station. Repeating the point that Malcolm's death resulted from his preaching war, Muhammad said that the Nation of Islam had "no guns, bombs, or artillery pieces to field." Likewise, he denied that the Nation of Islam had any involvement in Malcolm's assassination. "If the authorities discovered that one of his followers had killed him," he said, he would disavow him since the Koran taught only to kill on Allah's orders."[105]

War Clouds

Harlemites reacted to Malcolm's assassination with "mute shock." While some gathered on street corners in small clusters to discuss it, others congregated outside Louis Michaux's bookstore — the center of Harlem's black nationalist activity. In deep grief, OAAU members sat in their headquarters refusing to make any statements to reporters.[106] His death, said Benjamin 2X, had "emptied our souls."[107]

As fifty detectives began interviewing everybody that was at the Audubon Ballroom on the day of the assassination, police officials, fearing war between the Nation of Islam and Malcolm's followers, ordered its elite tactical force into Harlem. Its commanders set up their command post in the main recreation building in Harlem's Mount Morris Park, putting them in touch with every policeman in Harlem. Outside the building, they had parked a tow truck, two emergency trucks, a communications truck, and two trucks loaded with wooden barricades.[108]

In the next few days, an ominous mood of threats and trouble prevailed throughout Harlem. Someone called in a bomb threat to the *New*

York Times because it had written "a bad article" about Malcolm. In separate incidents, police arrested two men for carrying rifles, but the authorities released them after questioning established their innocence of any unlawful intent.[109]

Earlier, only hours after Malcolm's assassination on Sunday, Chicago firemen responded to a fire call at Muhammad Ali's south side third floor apartment. By the time they arrived, however, although he was unhurt, the fire had gutted his entire apartment. The police said that a second floor resident had accidentally set it, but the assumption remained among the Nation's Muslims that Malcolm's followers had started it.[110]

Despite the presence of a four man police guard, early Monday morning arsonists torched the Nation of Islam's four story building, which housed Mosque Number Seven, the Shabazz Restaurant, and various small shops rented out on the first floor, located at 116th Street and Lenox Avenue. More than a hundred firemen responded to the three alarm blaze. As they assembled to put it out, the fourth floor crumbled to the third floor until the whole building's structure fell to the ground. In the process, several firefighters were hurt when a part of a burning wall fell on them.

As an omen of things to come, a white policeman, who had been pounding a Harlem beat for ten years, called the fire the beginning of Harlem's "long hot summer."[111]

On an adjacent roof, police searchers found an empty five-gallon gasoline can, a brown gasoline-stained shopping bag, and oil rags. From there, they speculated that the arsonists threw their firebombs through the mosque's semi-barred fourth floor windows, the blaze's center.[112] "We expected something like this," said a Harlem resident to reporters. "These cats are going to be scratching until there's not one of them left."[113]

Blaming Malcolm's followers for firebombing the building, Captain Joseph called their action "a vicious sneak attack," and that it held "one of the Nation's religious sanctuaries" made the act worse.[114] His accusation, said Earl Grant, was false and insulting. "Certainly," he added, "give us the credit of having the good sense to attack a building filled with the alleged enemy."[115]

On February 23, when Leon 4X Ameer, a former FOI karate instructor, arrived in New York City from Boston where he had been trying to organize an OAAU chapter, he told reporters that Elijah Muhammad would not live out the month.[116] Similarly, at a press conference in Boston on the same day, Ella Collins said that "whether it is through justice, by law, or divine justice, Malcolm would be avenged."[117]

Counseling caution, however, OAAU Lieutenant James Shabazz said that the only people who would benefit from "a war of black man against black man" were those elements who had "enslaved us."[118]

On February 25, for its three day annual Saviour's Day convention, over 2,500 members of the Nation of Islam assembled at Chicago's Coliseum, an old sports palace south of the Chicago business district. Earlier, a man phoned police to warn them that someone had placed a time bomb in the coliseum set to go off during the convention. After searching it, however, the bomb squad found no bomb. Then, a second caller warned that one hundred men were coming to Chicago from New York City to kill Muhammad, and hours before the convention, a third caller said, "We have arrived."[119]

As a result, security was tight at the coliseum. While two FOI teams searched everyone entering it, black detectives fanned out inside among the audience; fifty uniformed policemen stood guard outside; the fire department stationed fire trucks near hydrants ready for use, and throughout the city, the police routinely stopped cars with New York license plates as well as watched the airport and train depots.[120]

Malcolm's defection and death dominated Elijah Muhammad's hour and a half keynote address. At first, he said, Malcolm was "a light, a star among his people"; but he departed from the Nation's beliefs, "sank into the grave," and became a hypocrite, who had lost his mind by adopting "bloodbath teachings." Muslims, however, would "fight to protect themselves," said Muhammad.

At times, Muhammad got so emotionally worked up that he would begin coughing while the audience would plead with him to take it easy. Yet they cheered him when he called Malcolm foolish and ignorant, and Muhammad Ali, sitting in the front row, would jump up yelling, "Yes sir!" or "Sweet words Apostle!"

Although repeating his frequent assertion that the Nation did not kill Malcolm, Muhammad implied in his concluding remarks that it did. "If you seek to snuff out the life of Elijah Muhammad," he said, "you are inviting your own doom." He added, "I am not going to let crackpots destroy the good things Allah sent you and me."[121]

Among the rally's speakers were Philbert and Wilfred, repeating the Nation's official line on their brother's assassination. While Philbert denounced him for "deviating from Muhammad's teachings," Wilfred said that his brother had traveled "on a very reckless and dangerous road," leading to his early death.[122] Both men, to be sure, were walking a thin line, fearing the wrath from the Nation's zealots if they said the wrong word. As Wilfred said later, they had their "hands in the lion's mouth."[123]

The Funeral

Before the funeral, scheduled for Saturday, February 26, at Bishop Alvin S. Child's Amsterdam Avenue Temple Church of God, Harlem's Unity Funeral Home placed Malcolm's body on view from Tuesday, February 23 to Friday, February 26. Throughout the week, several callers phoned in bomb threats to the Unity Funeral Home's director, Joseph E. Hall. In one instance, the caller warned that "Malcolm won't be buried, he'll be cremated," and another, from a woman with a West Indian accent, said that she overheard "three men threatening to blow up the place."[124] The bomb squad swept the funeral home, but it failed to discover any bombs. Nonetheless, police officials assigned fifty policemen to patrol it.

For the viewing, morticians had dressed Malcolm's body in a business suit and placed it in a six-foot, nine-inch bronze casket lined with eggshell velvet with a glass shield over it. Above that, an oblong brass plate hung, which read: El-Hajj Malik El-Shabazz — May 19, 1925 to February 21, 1965.

Early Tuesday evening, after Betty and a few close friends viewed Malcolm's body, funeral officials opened their doors to the general public. Before the week was over, twenty-two thousand people filed past it to say their good-byes. "He made all of us feel alive," said Aliva Johnson, a gray-haired housewife clutching her coat to her throat as tears ran down her cheeks.[125] "He was a man we could follow," said Ozzie Cuvilge, a Queens taxi driver.[126] "He wasn't afraid of nothing," said a high school student. "That's why they killed him."[127]

Yet, for some of Malcolm's closest followers, so "overwhelmed with feelings of sadness" and grief, they either stayed away from the funeral home, or they waited "until the last day and the last hour that he lay in state."[128]

On Friday afternoon, funeral home officials temporarily interrupted the public viewing of Malcolm's body so that his spiritual advisor, Sheik Ahmed Hassoum, who had arrived with a hand-picked retinue of twelve mourners, could prepare it for burial in accordance with Muslim tradition. After sheathing it from head to foot in white linen, leaving only Malcolm's face exposed, the Sheik read selected passages from the Koran; then funeral officials allowed viewing to resume.[129]

At 1:35 A.M. the following morning, funeral home officials placed Malcolm's body in a hearse, flanked by a dozen police cars, for the twenty block drive to the Faith Temple Church of God.

Earlier that week, as an honor to Malcolm, a few of his admirers, led by political activist Jesse Gray, threatened to boycott and picket Harlem's merchants along 125th Street unless they closed their businesses on the day of his funeral. Undercutting the boycott movement, however, Harlem's merchants adopted a compromise resolution whereby they would stay open but agreed to allow their employees to attend the funeral with full pay.[130]

On Saturday morning, the day of the funeral, as police blocked all traffic from 145th Street to 149th Street, thousands of mourners assembled along the east side of Amsterdam Avenue. Five-hundred policemen were on hand to watch the crowds. While some policemen stood off to the side, others mixed among the people or watched indiscreetly from the rooftops.

While thousands stood outside, six hundred people attended Malcolm's funeral service. These included civil rights leaders Andrew Young, James Farmer, Bayard Rustin, Dick Gregory, and SNCC's John Lewis. Some Nation of Islam members and a few whites were there, too, describing themselves as "truly saddened" by his death.[131] Also, to the rear of the church's altar, fifty reporters, photographers, and television cameramen assembled, and eight policemen and two black policewomen guarded the coffin, which faced eastwards toward Mecca. In the second row, two black detectives sat near Betty and Malcolm's half-sister Ella Collins.

Opening the fifty-five minute funeral service, Ossie Davis, playwright and actor, and his actress wife, Ruby Dee, read the notes, telegrams, and cables of condolences. They came from the executive director of the National Urban League, Whitney M. Young; the West Indian Society of the London School of Economics; the Michigan Committee of the Freedom Now Party; the NAACP's Los Angeles Youth Group; the Pan-African Congress of Southern Africa, which hailed Malcolm as "anti-imperialist, anti-colonialist, and anti-racist"; and the president of Ghana, Nkrumah, who wrote that Malcolm's "work for the cause of freedom shall not be in vain."[132]

After a short talk by the director of New York City's Islamic Center, Omar Osman, who described himself as one of Malcolm's teachers, Davis gave the eulogy. He neither played upon emotions nor called for retribution. Instead, speaking slowly and with his voice often cracking, he called Malcolm Harlem's "living black manhood," and said that it had never produced "a braver, more gallant young champion" who laid before them "unconquered still."

Davis said that people would say that Malcolm was a fanatic and a racist and revile him. But did they ever talk to him or know him to commit an act of violence or public disturbance? After his visit to Mecca, said Davis, Malcolm came to believe that all men of color could live in peace, and that no matter how much American blacks disagreed with each other, "now was the time to come together."

Now that Malcolm's mortal remains were consigned to earth, Davis hoped that out of them would grow a seed which would come forth again to meet the living. "And we will know him then for what he was and is," concluded Davis, "a prince, our own black shining prince, who didn't hesitate to die, because he loved us so."[133]

When Davis finished, a young Islamic priest, Iman Alhajj Heshaam Jaaber, said a brief prayer. Then, while one woman in the back "moaned loudly" and another "shrieked," Betty slowly came forward for one last look at her husband. Stopping in front of the bronze coffin, she shook her head, wept, and pressed her lips against the glass surface that shielded her husband's body. As she turned back to her seat, the funeral directors closed the lid on Malcolm's coffin and loaded it onto a two-tone blue hearse.[134]

The funeral procession, consisting of the hearse, three family cars, eighteen mourner's cars, twelve NYPD police cars, six press cars, and fifty other cars, proceeded through Harlem to the Major Deegan Expressway and traveled north from New York City to the city line. From there, the state police took over the procession en route to Ferncliff Cemetery in Hartsdale, New York.[135]

At the Ferncliff Cemetery's grave site, while the grave keeper lowered Malcolm's coffin into the earth, his Muslim followers knelt beside the grave, pressing their foreheads to the earth and chanting Islamic prayers. Afterwards, they wrested the shovels from the grave diggers. "We won't let white men bury him," said one Muslim. Another, shovel in hand, raising his face to the sun, said "Let it be known to one and all that the falling of one is the rising of another."[136]

To Earl Grant, the last year of his life was at an end. Returning home, he fell into "a deep sleep." He said that this was the first rest that he had been able to get in months and that there was "no longer any reason to jump when the phone rang or to sleep with a loaded gun."[137]

CHAPTER 13

Arrests, Convictions, and Theories

Police officials assigned fifty detectives to the Malcolm X murder case. Under the direction of sixty-one year old Joseph W. Coyle, they went under the assumption, which they never deviated from, that the Nation of Islam was behind the assassination because of an interrelated set of motives, including jealousy, desertion, rivalry, and public accusations.[1] Yet, for reasons that were unclear, they chose not to pursue those individuals within the Nation who might have ordered it; instead, the detectives would concentrate their efforts on apprehending the actual gunmen.

Shortly after the shooting, the detectives combed the Audubon Ballroom for evidence. They found a sawed-off double-barreled shotgun containing two discharged Remington express shells; six nine millimeter shells and two slugs; and three thirty-two caliber slugs and ten pieces of lead, presumably fired from the shotgun. Although the luger never resurfaced and its disappearance remained one of the mysteries of the case, the detectives obtained the forty-five automatic from an OAAU member who had picked it up after Hayer had dropped it while trying to escape.[2]

The capture of Talmadge Hayer convinced detectives that they had collared one of the assassins. Although he refused to talk with them, an eyewitness newsman, Charles Moore, told them that after hearing gunshots, he saw Hayer pointing a pistol at Malcolm. Ballistics technicians, too, dusting a piece of unraveled film inside the smoke bomb, lifted Hayer's left thumb print off it. The detectives had eyewitness identification by one of the Hilton Hotel's security officers who placed him in the hotel on the night before the assassination, trying to find out what room Malcolm occupied.[3]

By the end of the first day, the detectives were certain that Hayer was part of a five man murder team, including two for the diversionary incident and three for the actual shooting.[4] Moreover, although he had denied that he was a member of the Nation of Islam, they came up with two photos showing a group of young black men wearing karate suits and standing in New Jersey's Newark Mosque, and Hayer was among them.[5]

Putting in long hours, the detectives bought information from informers, interviewed witnesses, and educated themselves on Malcolm X and the Nation of Islam. From New York City and New Jersey mosques, they made a list and picture file on known FOI "enforcers," which grew to over sixty names.

A major break in the case came when detectives recognized similarities between Malcolm's assassination and the January 6, 1965, shooting of Benjamin Brown, a Nation of Islam defector. Although the FOI had warned him not to do so, he had left Mosque Number Seven and set up his own mosque in a Bronx storefront. As he talked with friends outside his mosque on January 6, a bullet from a twenty-two caliber Winchester rifle hit him in the shoulder.

After Brown named Willie 8X Gaines, Thomas 15X Johnson, and Norman 3X Butler as the shooters, the police, finding the Winchester rifle in Johnson's home, arrested the three men, charging them with felonious assault. On the day of the assassination, all three men were out on bail, and the twenty-six year old Butler and the thirty-year old Johnson fit the eyewitness descriptions of the shooters.[6]

Late in the evening of February 25, two carloads of detectives converged on the Soundview Housing Project in the Bronx where Butler lived with his wife and four children. Upon opening the door, his wife, surprised by the police, who came crowding through with guns at the ready, stood aside. Apparently, they feared that her husband would resist arrest as he did when police officers came for him in the Brown shooting. Because of leg injuries sustained during his previous arrest, however, he was resting his legs on the living room couch and submitted to arrest without a struggle.[7]

The detectives took Butler downtown to criminal court, arraigned him without bail for Malcolm's murder, and interrogated him for four hours. They used the good guy and bad guy approach; while one detective sympathized with him, the other threatened him. But this approach got nowhere with Butler, who kept insisting that his badly injured legs prevented him from participating in Malcolm's assassination. In fact, he said, he had visited the hospital that Sunday morning because they had bothered him so much.[8]

Unconvinced by Butler's statements, the detectives placed him in a lineup where two eyewitnesses picked him out as one of the killers.[9] At that point, they transported him to the Tombs, the old city prison.

Unlike Butler, Johnson had a long arrest record, including narcotics possession, grand larceny, and possession of burglary tools. But detectives postponed his arrest since they had less evidence on him than they did on Butler. Not long afterwards, however, one of Malcolm's bodyguards, Cary 2X Thomas, decided to come forward with his eyewitness account of the shooting. Although he was carrying a three-fifty-seven magnum on the day of the assassination, he froze, he said, when the shooting broke out and ducked for cover. Yet, he said that he saw enough of it to positively identify Hayer, Butler, and Johnson as Malcolm's killers.[10]

Although Thomas did not commit a crime, detectives decided to hold him as a material witness to ensure that he would neither leave the city nor allow the Nation of Islam's enforcers an opportunity to kill him.

On March 3, at the Bronx County Courthouse, detectives arrested a "surprised" Johnson when he appeared on the assault charge in the Benjamin Brown shooting.[11] With his arrest, the detectives who had agreed that a five man team had carried out the assassination stopped their investigation of any more suspects. For reasons that the detectives never made clear, they were satisfied to arrest only three of the five, and the other two were free to go about their business without fear of arrest.

Both Johnson and Butler, members of Mosque Number Seven's FOI, denied being in the Audubon Ballroom on the day of the assassination, and Malcolm's bodyguards, most of whom were former members of it, denied seeing the two men there. "No way I could have walked in there," said Johnson.[12] "Was no doubt in anybody's mind who I was," added Butler.[13] Both men would have been "held at the door," said Benjamin 2X.[14] The only way those two men could have gotten through the door that day, said Herman Ferguson, was if Malcolm's security had undergone "a total breakdown."[15] To Peter Goldman, that these two well-known followers of Elijah Muhammad could have gotten past Malcolm's bodyguards was the most "puzzling anomaly" of the police's version of events.[16]

Seventeen days after the assassination, a grand jury indicted Hayer, Butler, and Johnson for "willfully, feloniously, and with malice aforethought" killing Malcolm X. At the same time, it issued a second indictment against thirty-three year old Reuben Francis on one count of first degree felonious assault for "aiming and discharging a pistol" at Hayer; two counts of second degree assault; and a fourth count for possessing a pistol. The court freed him after he posted ten-thousand dollars bail, but he skipped town soon thereafter, disappearing until his arrest on February 2, 1965.[17]

The Trial

On January 12, 1966, in front of seventy-one year old Judge Charles Marks, Hayer's, Butler's, and Johnson's trial began for the murder of Malcolm X. The court spent the first week selecting twelve jurors, nine whites and three blacks. While Hayer's family retained lawyers Peter L. Sabbatino and Peter Yellin, both whites, for their son, the other defendants had court appointed attorneys: William C. Chance and Joseph B. Williams for Butler and Joseph Pinckney and Charles T. Beavers for Johnson. All four of them were black. Considered one of the best murder-trial men in New York City, Vincent J. Dermody, a twenty-five year veteran, was the prosecutor.[18]

In opening statements to the jury, although Dermody vowed to show that the three defendants were members of the Nation of Islam, he neither pushed the popular allegation that it was behind the plot to assassinate Malcolm nor that they were part of a larger assassination team. Instead, he merely said that they acted together "in a carefully laid plan to kill Malcolm."[19]

Dermody carefully outlined the prosecution's version of events. Armed with automatic pistols, he said, Butler and Hayer sat next to each other while Johnson sat by himself, concealing a sawed-off shotgun. Following their pre-arranged plan, Butler and Hayer created a disturbance to attract the crowd's attention while Johnson rushed to the stage, pulled out the sawed-off shotgun from under his coat, and fired two blasts which felled Malcolm. At that point, Hayer and Butler ran to the stage and emptied their pistols into Malcolm's prone body. While Johnson and Butler were able to escape in the confusion, Francis Reuben shot Hayer and the angry crowd mobbed him until police rescued him outside the Audubon Ballroom.[20]

In their opening statements, the defense attorneys implied that dissident members of the OAAU led by Francis Reuben were responsible for Malcolm's assassination. Butler and Johnson, said the attorneys, were not at the Audubon Ballroom on February 21, and Hayer was there only out of curiosity. Moreover, he was not a member of the Nation of Islam. Reuben shot him, they said, to protect himself, and the mob wrongly identified Hayer as the assassin.[21]

In the next thirty days, Dermody would call twenty-four witnesses against the three defendants. They were either eyewitnesses to the assassination, fingering Hayer, Johnson, or Butler as one of the killers, or else policemen testifying to the evolving sequence of the investigation that pointed to them as the suspects.

The prosecution's main witness, however, was thirty-five year old Cary Thomas, who placed the three men at the murder scene with guns in their hands. Moments after he heard two shotgun blasts, he said he saw both Johnson holding a shotgun and Butler and Hayer running to the stage, although Thomas did not see their guns, only "a pumping motion."[22]

On cross-examination, defense attorneys attempted to undermine Thomas' credibility. They got him to admit that while serving in the Army between 1947 and 1953, he had been court-martialed several times before being dishonorably discharged, that he was a former heroin addict who had received a two-year suspended sentence in 1961 for narcotics possession, and that for reasons not adequately explained, he had spent three weeks in one of New York State's mental hospitals in 1963.

Although Thomas carried a .357 magnum pistol with him to the Audubon Ballroom, he failed to use it against Malcolm's attackers. Pressed by the defense attorneys to explain his failure to use it, he said that he was afraid of hitting women and children. "I wasn't sure which way the shots were going or who would start shooting next," and "I just took cover."[23]

Next, attempting to prove that Malcolm was the victim of a conspiracy by his own guards, the defense attorneys asked Thomas, as they did Malcolm's other bodyguards, if he had conspired in the assassination. At this question, he gripped the microphone, brought it up to his mouth, and said, "No!"[24]

Finally, the defense attorneys questioned Thomas about the discrepancies between his testimony in the trial and that of what he had earlier told the grand jury, which was that Johnson and Butler had rushed the stage together while Hayer ran interference. Since three gunmen had shot Malcolm, the inference was that an unidentified third gunman had gotten away. But the way Thomas had presented his version at the trial was that only three men, not four, had both created the diversion and done the shooting — the prosecution's contention.[25] Nonetheless, although the defense attorneys got the discrepancy into the record, they let it pass with little questioning.

Backing up Thomas' account, the prosecution presented a series of eyewitnesses that placed the three defendants both in the Audubon and as the shooters, yet not all of them were totally reliable. Twenty-three-year-old Venal Temple, for example, said that when he arrived at the Audubon, he saw Johnson seated in the back and identified Hayer as the man causing the commotion. But under cross examination, he said that he had seen Johnson at a Nation of Islam rally in Chicago, although he could not remember the "time, date, or place" of the event. Likewise, he admitted that he had seen pictures of Johnson, Butler, and Hayer before giving similar testimony before the grand jury.[26]

But defense attorneys could not easily shake the other eyewitness accounts that fingered the three defendants as the shooters. Among those identifying Butler included George Whitney, a former member of Mosque Number Seven and Jasper Davis, a department store superintendent. Fred Williams, who had driven Malcolm the final twenty blocks to the Audubon the day of the assassination, named Johnson as the man that he saw facing away from the stage holding the shotgun.[27] Charles X Blackwell, who was also in Williams' car when they picked up Malcolm that day, identified both Hayer and Butler as causing the commotion, and along with Charles Moore, a public relations man, saw Johnson escaping through the ladies' lounge, which led to a back way out of the Audubon.[28]

For one eyewitness, Ronald Timberlake, who feared for his life as a result of his testimony, Judge Marks cleared the courtroom of all spectators. Picking up Hayer's forty-five pistol when he dropped it on the steps while trying to flee the crowd, Timberlake said that he tried to fire it at him, but the safety lock was on. Later, he gave it to the FBI, who handed it over to the NYPD.[29]

On February 17, the twenty-sixth day of the trial, Dermody called Malcolm's wife to the stand. Dressed in black with a single strand of white pearls around her neck, she told her story of shots firing, people hollering, chairs falling, and pushing her children to the floor and covering them with chairs. Although she could not identify any of the killers since she had not seen her husband killed, her presence added an emotional aspect that proved helpful to the prosecution.

After defense attorneys declined to cross-examine Betty, Judge Marks dismissed her from the stand. On her way to the exit, however, she stopped abruptly by the table where the three defendants were sitting, and in a low "quavering" voice, she said to them that they had no right to kill her husband. While court attendants grabbed her hands and escorted her out of the courtroom, the defense attorneys jumped up and demanded a mistrial. Denying it, Judge Marks noted that she had not pointed her fingers at any of the three defendants, and he asked the jury to disregard her outburst.[30]

Dermody had hard evidence against Hayer. Detective Joseph Reisch, a ballistics expert, testified that two of the slugs retrieved from Malcolm's body matched the cartridges found in the forty-five clip confiscated from Hayer by the police at the time of his arrest. Also, a fingerprint expert testified that Hayer's thumb print matched latent prints taken from the film found in the smoke bomb that went off the day of the assassination.[31]

On February 23, Hayer took the stand on his behalf. He denied being a member of the Nation of Islam, knowing Butler and Johnson, or having on his person a forty-five pistol at any time during the day of the assassination. Although he could not account for the fact that the police found his thumb print on a piece of film that formed part of the smoke bomb, he said that he found the forty-five cartridge clip in the men's room before the rally began.[32]

Unlike Hayer, for whom detectives had gathered concrete evidence placing him at the Audubon on February 21, Dermody only had eyewitness testimony placing Butler and Johnson there that day. Yet, their wives said that they were home with them that day. Collaborating the testimony of Butler's wife, two Nation of Islam women testified that her husband had been at home on February 21 when they called him to pass the news of Malcolm's assassination, which they had heard on the radio. Earlier that day, Dr. Kenneth Seslove testified that he had diagnosed Butler with an inflammation of the veins, giving him bandages and telling him to keep his legs elevated.

What's more, the luger, which several witnesses had placed in Butler's hands, had disappeared and the shotgun had neither fingerprints on it nor a traceable history tying it to Johnson.[33]

On February 28, taking the stand again, Hayer, to the court's astonishment, admitted to firing shots from the forty-five automatic pistol into Malcolm's body after another shooter had felled him with two shotgun blasts. He insisted, too, that neither Johnson nor Butler had anything to do with the assassination. Stating that he had three accomplices, Hayer both refused to name them and denied that the Nation of Islam had any part in it.[34] Instead, he said that someone had offered him money to shoot Malcolm, but again, he refused to say who or how much. Also, he left unanswered the question of motive.

According to Dermody's version, a three man hit team carried out the assassination. Hayer and Butler created the disturbance, and after Johnson felled Malcolm with two shotgun blasts, they rushed the stage and emptied their pistols into his prone body. In Hayer's four man version, however, one man, sitting in the back, created the disturbance while another shot Malcolm with two shotgun blasts. Then Hayer and another man, both sitting in the front, jumped up and pumped bullets into his fallen body.[35]

Under cross-examination, Dermody repeatedly pressed Hayer to name his accomplices. Although steadfast in his refusal to do so, he said that the man who fired the shotgun was a "husky, dark-skinned Negro who wore a beard," matching one of the defense witnesses' description.[36]

Fearing that Hayer's confession might influence the jury to acquit Johnson and Butler, Dermody argued that because there was so much evidence against him, his confession was an attempt to save his fellow conspirators.

His lawyers, too, tried to get the jury to ignore their client's confession. They said that he was trying to save his co-defendants for no other reason than from "a high sense of Christian charity."[37] Apparently, they either did not realize or were insensitive to the fact that their client was a Muslim.

On March 7, Johnson's and Butler's lawyers made their closing statements to the court. They asked the jury not to convict their clients "merely because of their membership in the Nation of Islam." Waving the gray-jacketed records folder from Bellevue Hospital's psychiatric division, they asked the jury to exclude Cary Thomas' testimony because he suffered "from an impaired mentality." Likewise, they tried to undermine Dermody's other witnesses by noting their criminal records, advanced age, poor vision, and "defective" memories.[38]

Presenting the closing statements for Hayer was Sabbatino, who said that Malcolm was the victim of "a vast conspiracy." Led by the "arch-boss" Reuben Francis, it included Malcolm's security guards and several prosecution witnesses. Accordingly, dismissing all the evidence the prosecution had against Hayer, Sabbatino said that somebody had placed the forty-five caliber cartridge clip in the Audubon's toilet, watching who took it and making sure to divert police attention to that person. The weight of this "rigged evidence," moreover, had persuaded his client to confess and absolve his co-defendants.[39]

On the matter of the thumb print on the smoke bomb, said Sabbatino, looking with "solemn faith" at every juror, "I leave that for you to explain."[40]

Just before presenting his closing arguments, Dermody, over the objectives of the defense lawyers, had persuaded Judge Marks to label the trial a conspiracy, meaning that any evidence that the prosecution presented against one defendant would also pertain to all three. At that point, Sabbatino, so that he could defend Hayer without hurting the other two defendants, asked Judge Marks for a mistrial, which he denied.

For four hours and twenty minutes, Dermody presented the prosecution's closing arguments. As to Butler's and Johnson's claim that they had spent the day of the assassination with their families, he said that either the two defendants, their wives, and the two Muslim women, claiming to have spoken to Butler on the telephone right after the shooting, were lying or the numerous witnesses who testified that they saw the two men in the Audubon participating in the killing of Malcolm X were not telling the truth. "The first group had every reason to lie," said Dermody, while "the second group none."

Throughout the trial, although Dermody had emphasized that the three defendants were members of the Nation of Islam, he said that he never sought to prove that Elijah Muhammad had ordered them to kill Malcolm or that the Nation was on trial. Dermody added, however, that from the time Malcolm had split from the Nation in March 1964 to the time of his death in February 1965, he often "stated as a certainty that the Muslims would murder him." Then, facing the jury with downward thrusts of his right hand, Dermody said that there must have been some reason why they killed him with such "brazenness." It was, he said, an "object lesson" to Malcolm's followers that this could also happen to them.

Describing Hayer's avowal that his co-defendants were innocent as "a futile, desperate gesture" by a man buried under "a mound of evidence" to do "the noble thing" was Dermody's way of explaining it. Somewhere along the line, he said, someone decided, he could not say who, that Hayer was "a dead duck" and "that he should take the fall."[41]

On March 11, after deliberating more than twenty hours, the jury returned a verdict of murder in the first degree against all three defendants. According to one juror, the greatest difficulty was in placing Butler and Johnson in the ballroom, but once they had resolved the credibility of the witnesses, the rest fell into place. As to Hayer, said another juror, when he realized that the evidence overwhelmingly identified him as one of the assassins, he confessed "to save the other two."[42]

On April 14, Judge Marks sentenced each of the three men to life imprisonment. In New York, a life sentence was tantamount to a forty-year sentence, which meant that they would become eligible for parole after serving twenty-six years and eight months. Their attorneys immediately launched an appeal on the grounds that Timberlake's secret testimony deprived the three men of their constitutional right to a public trial. In 1969, however, the New York Court of Appeals upheld Judge Marks' decision, ruling that he could close a trial to manage it.[43]

To some, that the FBI encouraged, monitored, and unofficially sanctioned Malcolm X's murder was a fact. By "forging Malcolm's signature and sending inflammatory letters to Muhammad and his followers," said newsman Dan Rather, FBI agents caused "disruption" and "deepened the dispute."[44] While the "fire pre-existed the gasoline," said Peter Goldman, they threw "gasoline on it."[45] They "egged it on," said Yuri Kochiyama.[46] According to Herman Ferguson, "the FBI was the puppeteer and the Nation of Islam its puppet."[47] And to William Kunstler, while FBI agents "didn't actually pull the trigger," they "figuratively loaded the guns and placed them in the hands of the assassins."[48]

Although the FBI was hostile to the Nation of Islam and Malcolm X, said biographer Michael Friedly, its main target was Dr. Martin Luther King,

Jr., and "its desire and willingness to actually murder Malcolm X cannot be demonstrated."[49] Yet, if its agents had played a direct role in his assassination, they would have destroyed any evidence linking the FBI to it. According to scholar Paul Lee, FBI director J. Edgar Hoover kept the agency's undocumented "soft files" in his personal desk and "routinely destroyed them."[50] Despite the FBI's "thousands of hours" of monitoring Malcolm's life, said William Kunstler, most revealing was that it played no role in the investigation of his death."[51]

That the CIA was behind Malcolm's assassination was another theory. Its agents, according to this view, were unconcerned with him until he broke away from the Nation of Islam and began stirring up anti–American feelings during his travels abroad. As a result, they tried to poison him while he was abroad in 1964 and planned to assassinate him during his visit to Paris in February 1965, but the French learned of it and barred him from entering the country. Thus, although members of the Nation of Islam had killed him, the CIA was somehow behind it.[52]

Another theory placed a large measure of responsibility in Malcolm's assassination on the NYPD. Although only a week before the assassination, someone had firebombed his house, its officers failed to mount a serious investigation of the crime. Knowing too that he was in imminent danger from the Nation of Islam, whose members had been both stalking him and threatening his life during his recent trips to Los Angeles and Chicago, the NYPD failed to ensure his safety, which allowed them a window of opportunity to kill him.

According to NYPD officials, they offered Malcolm police protection several times in the three weeks before his assassination, but he repeatedly refused it.[53] Although they offered him protection, said Peter Goldman, they knew that "for reasons of pride and politics" that he would reject it.[54] Still, while Malcolm may have declined some police offers for protection, he sought it at other times, but whether the NYPD took these requests seriously was unclear. In fact, its behavior throughout the period leading to his death suggested an indifference to it.

At any rate, NYPD officials said that at least three undercover BOSS agents were among the crowd inside the Audubon Ballroom on February 21. According to one police official, "If we had not had them there, we certainly would have been very careless."[55] Yet, even if the killer's diversion had thrown the BOSS agents off guard, they failed to respond until the shooting was over.

Nonetheless, Gene Roberts, BOSS' closest undercover agent to Malcolm, acted heroically. Dodging a bullet in the process, Roberts floored Hayer with a chair as he was running for the door. Then, after Francis shot

Hayer in the leg and the crowd began to mob him, Roberts ran on the stage and gave Malcolm mouth-to-mouth resuscitation. These actions were not those of a man who was part of a police conspiracy to kill Malcolm.

The events surrounding the assassination were confusing, and the press may not have always reported them accurately. Besides Hayer, some press accounts reported that the NYPD arrested another gunman at the scene, which the police later denied. Writing for the SWP's *Militant,* however, George Breitman insinuated that the NYPD saved the second suspect from the mob and then let him go because he was part of a police conspiracy to kill Malcolm.[56] According to eyewitness accounts, however, first Hoy, then Aronoff and Angelos, grabbed hold of the same suspect, Talmadge Hayer. According to Goldman, "conspiratorialists doubt everything in the establishment press except its mistakes."[57]

In court, the defense attorneys for the three convicted killers developed the theory that a conspiracy had developed among Malcolm's followers because they feared that he was going soft on whites. By killing him, then, they could redeem themselves with Elijah Muhammad.

To buttress their case, the defense attorneys pointed to the strange behavior of Malcolm's security guards on the day of the assassination. While under orders not to frisk people entering the ballroom, they could easily have ignored them for those eliciting suspicious behavior. When the commotion in the audience commenced, the security guards rushed to it, leaving their man unprotected behind the lectern. The proper response, said the defense attorneys, was for them to rush the stage, form a protective wall around Malcolm, and get him off the stage.

Also, once the shooting started, said the defense attorneys, although some of Malcolm's security guards were carrying guns, they failed to use them while others froze in their tracks. After he went down, too, few of his guards either aided him or actively pursued the killers who were making their escape.

That Malcolm's security guards were incompetent may have explained their mistakes. Yet, knowing the imminent threat on Malcolm's life and their professed loyalty towards him, their bungling efforts to protect him on the day of the assassination remained a mystery.

Calling Malcolm's assassination "a political killing with international implications," James Farmer, Congress of Racial Equality's (CORE) director, developed the theory that Harlem's drug dealers, who were tied to New York City's mob syndicate and it to the international drug trade, killed him because his exhortations at Harlem's street rallies urging his followers to "chase the pushers out of Harlem" was hurting their business.[58] Yet, Farmer neither presented any evidence to back up his accusations nor did Malcolm's public lectures or private criticism of drug dealers make any dent in Harlem's drug trade.[59]

So far, conspiratorial theorists have yet to prove that government agencies, police departments, drug dealers, or OAAU dissidents had any direct involvement in Malcolm's assassination. Substantial evidence, on the other hand, pointed to Elijah Muhammad and the Chicago leadership, whose motives included jealousy, rivalry, resentment, and public accusations.

Since Malcolm's departure from the Nation of Islam on March 8, Muhammad's followers had been either stalking, threatening, or trying to kill him in Boston, Los Angeles, Chicago, and New York City. *Muhammad Speaks'* editorials had repeatedly referred to Malcolm as the Nation's chief hypocrite; its cartoons showed him with his head cut off; its articles by Louis X stated that Malcolm was "worthy of death." Phone taps by the FBI, moreover, had recorded Muhammad telling his followers that Malcolm's "tongue should be cut off."

Granted, the FBI added to the conflict by sending Malcolm poison pen letters, signed by the other, the NYPD showed a measure of indifference to threats against Malcolm's life, and the CIA had kept tabs on him throughout his two visits to the Middle East and Africa. Nevertheless, involvement by outside agencies was secondary to the conflict between the two men. "Even without outside interference," said Charles Kenyatta, "the Nation of Islam would still have killed Malcolm."[60] And according to Benjamin 2X, "neither the FBI nor any other federal agency or criminal organization had to contrive Malcolm's assassination" since "the Nation of Islam did it for them."[61]

While no concrete evidence existed linking Elijah Muhammad directly to Malcolm's death, circumstantial evidence tied him to it. To be sure, Muhammad allowed his followers to create a climate that led to it, which would not have occurred without his consent. "The FBI and the CIA had nothing to do with the climate," said Captain Joseph. "It was strictly between Malcolm and the zealots."[62]

Although "doubting" that his father or "senior courtiers" around him "pushed the button," Wallace Muhammad said that the "leadership created a volatile, fiery climate in which violence against Malcolm became acceptable."[63] "Where we are responsible for creating this climate," said Louis X much later, after he had changed his name to Louis Farrakhan, "where our hands are a part of this, we beg God's mercy and forgiveness."[64]

If Elijah Muhammad did give an order to have Malcolm assassinated, he would have wrapped it in symbol and suggestion. His main lieutenants, however, would understand its real implication and interpret it as such. Like the FBI, said Paul Lee, the Nation of Islam's culture was "designed to keep its members from getting caught" and "showing their fingerprints."[65]

Later, while in New York's Sing Sing Prison, Hayer told Goldman that he recalled a member of Newark's FOI telling his fellow Muslims "to go out thee to Malcolm's home" and "cut the nigger's tongue out, put it in an envelope, send it to me, and I'll stamp it approved and give it to Elijah Muhammad." Although the FOI lieutenant was speaking "metaphorically," said Hayer, to believers that was an order, and attempts on Malcolm's life followed.[66]

John Ali may have played some role in Malcolm's murder. Ironically, prior to becoming Chicago's national secretary, he was one of Malcolm's closest friends and advisors. Once becoming national secretary, however, he began to undermine his former mentor. He took *Muhammad Speaks* away from Malcolm, moving it to Chicago, where it gave his activities minimal coverage thereafter. In June 1964, Ali stated that Malcolm "deserved death," and on February 19, 1965, Ali flew to New York City, returning to Chicago on the evening of the assassination. According to newsman Jack Newfield, Ali met with Hayer the night before the assassination, but he presented no evidence to back up his claim.[67]

Also, on the day of the assassination, Louis X was visiting with Hayer at his mosque in Newark, New Jersey. "This was the man," said political observer John Henrik Clarke, "who was a former friend of Malcolm's but joined his detractors and helped create the climate that got Malcolm murdered."[68]

Hayer's 1977 Confession

After being processed in Sing Sing Prison, authorities shipped Hayer, Johnson, and Butler upstate to Dannemora Prison. Upon arrival, its warden, fearing that their presence among pro–Malcolm black inmates might cause trouble, placed them in solitary confinement. At first, he kept them eight cells apart on an otherwise vacant tier, but he later permitted them adjoining cells so that they could communicate with each other. Although Butler and Johnson were casual friends, they claimed not to have known Hayer. With endless time on their hands, however, all three men became close friends.

Doing time was hard on the three men. Their hair thinned and faces weathered and Butler's and Hayer's wives left them. Even though Johnson wanted his wife to divorce him and make something of her life while she was still young, she refused to do so. Meanwhile, the men took college courses and practiced their Muslim faith. Eventually, Butler and Hayer wound up at Attica Prison where they acted as peacemakers during its famous 1971 riot.[69]

With Elijah Muhammad's death in 1975, Wallace Muhammad took over the Nation of Islam and moved it towards adopting Orthodox Islam. Later, he publicly admitted that his father had committed infidelities, fathering several illegitimate children. Wallace's revelation "broke down" Hayer's "whole concept of things," and he began to have second thoughts about the assassination of Malcolm.[70]

In late 1977, Hayer persuaded Kunstler, who had earlier refused his case out of respect for Malcolm, to take it now. Supplying him with two affidavits, Hayer, who had earlier said that he was just a hired gun, admitted that he had been a member of Newark's Mosque Number Twenty-Five and that his accomplices had belonged to it, too. He listed them as twenty-seven year old William Bradley, who was then serving a seven to fifteen year sentence in New Jersey's Caldwell State Prison; twenty-one year old Leon Davis from Paterson, New Jersey; Benjamin Thomas, who at that time was assistant secretary of Newark's mosque; and Wilbur McKinley, who had died during the early 1970s.[71]

Shortly thereafter, Kunstler filed a motion to vacate the judgments against Butler and Johnson on the grounds that new evidence had surfaced. Hayer told Kunstler that he "felt guilty about letting Butler and Johnson sit in jail for something they had not done."[72] And to newsman Mike Wallace, Hayer said, "I realized I made this mistake, but I can't change what happened."[73]

In a prison interview with Peter Goldman, Hayer said that while he did not know who had initiated the order to have Malcolm killed, the members of Newark's mosque knew "that was what the leader wanted."[74] According to Hayer, when Leon Davis and Benjamin Thomas asked him to become a member of a five-man assassination team, a major influence on his decision to join it was seeing the cartoon printed in *Muhammad Speaks* which showed Malcolm's severed head bouncing down a roadway while shouting blasphemies against Elijah Muhammad. According to Goldman, Hayer "wasn't a terribly literate guy," and he was "more powerfully moved by that cartoon than by the acres of prose."[75]

According to Hayer's affidavits, after the five-man team obtained guns from a street hustler, they scouted the Audubon twice, once to ascertain that Malcolm's guards were not frisking people at the door and again at a dance on the night before the assassination to check exit routes. On the following day, they divided up their assignments, drove to the Audubon in Wilbur

McKinley's Cadillac, walked past Malcolm's loose security with their guns hidden under their winter topcoats, and took their assigned positions.

Armed with a forty-five and a luger pistol, Hayer and McKinley sat in the front row. Behind them sat Bradley, holding the sawed-off shotgun under his coat, and Thomas to make noise and run interference. Halfway back sat McKinley with the smoke bomb and the rehearsed diversionary statement that someone was picking his pocket.[76]

Hayer's accomplices, however, refused to come forward to collaborate his testimony, and New York City's district attorney refused to put pressure on them to do it. As a result, Kunstler filed a motion with the New York Supreme Court to reopen the case, but it ruled that there was insufficient evidence to reopen the case.[77]

Refusing to give up, Kunstler obtained the help of Harlem's Democratic Congressman, Charles Rangel, who submitted Hayer's affidavits to the U.S. House of Representatives' Black Caucus so that it could present them to the House select committee on assassination. Yet, Malcolm's wife, for reasons that remained unclear, objected to reopening the case, and its members would not support any attempt by Kunstler to reopen it unless she changed her mind.[78]

By June 1985, the New York Parole Board had awarded parole to Hayer, Johnson, and Butler. They assumed private lives and tried to stay out of the public eye.

CHAPTER 14

Recapitulation and Reflection

As a child, Malcolm X experienced grief, hunger, and isolation from his family. When he was only six years old, his father was either murdered by racists or accidentally fell under the wheels of a trolley car. Only thirty-four years old and left with seven children amid the Great Depression, his mother could not always feed her children. Nonetheless, a proud woman, she would whip Malcolm whenever store owners caught him stealing food. These whippings led neighbors to inform welfare agents that she was abusing her son; to protect him, they placed him in a foster home.

Not long afterwards, Malcolm's mother suffered a mental breakdown. In 1939, the courts sent her to the state's mental hospital in Kalamazoo, Michigan, and placed the younger children in foster homes. Meanwhile, bound for reform school because of some minor misbehavior, Malcolm wound up in a detention home. Impressed by his good behavior, the Swerleins, who ran it, blocked his transfer to reform school and enrolled him in Mason Junior High School, making him the first boy in the detention home to have that privilege.

Because Malcolm had no other place to live and liked the Swerleins, he tolerated their racial prejudices. Likewise, despite being the only black student at a school where racism was endemic, he rose to the head of his class, played sports, and became class president. But after visiting with his half-sister, Ella Collins, in Boston during the summer of 1940 and feeling a part of a vibrant black community, continuing to live with a white family and attending an all white school became intolerable for him. Sensing his unhappiness from his letters, Ella persuaded the Michigan authorities to transfer him to her custody.

Arriving in Boston's black ghetto in February 1941, fifteen-year-old

Malcolm rejected Ella's attempts to persuade him to stay in school and became a small time hustler. Developing alcohol, tobacco, and marijuana habits, he bought a zoot suit, conked his hair, learned the Lindy, started gambling, and met Beatrice Bazarian, an attractive white woman. Although he may have initially looked upon her as a status symbol, his feelings grew for her, and their relationship continued for five years.

As a waiter at Small's Paradise in Harlem, Malcolm refined his hustling techniques by listening to the professional hustlers who hung out there. But whether he became the sophisticated hustler that he had portrayed himself to be in his autobiography was open to question.

While Malcolm described his gang's burglaries as well planned jobs, Shorty said that they were not only unplanned, but also committed for fun, not money. Malcolm's description of the gang's method of operation, in fact, was stuff that he may have learned from his prison friendship with Bembry. Unlike a professional criminal, too, Malcolm acted like a man who wanted to get caught. By late 1945, he probably realized that he was out of control, and that his choices had narrowed to either prison or death. Wisely, he chose the former.

Although Sammy McKnight and the other hustlers may have influenced Malcolm's cynical view of women, that Beatrice testified against him at the trial, and that the judge had given Shorty and him harsher sentences than their female accomplices, may have further soured Malcolm's view of women. Still, he was the one who had informed on his gang, including Beatrice, to the detectives, and the court's racism, not the women, was responsible for the harsher sentences.

Blessed with quick intelligence and a love of learning, which his Garveyite parents had instilled in him, Malcolm had suppressed it during his hustling years. Upon entering Charleston State Prison, however, Bembry told him to use his brains and make something of himself. This was the kind of advice Malcolm was looking for, and he immediately mapped out a self-education program for himself, including writing out every word from the dictionary.

At this time, however, Malcolm said that he was engaged in self-education, not moral rehabilitation. That he continued to express a tough and cynical attitude only masked the substantive changes that were occurring within him. With his reading and writing, for instance, he was discovering new insights about both the world around him and into his personality. Thus, his conversion to the Nation of Islam did not, as he insinuated in his autobiography, come as a blinding light after his siblings had introduced him to Elijah Muhammad's teachings, but was part of an ongoing process that began with Bembry's friendship.

Nonetheless, joining the Nation of Islam increased Malcolm's motivation for self-improvement. To spread the Nation's message, he participated in the prison's debate team and improved his timing, delivery, and cadence by listening to black speaker Paul Robeson on the radio. Embarking on a letter writing campaign, too, Malcolm hoped to both improve his writing skills and win over converts to the Nation.

The Middle Years

Upon leaving prison in 1952, Malcolm became a frequent visitor to Muhammad's home in Chicago. Soon, the two men bonded. To Muhammad, Malcolm became his seventh son, while Malcolm looked upon him as father figure.

Because of his speaking and organizing abilities as well as his tireless enthusiasm, Malcolm rose to prominence and position in the Nation. He traveled throughout the country, spoke at temples, set up new ones, conducted fund raising campaigns, and served as both Muhammad's trouble shooter and spokesman. As a result, Malcolm was responsible for the Nation's phenomenal growth from a few hundred members and a number of storefronts in 1952 to several thousand and over thirty temples by 1959.

Describing women as deceitful and untrustworthy, Malcolm's negative attitudes towards them went beyond the Nation's patriarchal male chauvinism. As stated previously, he developed these attitudes from other hustlers on the streets as well as from his complex relationship with Beatrice Bazarian. Despite his stated belief in the hustler's code to keep women at a distance, that she betrayed him not only during the trial, but also by marrying a soldier during their relationship, hurt him and strengthened his distrust of women.

Marrying Betty in 1958 was a big step for Malcolm. When he said that she was the first woman he had slept with since his hustling days, he was probably telling the truth. With time, he came to trust her more than anyone else. Yet, their marriage was not without problems. That Malcolm would not save money for their children's future bothered her. Also, she disapproved of his non-stop schedule and his unfavorable opinion concerning her desire to continue her nursing career. She left him three times over these issues, yet she always returned.

By 1961, Malcolm's command of the language and charisma had brought him greater publicity than Muhammad. The general public, in fact, began to think of Malcolm as the Nation of Islam's central figure. At the same time, impressed by the non-racist attitudes of white college students, he began to modify his views towards them. As a result, Muhammad became both concerned with the degree of news attention Malcolm was receiving and feared that he was losing his enthusiasm for the Nation's white devil theory.

By this time, too, Muhammad and the Chicago leadership considered Malcolm a threat to their power and prestige in the movement. Like Muhammad, living in large homes, driving big cars, and wearing expensive clothes, the Chicago leadership became more interested in their materialist lifestyles than in promoting the Nation's religious ideals. In contrast to their extravagant lifestyles, Malcolm practiced thrift and simple living, allocating to himself only about one hundred and seventy-dollars a week for living expenses.

Regarded by Elijah's followers as his likely successor, Wallace Muhammad, like Malcolm, eschewed wealth and lived up to the Nation's religious ideals. With Wallace at the Nation's helm, the Chicago leadership feared that Malcolm would influence him to clean house and return to the Nation's ideals. Consequently, they began spreading rumors that Malcolm was promoting himself over Muhammad, and that he was amassing a core of ministers primed to aid a "succession coup."

Meanwhile, Malcolm, whose restless nature and love of learning would not allow him to remain confined within the Nation's narrow doctrines, began to rely more on his own judgments. With blacks demonstrating in the streets for civil rights, moreover, Muhammad's nonengagement policy seemed irrelevant to Malcolm. As a result, he started shifting his speeches away from religion to politics, talking less about God bringing justice to blacks and more about them getting it for themselves.

The Last Years

In February 1963, according to Malcolm, Wallace Muhammad's confirmation of his father's infidelities for him precipitated an emotional crisis. Yet, since rumors of them had been circulating throughout the Nation for years, by 1963, Malcolm's problems associated with Elijah Muhammad and the Chicago leadership had become unbearable. In this changed environment, Muhammad's infidelities, formerly blotted out by Malcolm, now became significant for him.

In early November 1963, Malcolm endorsed a boycott in Queens of store owners who refused to hire blacks, defying the Nation's ban on political activism. Also, he implied a willingness to ally himself with non–Muslim militants in his "A Message to the Grass Roots" speech at a black leadership conference in Detroit. To Muhammad and the Chicago leadership, these two actions were additional signals of Malcolm's growing independence from their control.

Shortly thereafter, Malcolm's "chickens coming home to roost" statement, given at New York City's Manhattan Center on December 1, 1963, violated Muhammad's orders to remain silent on Kennedy's assassination nine days earlier. In an act of rebellion, Malcolm was both challenging Muhammad's power and daring him to do something about it. Consequently, he suspended Malcolm for ninety days, changing it shortly thereafter to an indefinite period and stripping him of all power by appointing Minister James Shabazz of Newark's mosque to head Mosque Number Seven.

On March 8, 1964, Malcolm's declaration of independence from the Nation of Islam was anticlimactic, for Muhammad had already retired him three months earlier.

Once out of the Nation, Malcolm adopted the battle cry "by any means necessary." For him, along with rent strikes and electoral campaigns, it included using both defensive and offensive violence. In this way, he was articulating the growing impatience of Northern blacks with Dr. King's nonviolent strategy.

Still, although civil rights leaders rejected Malcolm because of his willingness to use violence, he never gave up trying to find some common ground with them. He was not, however, as some have suggested, moving in the direction of integration. For Malcolm, America's black freedom struggle had more to do with human rights than civil rights, and since that went beyond Washington's authority, he sought to internationalize America's race problem by first linking it to the worldwide struggle against colonialism and then presenting it to the U.N. as a human rights problem.

While Malcolm no longer regarded whites as devils, his attitude towards them remained ambivalent. To blacks, he said that he never really changed his attitude towards whites, but since they cannot help being white, blacks should give them a chance, which they probably would not take — "the snakes."

By mid 1964, describing Malcolm's philosophy was difficult to do. He wanted to "turn the corner" and develop a concrete direction, yet the Nation of Islam would not allow him the peace of mind to do it.

Breaking from the Nation had made Malcolm an even more dangerous rival to Muhammad and the Chicago leadership. It increased the rise in the possibility that Malcolm might go public with Muhammad's extramarital affairs, the Chicago leadership's corruption, or the Nation's dealings with the Ku Klux Klan and the Nazi party. By going public with any one of these three issues, Malcolm could do irreparable harm to the Nation.

Accordingly, Malcolm and the Chicago leadership used all of the Nation's resources, including scores of FOI soldiers and a newspaper whose subscribers numbered in the thousands, to create a climate among its members where killing Malcolm became a holy obligation. In contrast, although Malcolm received widespread media attention and the support of young blacks disenchanted with nonviolence, he did not have the materials to counter the Nation's carefully constructed holy war against him.

By establishing permanent residence abroad, Malcolm might have saved his life. During his travels, throughout the Middle East and Africa, he received offers of employment from Presidents Nassar of Egypt and Nkrumah of Ghana, and for as long as necessary, his expatriate friends in Accura offered to share their lodgings with him and his family. Nevertheless, knowing that it would cost him his life, he chose to return to the United States. Fighting for American blacks' human rights was more important to him than living a long life.

Throughout 1964 and early 1965, Malcolm received frequent death threats by mail and over the phone, rumors of assassination plots abounded, and stalking incidents occurred in Boston, Los Angeles, Chicago, and New York City. Yet, not until the firebombing of his home on February 14, 1965, did he begin to unravel from the pressure. Still, he would not allow his deteriorating psychological condition to slow him down, and he kept appointments and made appearances to speak right up to the day of his assassination on February 21.

Conclusion

Although there was little evidence that the CIA, international drug dealers, or a conspiracy by Malcolm's followers played a role in his death, it was clearer that the NYPD and the FBI shared some responsibility for it. While the NYPD failed to provide adequate measures to help ensure his safety, the FBI aggravated the conflict by forging Malcolm's signature to inflammatory letters and sending them to the Nation's leadership.

Nevertheless, neither neglect nor outside agitation had much, if anything, to do with Malcolm's ultimate assassination. Substantial evidence indicated that Elijah Muhammad and the Chicago leadership, whose motives included jealousy, rivalry, resentment, and public accusations, created a climate of hate that motivated their followers to kill Malcolm.

Not long after Malcolm's death, young blacks, influenced by his life and message, started the "Black Power Movement." Its leaders included Stokely Carmichael, a former member of SNCC, and Huey Newton and

Bobby Seale, founders of Oakland, California's Black Panther party. Calling for black nationalism and armed defense, black power advocates referred to themselves as African Americans, promoted "Afro" hairstyles and dress, shed their "white" names for African identities, and demanded black studies programs in schools and universities.

Malcolm's prediction that the United States' black ghettos, burdened with poor schools, dilapidated housing, and high youth unemployment, would rise in violent protest proved accurate. Between 1965 and 1967, one hundred and one major riots had left one-hundred thirty people dead and nearly four thousand injured, and the economic loss was over seven hundred million. More riots took place after a sniper's bullet killed Dr. King in Memphis, Tennessee, on April 4, 1968. The resulting violence cost over forty lives. During the riots, blacks directed most of their anger at ghetto white-owned stores and property, and the police and military troops did much of the shooting.

On February 25, 1975, Elijah Muhammad died of a heart attack. With his death, Wallace Muhammad became the leader of the Nation of Islam. Rejecting the racism of his father, he renamed it the World Community of Islam and aligned it with Orthodox Islam. Two years later, Louis X, formerly Louis Walcott, renamed himself Louis Farrakhan and reestablished the Nation of Islam.

By the mid 1980s, because of Farrakhan's charisma and organizational abilities, the Nation's membership increased and his followers set up mosques and study groups throughout the United States. What's more, he was able to attract larger audiences than other black leaders. His largest gathering of blacks occurred in Washington on October 16, 1995. Billed as a "Million Man March" to affirm black manhood, over five hundred thousand black men assembled on the mall in front of the Washington Monument to hear him speak on atonement and renewal. That so many blacks attended the event illustrated how far America had yet to travel to achieve Malcolm X's demand for human rights and freedom for black Americans.

Notes

Introduction

1. Craig W. Wade, *The Fiery Cross: The Ku Klux Klan in America* (New York: Oxford University Press, 1987), p. 218.

2. C. Eric Lincoln, *The Black Muslims in America* (Boston: Beacon Press, 1961), pp. 63–64.

3. Louis A. DeCaro, Jr., *On the Side of the People: A Religious Life of Malcolm X* (New York: New York University Press, 1996), p. 13.

4. Claude Lewis, "The Many Heirs to Malcolm's Mantle," *New York Herald Tribune*, February 28, 1965.

5. Victor Wolfenstein, *The Victims of Democracy: Malcolm X and the Black Revolution* (New York: Guilford Press, 1973), p. 42.

6. DeCaro, *Side of the People*, p. 39.

7. Hans J. Massaquoi, "Mystery of Malcolm X," *Ebony*, September 1964, pp. 38–40.

8. Alex Haley, *The Autobiography of Malcolm X* (New York: Ballantine Books, 1992), pp. 6–7.

9. Wilfred Little, in *Malcolm X: Make It Plain*, ed. Cheryll Y. Greene (New York: Penguin Books, 1994), p. 23.

10. Haley, *Autobiography*, p. 7.

11. Robert Penn Warren, "Malcolm X: Mission and Meaning," in *Malcolm X: As They Know Him*, ed. David Gallen (New York: Carroll and Graf, 1992), p. 204.

12. Bayard Rustin, "Making His Mark, *New York Times*, November 14, 1965.

13. Bruce Perry, *Malcolm: The Life of a Man Who Changed Black America* (New York: Station Hill Press, 1991), p. 5.

14. Wolfenstein, *Victims of Democracy*, p. 43.

15. DeCaro, *Side of the People*, pp. 44–45.

16. Wilfred Little, in Greene, *Malcolm X*, p. 2.

17. Louis E. Lomax, *When the Word is Given* (Cleveland, Ohio: World Publishing, 1963), p. 56.

18. Philbert Little, in Greene, *Malcolm X*, p. 21.

19. DeCaro, *Side of the People*, p. 45.

20. Wilfred Little, in Greene, *Malcolm X*, p. 22.

21. Spike Lee and Ralph Wiley, *By Any Means Necessary: The Trials and Tribulations of the Making of Malcolm X* (New York: Hyperion, 1992), pp. 46–47.

22. Archie Epps, ed., *Malcolm X: Speeches at Harvard* (New York: Paragon House, 1991), p. 18.

23. Haley, *Autobiography*, pp. 14–15.

24. Ibid., p. 449.

25. Ibid., p. 17.

26. Philbert Little, in Greene, *Malcolm X*, p. 26.

27. Perry, *Malcolm*, p. 35.

28. Yvonne Woodward, in Greene, *Malcolm X*.

29. Haley, *Autobiography*, pp. 22–23.

30. Woodward, in Greene, *Malcolm X*.

31. Haley, *Autobiography*, pp. 26–27.

32. Ibid., pp. 33–34.

33. Hans J. Massaquoi, "Mystery of Malcolm X," *Ebony*, September 1964, p. 45.

34. Haley, *Autobiography*, pp. 32–33.

35. Ibid., pp. 36–37.

36. DeCaro, *Side of the People*, p. 54.

37. Rodnell P. Cullins and Peter Bailey, *Seventh Child: A Family Memoir of Malcolm X* (Secaucus, N.J.: Birch Lane Press, 1998), pp. 19–20.

38. Haley, *Autobiography*, p. 42.

39. Rustin, *New York Times.*
40. Ibid.
41. Haley, *Autobiography,* p. 41.
42. Ibid., pp. 55–56.
43. Malcolm Jarvis, in *Malcolm X: An Intimate Portrait of the Man,* prod. and dir. Andrew Lack and Brett Alexander, 60 min., Fox Video, 1992, videocassette.
44. Haley, *Autobiography,* p. 64.
45. Malcolm Jarvis, in Greene, *Malcolm X,* p. 49.
46. Haley, *Autobiography,* p. 74.
47. Collins and Bailey, *Seventh Child,* p. 45.
48. Haley, *Autobiography,* p. 80.
49. Massaquoi, *Ebony,* pp. 45–46.
50. Haley, *Autobiography,* p. 89.
51. Wolfenstein, *Victims of Democracy,* pp. 167–168.
52. Haley, *Autobiography,* p. 101.
53. Rustin, *New York Times.*
54. Haley, *Autobiography,* p. 126.
55. Ibid., p. 450.
56. Peter Goldman, interview by author, February 27, 1999.
57. Lee and Wiley, *By Any Means Necessary,* p. 46.
58. Ibid., p. 45.
59. Haley, *Autobiography,* p. 150.
60. DeCaro, *Side of the People,* p. 70.
61. Haley, *Autobiography,* pp. 123–124.
62. Perry, *Malcolm,* p. 75.
63. Haley, *Autobiography,* p. 130.
64. Perry, *Malcolm,* pp. 80–81.
65. Haley, *Autobiography,* p. 141.
66. Ibid., p. 145.
67. Perry, p. 87.
68. Haley, *Autobiography,* p. 146.
69. Epps, *Speeches at Harvard,* p. 25.
70. Haley, *Autobiography,* pp. 159–160.
71. Ibid., pp. 164–165.
72. DeCaro, *Side of the People,* pp. 72–73.
73. Louis A. DeCaro, Jr., interview by author, March 4, 1999.
74. Perry, *Malcolm,* p. 94.
75. Malcolm Jarvis, in *Malcolm X: Biography,* prod. and dir. Ron Steinman and Lisa Zeff, 50 min., New Video Group, 1995, videocassette.
76. Wolfenstein, *Victims of Democracy,* p. 201.
77. Haley, *Autobiography,* pp. 170–171.
78. Perry, *Malcolm,* p. 99.
79. Haley, *Autobiography,* p. 172.
80. DeCaro, *Side of the People,* p. 73.
81. Haley, *Autobiography,* p. 173.
82. Jarvis, in Greene, *Malcolm X,* p. 58.
83. Ella Collins, in *Malcolm X: Make It Plain,* prod. and dir. Orlando Bagwell, 136 min., MPI Home Video, 1995, videocassette.
84. DeCaro, *Side of the People,* p. 74.

85. Malcolm Jarvis, in Bagwell, *Make It Plain.*
86. Haley, *Autobiography,* p. 436.

Chapter 1

1. Malcolm Jarvis, in *Malcolm X: Biography,* prod. and dir. Lisa Zeff and Ron Steinman, 50 min., New Video Group, 1995, videocassette.
2. Alex Haley, *The Autobiography of Malcolm X* (New York: Ballantine Books, 1992), p. 176.
3. Louis A. DeCaro, Jr., *On the Side of My People: A Religious Life of Malcolm X* (New York: Ballantine Books, 1992), p. 176.
4. Ibid., p. 75.
5. Bruce Perry, *Malcolm: The Life of a Man Who Changed Black America* (New York: Station Hill Press, 1991), p. 106.
6. James H. Cone, *Martin and Malcolm and America: A Dream of a Nightmare* (Maryknoll, N.Y.: Orbis Books, 1991), p. 50.
7. DeCaro, *Side of the People,* pp. 78–79.
8. Louis A. DeCaro, Jr., interview by author, March 4, 1999.
9. Malcolm Jarvis, in *Malcolm X: Make It Plain,* ed. Cheryll Y. Greene (New York: Penguin Books, 1991), p. 50.
10. Perry, *Malcolm,* p. 109.
11. Philbert and Wilfred Little, in *Malcolm X: Make It Plain,* prod. and dir. Orlando Bagwell, 136 min., MPI Home Video, 1995, videocassette.
12. Abdul Aziz Omar, in Bagwell, *Make It Plain.*
13. Haley, *Autobiography,* p. 183.
14. Ibid., p. 186.
15. C. Eric Lincoln, *The Black Muslims in America* (Boston: Beacon Press, 1961), p. 75.
16. James Turner, in *A History of the Civil Rights Movement,* prod. and dir. Jerry Baber and Rhonda Fabian, 30 min., Schlesinger Video Productions, 1994, videocassette.
17. Lincoln, *Black Muslims,* p. 76.
18. Peter Goldman, *The Death and Life of Malcolm X* (Urbana, Ill.: University of Illinois Press, 1979), p. 33.
19. Victor Wolfenstein, *The Victims of Democracy: Malcolm X and the Black Revolution* (New York: Guilford Press, 1993), pp. 214–215.
20. Haley, *Autobiography,* p. 437.
21. Jarvis, in Bagwell, *Make It Plain.*
22. Stanley Jones, in Bagwell, *Make It Plain.*
23. Wolfenstein, *Victims of Democracy,* p. 225.
24. Haley, *Autobiography,* pp. 198–199.
25. Ibid., p. 197.
26. Cone, *Martin and Malcolm,* pp. 52–53.

27. Wilfred Little in Bagwell, *Make It Plain.*
28. Lincoln, *Black Muslims,* p. 114.
29. Haley, *Autobiography,* p. 214.
30. DeCaro, *Side of the People,* pp. 86–87.
31. Haley, *Autobiography,* p. 215.
32. Wolfenstein, *Victims of Democracy,* pp. 221–222.
33. Perry, *Malcolm,* pp. 127–128.
34. DeCaro, *Side of the People,* pp. 36–37.
35. Ibid., p. 87.
36. Wolfenstein, *Victims of Democracy,* pp. 222–223.
37. Perry, *Malcolm,* pp. 134–135.
38. Report: "Malcolm K. Little," Special Agent in Charge (SAC) Boston to Federal Bureau of Investigation (FBI) director, February 17, 1953, Section 1, Microfilm Roll 1, FBI file on Malcolm X, Scholarly Resources, Wilmington, Delaware.

Chapter 2

1. Claude A. Clegg III, *An Original Man: The Life and Times of Elijah Muhammad* (New York: St. Martin's Press, 1997), p. 6.
2. Ibid., p. 9.
3. C. Eric Lincoln, *The Black Muslims in America* (Boston: Beacon Press, 1961), pp. 10–11.
4. Report: "Elijah Poole," Special Agent in Charge (SAC) Chicago to Federal Bureau of Investigation (FBI) director, December 27, 1956, Section 1, Microfilm Roll 1, FBI file on Elijah Muhammad, Scholarly Resources, Wilmington, Delaware.
5. Report: "Nation of Islam," (SAC) Chicago to FBI director, August 12, 1964, Section 5, Microfilm Roll 2, FBI file on Muslim Mosque Inc. (MMI), Scholarly Resources.
6. Louise E. Lomax, *When the Word is Given* (Cleveland, Ohio: World Publishing, 1963), pp. 51–52.
7. Alex Haley, *The Autobiography of Malcolm X* (New York: Ballantine Books, 1992), p. 240.
8. Lincoln, *Black Muslims,* p. 204.
9. Clegg, *An Original Man,* p. 33.
10. Louis A. DeCaro, *On the Side of the People: A Religious Life of Malcolm X* (New York: New York University Press, 1996), p. 25.
11. Lincoln, *Black Muslims,* pp. 181–182.
12. Ibid., p. 73.
13. U.S. Department of Justice, J. Albert Woll to Wendell Berge, September 23, 1942, Litigation Case Files: Nation of Islam, Folder: 146-28-264, Record Group 60, National Archives, College Park, Maryland.
14. Report: "Elijah Poole," SAC Detroit to FBI director, August 9, 1957, Section 2, Microfilm Roll 1, FBI file on Elijah Muhammad.

15. Clegg, *An Original Man,* p. 96.
16. Ibid., pp. 97–98.
17. Karl Evanzz, *The Judas Factor: The Plot to Kill Malcolm X* (New York: Thunder's Mouth Press, 1992), p. 26.
18. Haley, *Autobiography,* p. 222.
19. Philbert Little, in *Malcolm X: Make It Plain,* prod. and dir. Orlando Bagwell, 136 min., MPI Home Video, 1995, videocassette.
20. Haley, *Autobiography,* pp. 225–226.
21. Bruce Perry, *Malcolm: The Life of a Man Who Changed Black America* (New York: Station Hill Press, 1991), p. 142.
22. Haley, *Autobiography,* p. 227.
23. Wallace Muhammad, in Bagwell, *Make It Plain.*
24. Haley, *Autobiography,* p. 228.
25. Alfred Balk, "Muslim Chief Rose from Squalor," *New York: World Telegram and Sun,* March 13, 1964.
26. Abdul Aziz Omar, in *Malcolm X: Make It Plain,* ed. Cheryll Y. Greene (New York: Penguin Books, 1994), p. 118.
27. Lincoln, *Black Muslims,* p. 110.
28. Charles Kenyatta, interviewed by author, March 6, 1999.
29. Wallace Muhammad, in Bagwell, *Make It Plain.*
30. Victor Wolfenstein, *The Victims of Democracy: Malcolm X and the Black Revolution* (New York: Guilford Press, 1993), p. 248.
31. Lomax, *Word is Given,* p. 58.
32. Haley, *Autobiography,* p. 444.
33. Alex Haley, in Bagwell, *Make It Plain.*
34. Lincoln, *Black Muslims,* p. 115.
35. Elijah Muhammad, in Bagwell, *Make It Plain.*
36. Balk, *New York World Telegram and Sun.*
37. Haley, *Autobiography,* p. 234.
38. Evanzz, *The Judas Factor,* pp. 34–35.
39. Wolfenstein, *Victim of Democracy,* p. 24.
40. Haley, *Autobiography,* pp. 230–231.
41. Rodnell P. Collins and Peter Bailey, *Seventh Child: A Family Memoir of Malcolm X* (Secaucus, N.J.: Birch Lane Press, 1998), p. 85.

Chapter 3

1. Whitney M. Young, Jr., "Malcolm's Death Solves Nothing," *New York World Telegram and Sun,* March 4, 1965.
2. C. Eric Lincoln, "Malcolm X: Authority on Muslims Fears Frightening Legacy," *New York Journal,* February 28, 1965.
3. Peter Goldman, *The Death and Life of Malcolm X* (Urbana, Ill.: University of Illinois Press, 1979), pp. 49–50.
4. Maya Angelou, in *Malcolm X: Make It*

Plain, ed. Cheryll Y. Greene (New York: Penguin Books, 1994), p. 111.

5. Alex Haley, *The Autobiography of Malcolm X* (New York: Ballantine Books, 1992), p. 250.

6. Goldman, *Death and Life,* pp. 54–55.

7. Haley, *Autobiography,* pp. 250–251.

8. William Defossett, in Greene, *Make It Plain,* p. 101.

9. Lewis Michaux, in *Malcolm X: Make It Plain,* prod. and dir. Orlando Bagwell, 136 min., MPI Home Video, 1995, videocassette.

10. C. Eric Lincoln, *The Black Muslims in America* (Boston, Mass.: Beacon Press, 1961), p. 116.

11. Victor Wolfenstein, *The Victims of Democracy: Malcolm X and the Black Revolution* (New York: Guilford Press, 1993), pp. 253–254.

12. Haley, *Autobiography,* p. 253.

13. Ibid., p. 254.

14. "Malcolm X—Man of Violence," *Chicago Tribune,* February 22, 1965.

15. John Henrik Clarke, in Bagwell, *Make It Plain.*

16. Benjamin Karim, Peter Skutches, and David Gallen, *Remembering Malcolm* (New York: Carroll and Graf, 1992), pp. 84–85.

17. Spike Lee and Ralph Wiley, *By Any Means Necessary: The Trials and Tribulations of the Making of Malcolm X* (New York: Hyperion Press, 1992), pp. 50–51.

18. Rodnell P. Collins and Peter Bailey, *A Family Memoir of Malcolm X* (Secaucus, N.J.: Birch Lane Press, 1998), p. 137.

19. Louis A. DeCaro, Jr., *Malcolm and the Cross: The Nation of Islam, Malcolm X, and Christianity* (New York: New York University Press, 1998), p. 90.

20. Goldman, *Death and Life,* p. 48.

21. Amina Rabman, in Greene, *Malcolm X,* p. 114.

22. Sonia Sanchez, in Bagwell, *Make It Plain.*

23. James H. Cone, *Martin and Malcolm and America: A Dream or a Nightmare* (Maryknoll, N.Y.: Orbis Books, 1991), pp. 93–94.

24. Karim, Skutches, and Gallen, *Remembering Malcolm,* p. 109.

25. Ibid., p. 70.

26. Karl Evanzz, *The Judas Factor: The Plot to Kill Malcolm X* (New York: Thunder's Mouth Press, 1992), p. 36.

27. Malcolm X interview by Federal Bureau of Investigation (FBI) agents, January 10, 1955, in *Malcolm X: The FBI File,* ed. Clayborne Carson (New York: Carroll and Graf, 1991), pp. 114–115.

28. Claude A. Clegg, Jr., *An Original Man: The Life and Times of Elijah Muhammad* (New York: St. Martin's Press, 1997), p. 116.

29. Louis A. DeCaro, Jr., *On the Side of My People: A Religious Life of Malcolm X* (New York: New York University Press, 1996), p. 102.

30. James Hicks, "Station House Beating," *Amsterdam News,* April 24, 1957.

31. Ibid.

32. William DeFossett, in Bagwell, *Make It Plain.*

33. Hicks, *Amsterdam News.*

34. Robert Mangum, in Bagwell, *Make It Plain.*

35. Hicks, *Amsterdam News.*

36. Ibid.

37. Ibid.

38. John Hicks, "Muslims Ask Kennedy to Fire 2 Cops," *New York Amsterdam News,* November 9, 1957.

39. Hicks, *Amsterdam News,* April 24, 1957.

40. Karim, Skutches, and Gallen, *Remembering Malcolm,* p. 49.

41. Haley, *Autobiography,* p. 271.

42. Wolfenstein, *Victims of Democracy,* p. 266.

43. DeCaro, *Side of the People,* p. 115.

44. Robert Mangum, in Bagwell, *Make It Plain.*

45. DeCaro, *Side of the People,* p. 113.

46. Evanzz, *The Judas Factor,* p. 113.

47. Report: "Nation of Islam," Special Agent in Charge (SAC) Chicago to SAC Atlanta, August 10, 1961, Section 35, Microfilm Roll 6, FBI file on Malcolm X, Scholarly Resources, Wilmington, Delaware.

48. Karim, Skutches, and Gallen, *Remembering Malcolm,* pp. 73–74.

49. Charles W. Wiley, "Who was Malcolm X?" *National Review,* March 23, 1965, pp. 239–240.

50. James H. Cone, *Martin and Malcolm and America: A Dream or a Nightmare* (Maryknoll, N.Y.: Orbis Books, 1991), p. 275.

51. Bruce Perry, *Malcolm: The Life of a Man Who Changed Black America* (New York: Station Hill Press, 1991), p. 171.

52. Evanzz, *The Judas Factor,* p. 72.

53. Betty Shabazz, "Malcolm X: As a Husband and Father," in *Malcolm X: The Man and His Times,* ed. John H. Clarke (Trenton, N.J.: Africa World Press, 1990), pp. 133–134.

54. Haley, *Autobiography,* p. 339.

55. Betty Shabazz, in *The Real Malcolm X: An Intimate Portrait of the Man,* prod. and dir. Andrew Lack and Brett Alexander, 60 min., Fox Video, 1992, videocassette.

56. Haley, *Autobiography,* p. 339.

57. Betty Shabazz, "The Legacy of My Husband, Malcolm X," *Ebony,* June 1969, pp. 172–182.

58. Shabazz, in Clarke, *Man and His Times,* p. 142.

59. Collins and Bailey, *Seventh Child*, p. 95.
60. Shabazz, in Clarke, *Man and His Times*, p. 135.
61. Shabazz, *Ebony*, p. 178.
62. Peter Goldman, interview by author, February 27, 1999.
63. Shabazz, in Clarke, *Man and His Times*, p. 134.
64. Shabazz, *Ebony*, p. 178.
65. Ibid., p. 176.
66. Shabazz, in Bagwell, *Make It Plain*.
67. Attallah Shabazz, in Greene, *Malcolm X*, p. 125.
68. Clegg, *An Original Man*, p. 114.
69. Malcolm X, *Malcolm X: Speeches at Harvard*, ed. Archie Epps (New York: Paragon House, 1991), pp. 31–32.
70. Lincoln, *Black Muslims*, p. 189.
71. Alex Haley, in Bagwell, *Make It Plain*.
72. Bayard Rustin, "Making His Mark," *Washington Post*, November 14, 1965.
73. John Henrik Clarke, in *Brother Minister: The Assassination of El-Hajj Malik Shabazz*, prod. and dir. Jack Baxter and Jefri Aal Muhammed, 115 min., X-ceptional Productions Inc., 1997, videocassette.
74. DeCaro, *Side of the People*, pp. 116–117.
75. Ibid., p. 138.
76. Report: "Malcolm K. Little," SAC New York to FBI director, December 17, 1959, Section 5, FBI file on Malcolm X, in Carson, *FBI File*, p. 178.
77. DeCaro, *Side of the People*, p. 140.
78. Perry, *Malcolm*, p. 206.
79. "Arabs Send Warm Greetings to Our Brothers of Color in U.S.A.," *Pittsburgh Courier*, August 15, 1959.
80. DeCaro, *Side of the People*, p. 142.
81. *Pittsburgh Courier*, August 15, 1959.
82. Report: "Nation of Islam," SAC Chicago to FBI director, March 8, 1963, Section 48, Microfilm Roll 6, FBI file on Malcolm X.
83. Mike Wallace and Gary P. Gates, *Close Encounters: Mike Wallace's Own Story* (New York: William Morrow, 1984), p. 136.
84. Joseph X, in Greene, *Malcolm X*, p. 106.
85. Wallace and Gates, *Close Encounters*, p. 136.
86. Report: "Nation of Islam," SAC New York to FBI director, July 16, 1959, Section 1, Microfilm Roll 1, FBI file on Malcolm X.
87. Report: "Nation of Islam," SAC New York to FBI director, July 13, 1959, in Carson, *FBI file*, p. 161.
88. Wallace and Gates, *Close Encounters*, p. 137.
89. Ibid., pp. 137–138.
90. Robert Laird, "Malcolm X in Life and Death, the Center of Violence," *New York World Telegram and the Sun*, February 22, 1965.

91. Sonia Sanchez, in Bagwell, *Make It Plain*.
92. Haley, *Autobiography*, pp. 273–274.
93. Joseph X in Greene, *Malcolm X*, p. 106.
94. DeCaro, *Side of the People*, p. 135.
95. "Dr. King, Keating Blast Muslims Group," *Pittsburgh Courier*, August 29, 1959.
96. Clegg, *An Original Man*, p. 130.
97. Milt Freudenheim, "Myth Already Springing Up: Malcolm X Martyred Hero," *Chicago Daily News*, February 23, 1965.
98. Haley, *Autobiography*, p. 284.
99. Lincoln, *Black Muslims*, pp. 107–108.
100. Haley, *Autobiography*, p. 278.
101. Evanzz, *The Judas Factor*, p. 63.
102. Rosemari Mealy, *Fidel and Malcolm X: Memories of a Meeting* (Melbourne, Australia: Ocean Press, 1993), pp. 18–19.
103. John Henrik Clarke, in Greene, *Malcolm X*, p. 109.
104. Paul Lee, interview by author, March 1, 1999.
105. Report: "Malcolm K. Little," SAC New York to FBI director, September 22, 1960, Section 30, Microfilm Roll 6, Scholarly Resources.
106. "Malcolm X Explains Wee Visit to Castro at Theresa," *Pittsburgh Courier*, October 1, 1960.
107. Evanzz, *The Judas Factor*, p. 86.
108. Report: "Malcolm K. Little," SAC New York to FBI director, September 22, 1960, Section 30, Microfilm Roll 6, FBI file on Malcolm X.
109. "Malcolm Links Klan, Muslims," *New York Post*, February 16, 1965.
110. DeCaro, *Side of the People*, p. 181.
111. James Farner, *Lay Bare the Heart* (New York: Arbor House, 1985), p. 226.
112. Clegg. *An Original Man*, p. 154.
113. Dan Burley, "Why Nazis at Muslim Rally?" *The New Crusader* (Chicago), March 3, 1962.
114. Malcolm X, interview by Kenneth B. Clark, June 1963, in Clarke, *Man and His Times*, p. 180.
115. George Plimpton, "Miami Notebook: Cassius Clay and Malcolm X," *Liberator*, May 1964, p. 57.
116. Maya Angelou, in *The Real Malcolm X: An Intimate Portrait of the Man*, prod. and dir. Andrew Lack and Brett Alexander, 60 min., Fox Video, 1992, videocassette.
117. James Baldwin, in Bagwell, *Make It Plain*.
118. Dick Gregory, in *Malcolm X: Biography*, prod. and dir. Lisa Zeff and Ron Steinman, 50 min., New Video Group, 1995, videocassette.
119. Marlene Nadle, "Malcolm X: The

Complexity of a Man in the Jungle," *Village Voice*, February 25, 1965, p. 6.

120. Wiley, *National Review*, p. 239.

121. Karim, Skutches, and Gallen, *Remembering Malcolm*, p. 123.

122. Wiley, *National Review*, p. 239.

123. Ossie Davis in Bagwell, *Make It Plain*.

124. Plimpton, *Liberator*, p. 57.

125. "Malcolm X Publishes New Magazine," *Los Angeles Herald Dispatch*, May 21, 1959.

126. Haley, *Autobiography*, pp. 272–273.

127. Karim, Skutches, and Gallen, *Remembering Malcolm*, pp. 107–108.

128. Murry Kempton, "The Fruit of Islam," *New York World Telegram and the Sun*, February 23, 1965.

129. Lack and Alexander, *The Real Malcolm X*.

130. Joseph X in Greene, *Malcolm X*, p. 228.

131. Haley, *Autobiography*, p. 324.

132. David Gallen, ed., *Malcolm X: As They Knew Him* (New York: Carroll and Graf, 1992), p. 45.

133. Karim, Skutches, and Gallen, *Remembering Malcolm*, p. 131.

134. DeCaro, *Side of the People*, pp. 173–174.

135. Haley, *Autobiography*, pp. 324–325.

136. M.S. Handler, "Malcolm X Splits With Muhammad," *Washington Post*, March 9, 1964.

137. Haley, *Autobiography*, pp. 329–330.

138. Karim, Skutches, and Gallen, *Remembering Malcolm*, p. 131.

139. DeCaro, *Side of the People*, pp. 174–175.

Chapter 4

1. Claude A. Clegg III, *An Original Man: The Life and Times of Elijah Muhammad* (New York: St. Martin's Press, 1997), pp. 169–170.

2. Nelson Blackstock, *Cointelpro: The FBI's Secret War on Political Freedom* (New York: Anchor Foundation, 1988), p. 103.

3. "Black Muslim Riot: Jury Tries and Tries," *New York Herald Tribune*, June 9, 1963.

4. Ibid.

5. "Charge Muslim Was Murdered," *New Amsterdam News*, May 5, 1962.

6. "Black Muslim Riot," *New York Herald Tribune*.

7. Louis A. DeCaro, Jr., *On the Side of My People: A Religious Life of Malcolm X* (New York: New York University Press, 1996), p. 184.

8. Taylor Branch, *Pillar of Fire: America in the King Years 1963–65* (New York: Simon and Schuster, 1998), p. 10.

9. Samuel W. Yorty, "The Mayor From L.A. Calls Malcolm X Just a Hater," *New York Herald Tribune*, July 27, 1962.

10. Charles Davis, "Muslim Hatred Called Threat to Community," *Los Angeles Times*, May 7, 1962.

11. Frank Kofsky, "Malcolm X Denounces Police Killing of Muslim," *Los Angeles Herald-Dispatch*, May 10, 1962.

12. Ibid.

13. Bruce Perry, *Malcolm: The Life of a Man Who Changed Black America* (New York: Station Hill Press, 1991), p. 192.

14. Joseph X, in *Malcolm X: Make It Plain*, prod. and dir. Orlando Bagwell, 136 min., MPI Home Video, 1995, videocassette.

15. "Justifiable Homicide," *Los Angeles Dispatch*, May 17, 1962.

16. Haley, *Autobiography*, p. 334.

17. Benjamin Karim, Peter Skutches, and David Gallen, *Remembering Malcolm* (New York: Carroll and Graf, 1992), pp. 142–143.

18. "Malcolm X Raps L.A. Press as Favoring Cops in Trial," *The Chicago Defender*, May 25, 1963.

19. Fulton Lewis Jr., "Muslim Movement Prayers of Hate," *New York Mirror*, June 20, 1962.

20. Alex Haley, "Malcolm X: A Candid Conversation with the Militant Major-Domo of the Black Muslims," *Playboy*, May 1963, pp. 53–63.

21. Samuel W. Yorty, "Yorty Assails Boast of Black Muslim Chief," *Los Angeles Times*, June 7, 1962.

22. Alex Haley, *The Autobiography of Malcolm X* (New York: Ballantine Books, 1992), p. 453.

23. Gordon Parks, in *Malcolm X: Make It Plain*, ed. Cheryll Y. Greene (New York: Penguin Books, 1994), p. 134.

24. Pete Hamill, "Malcolm's Way," *New York Post*, December 5, 1965.

25. Zak A. Kondo, *Conspiracys: Unraveling the Assassination of Malcolm X* (Washington, D.C.: Nubia Press, 1993), p. 120.

26. Report: "Nation of Islam," Special Agent in Charge (SAC) Chicago to Federal Bureau of Investigation (FBI) director, March 11, 1963, Section 48, Microfilm Roll 7, FBI file on Malcolm X, Scholarly Resources, Wilmington, Delaware.

27. Herman Ferguson, interview by author, March 5, 1999.

28. Kondo, *Conspiracys*, p. 175.

29. Ted Poston, "Malcolm and the Muslims," February 22, 1965.

30. Spike Lee and Ralph Wiley, *By Any Means Necessary: The Trials and Tribulations of the Making of Malcolm X* (New York: Hyperion Press, 1992), p. 58.

31. Herman Ferguson, interview by author, March 5, 1999.

32. Peter Goldman, interview by author, February 27, 1999.

33. Lee and Wiley, *By Any Means Necessary,* p. 34.

34. Goldman, interview.

35. Karim, Skutches, and Gallen, *Remembering Malcolm,* p. 151.

36. Report: "Malcolm K. Little," SAC New York to FBI director, December 15, 1963, Section 9, Microfilm Roll 1, FBI file on Malcolm X, Scholarly Resources.

37. Clegg, *An Original Man,* p. 182.

38. Karim, Skutches, and Gallen, *Remembering Malcolm,* p. 153.

39. Haley, *Autobiography,* pp. 336–337.

40. Ibid., p. 336.

41. Betty Shabazz, "Malcolm X: As Husband and Father," in *Malcolm X: The Man and His Times,* ed. John H. Clarke (Trenton, N.J.: Africa World Press, 1990), p. 138.

42. Major Robinson, "Muzzling of Malcolm X for Indefinite Period," *New York Courier,* December 14, 1963.

43. Louis A. DeCaro, Jr., *On the Side of My People: A Religious Life of Malcolm X* (New York: New York University Press, 1996), p. 183.

44. "Elijah Losing Muslim Following Says Son," *Chicago American,* September 15, 1964.

45. Report: "Nation of Islam," SAC Chicago to FBI director, July 23, 1964, Section 66, Microfilm Roll 9, FBI file on Malcolm X.

46. Report: "Elijah Poole," SAC Chicago to FBI director, April 6, 1962, Section 7, Microfilm Roll 1, FBI file on Elijah Muhammad, Scholarly Resources.

47. Ferguson, interview.

48. Clegg, *An Original Man,* p. 113.

49. Ferguson, interview.

50. Benjamin 2X, in Bagwell, *Make It Plain.*

51. Haley, *Autobiography,* p. 259.

52. Goldman, interview.

53. Report: "Muslim Mosque Inc.," SAC New York to FBI director, September 27, 1964, Section 68, Microfilm Roll 9, FBI file on Malcolm X.

54. Yuri Kochiyama, interview by author, March 5, 1999.

55. Karim, Skutches, and Gallen, *Remembering Malcolm,* p. 138.

56. James H. Cone, *Martin and Malcolm and America* (Maryknoll, N.Y.: Orbis Books, 1991), pp. 185–186.

57. Wilfred Little, in Greene, *Malcolm X,* p. 139.

58. Paul Lee, interview by author, March 1, 1999.

59. Ferguson, interview.

60. Goldman, interview.

61. Haley, *Autobiography,* p. 444.

62. Alex Haley, "Alex Haley Remembers," in *Malcolm X: As They Knew Him,* ed. David Gallen (New York: Carroll and Graf, 1992), p. 244.

63. Haley, *Autobiography,* p. 445.

64. Ibid., p. 449.

65. Karim, Skutches, and Gallen, *Remembering Malcolm,* pp. 81–82.

66. Goldman, interview.

67. Lee, interview.

Chapter 5

1. Louis A. DeCaro, Jr., *Malcolm and the Cross: The Nation of Islam, Malcolm X and Christianity* (New York: New York University Press, 1998), pp. 53–54.

2. Report: "Nation of Islam," F.J. Baumgardner to W.C. Sullivan, July 14, 1962, Section 7, Microfilm Roll 1, Federal Bureau of Investigation (FBI) file on Malcolm X, Scholarly Resources, Wilmington, Delaware.

3. Alex Haley, *The Autobiography of Malcolm X,* (New York: Ballantine Books, 1992), p. 340.

4. Paul Lee, interview with author, March 1, 1999.

5. Betty Shabazz, in *Malcolm X: Make It Plain,* prod. and dir. Orlando Bagwell, 136 min., MPI Home Video, 1995, videocassette.

6. Report: "Muslim Mosque Inc." (MMI), Special Agent in Charge (SAC) Atlanta to FBI director, August 27, 1964, Section 68, Microfilm Roll 9, FBI file on Malcolm X.

7. Report: "Nation of Islam," SAC Boston to FBI director, June 15, 1964, Section 3, Microfilm Roll 1, FBI file on MMI, Scholarly Resources.

8. Lee, interview.

9. Louis A. DeCaro, *On the Side of My People: A Religious Life of Malcolm X* (New York: New York University Press, 1996), p. 190.

10. Haley, *Autobiography,* p. 12.

11. Wilfred X, in Bagwell, *Make It Plain.*

12. Charles Kenyatta, interview by author, March 6, 1999.

13. Lee, interview.

14. Report: "Malcolm K. Little," SAC New York to FBI director, May 16, 1963, Section 8, Microfilm Roll 1, FBI file on Malcolm X.

15. "Black Muslim Aide Berates Whites," *Chicago Daily News,* February 27, 1963.

16. Ibid.

17. Report: "Malcolm K. Little," SAC Chicago to FBI director, May 1, 1963, Section 8, in *Malcolm X: The FBI File,* ed. Clayborne Carson (New York: Carroll and Graf, 1991), p. 222.

18. Report: "Nation of Islam," SAC Boston to FBI director, June 15, 1964, Section 3, Microfilm Roll 1, FBI file on MMI.

19. "Malcolm X Criticism Began in 1961," *Chicago American*, March 4, 1965.

20. Report: "Nation of Islam," SAC Boston to FBI director, June 15, 1964, Section 62, Microfilm Roll 8, FBI file on Malcolm X.

21. Report: "Nation of Islam," SAC Boston to FBI director, June 15, 1964, Section 62, Microfilm Roll 8, FBI file on Malcolm X.

22. Louis A. DeCaro, Jr., interview by author, March 4, 1999.

23. Claude A. Clegg III, interview by author, September 6, 1997.

24. Haley, *Autobiography*, p. 345.

25. Report: "Nation of Islam," SAC New York to FBI director, May 23, 1963, Section 9, Microfilm Roll 1, FBI file on Malcolm X.

26. Lee, interview.

27. Claude A. Clegg III, *An Original Man: The Life and Times of Elijah Muhammad* (New York: St. Martin's Press, 1997), p. 175.

28. Report: "Elijah Poole," SAC Chicago to FBI director, April 6, 1962, Section 7, Microfilm Roll 7, FBI file on Elijah Muhammad, Scholarly Resources.

29. Report: "Nation of Islam," SAC Chicago to FBI director, July 31, 1962, Section 7, Microfilm Roll 1, FBI file on Elijah Muhammad.

30. Report: "Nation of Islam," F.J. Baumgardner to W.C. Sullivan, July 4, 1962, Section 7, Microfilm Roll 1, FBI file on Elijah Muhammad.

31. Lee, interview.

32. Report: "Natin of Islam," SAC Washington, D.C., to FBI director, February 4, 1963, Section 8, Microfilm Roll 1, FBI file on Malcolm X.

33. Malcolm X, in *A History of the Civil Rights Movement*, prod. and dir. Rhoda Fabian and Jerry Baber, 30 min., Schlesinger Video Productions, 1994, videocassette.

34. Benjamin Karim, Peter Skutches, and David Gallen, *Remembering Malcolm* (New York: Carroll and Graf, 1992), pp. 75–76.

35. Robert Mangum, in *Malcolm X: Make It Plain*, ed. Cheryll Y. Greene (New York: Penguin Books, 1994), p. 136.

36. Gene Roberts, in *The Real Malcolm X: An Intimate Portrait of the Man*, prod. and dir. Andrew Lack and Brett Alexander, 60 min., Fox Video, 1992, videocassette.

37. Joseph X, in Lack and Alexander, *The Real Malcolm X*.

38. John A. Salmond, *My Mind Set on Freedom: A History of the Civil Rights Movement, 1954–1968* (Chicago, Ill.: Ivan R. Dee, 1997), p. 77.

39. "Malcolm X, in D.C., Raps Jackie, Floyd, Dr. King," *Amsterdam News*, June 25, 1963.

40. "400 Hear Malcolm X Speak Here," *Washington Post*, May 13, 1963.

41. Clarence Hunter, "Muslim Leader Scorns King at D.C. Rally," *The Evening Star*, May 13, 1963.

42. Report: "Malcolm K. Little," SAC New York to FBI director, December 15, 1963, Section 9, Microfilm Roll 1, FBI file on Malcolm X.

43. Haley, *Autobiography*, pp. 320–321.

44. "Malcolm X Scores U.S. and Kennedy," *New York Times*, December 2, 1963.

45. Peter Bailey, in Bagwell, *Make It Plain*.

46. Zak A. Kondo, *Conspiracys: Unraveling the Assassination of Malcolm X* (Washington, D.C.: Nubia Press, 1993), p. 129.

47. Report: "Nation of Islam," SAC Boston to FBI file on Malcolm X.

48. David Remnick, *King of the World: Muhammad Ali and the Rise of an American Hero* (New York: Random House, 1998), p. 166.

49. James H. Cone, *Martin and Malcolm and America: A Dream or a Nightmare* (Maryknoll, N.Y.: Orbis Books, 1991), p. 114.

50. Peter Goldman, *The Death and Life of Malcolm X* (Urbana Ill.: University of Illinois Press, 1979), p. 117.

51. Malcolm X, "Message to the Grass Roots," in *Malcolm X Speaks: Selected Speeches and Statements*, ed. George Breitman (New York: Pathfinder Press, 1989), pp. 3–17.

52. DeCaro, *Side of the People*, p. 163.

53. Ibid., pp. 201–202.

Chapter 6

1. "Criticism Began in 1961," *Chicago American*, March 4, 1965.

2. Amina Rahman, in *Malcolm X: Make It Plain*, ed. Cheryll Y. Greene (New York: Penguin Books, 1994), p. 147.

3. "Malcolm X Scores U.S. and Kennedy," *New York Times*, December 2, 1963.

4. Joseph X, in *Malcolm X: Make It Plain*, prod. and dir. Orlando Bagwell, 136 min., MPI Home Video, 1995, videocassette.

5. Herman Ferguson, interview by author, March 5, 1999.

6. Report: "Nation of Islam," Special Agent in Charge (SAC) to FBI director, December 11, 1963, Section 55, Microfilm Roll 8, FBI file on Malcolm X, Scholarly Resources, Wilmington, Delaware.

7. Alex Haley, *The Autobiography of Malcolm X* (New York: Carroll and Graf, 1992), p. 156.

8. Benjamin Karim, Peter Skutches, and David Gallen, *Remembering Malcolm* (New York: Carroll and Graf, 1992), p. 156.

9. Report: "Nation of Islam," SAC Phoenix to FBI director, December 4, 1963, Section 8, Microfilm Roll 2, FBI file on Elijah Muhammad, Scholarly Resources.

10. Karim, Skutches, and Gallen, *Remembering Malcolm*, pp. 158–159.

11. Peter Goldman, in Bagwell, *Make It Plain.*

12. Claude A. Clegg III, interview with author, September 6, 1977.

13. Larry Van Gelder, "Malcolm X Trial Focuses on Religion," *New York World Telegram and Sun,* January 4, 1966.

14. Editorial, "Muzzling Malcolm X," *New York Courier,* December 21, 1963.

15. "A Split," *Chicago Sun Times,* January 3, 1964.

16. "Malcolm Expected to be Replaced," *New York Times,* December 6, 1963.

17. Report: "Nation of Islam," SAC Phoenix to FBI director, January 27, 1964, Section 8, Microfilm Roll 2, FBI file on Elijah Muhammad.

18. Zak A. Kondo, *Conspiracys: Unraveling the Assassination of Malcolm X* (Washington, D.C.: Nubia Press, 1993), p. 66.

19. Peter Goldman, *The Death and Life of Malcolm X* (Urbana Ill.: University of Illinois Press, 1979).

20. Report: "Nation of Islam," SAC Boston to FBI director, June 15, 1964, Section 62, Microfilm Roll 8, FBI file on Malcolm X.

21. Haley, *Autobiography,* p. 352.

22. "Malcolm X's New Insight," *Chicago American,* March 9, 1965.

23. Haley, *Autobiography,* p. 351.

24. Ibid., p. 349.

25. Rodnell P. Collins and Peter Bailey, *Seventh Child: A Family Memoir of Malcolm X* (Secaucus, N.J.: Birch Lane Press, 1998), p. 112.

26. Muhammad Ali, in Greene, *Malcolm X,* p. 166.

27. "Malcolm X's 'New Insight,'" *Chicago American,* March 9, 1965.

28. Haley, *Autobiography,* p. 353.

29. Report: "Nation of Islam," SAC Chicago to FBI director, March 25, 1964, Section 1, Microfilm Roll 1, FBI file on Muslim Mosque Inc. (MMI) Scholarly Resources.

30. Jimmy Cannon, "The Muslim's Prize," *New York Journal American,* February 23, 1965.

31. David Remnick, *King of the World: Muhammad Ali and the Rise of an American Hero* (New York: Random House, 1998), p. 169.

32. "X Marks the Champ," *The Miami News,* February 19, 1964.

33. George Plimpton, "Miami Notebook: Cassius Clay and Malcolm X," *Liberator,* May 1964, pp. 12–13.

34. Remnick, *King of the World,* pp. 170–171.

35. Report: "Nation of Islam," SAC New York to FBI director, February 5, 1964, Section 10, Microfilm Roll 2, FBI file on Malcolm X.

36. Haley, *Autobiography,* p. 354.

37. Bruce Perry, *Malcolm: The Life of A Man Who Changed Black America* (New York: Station Hill Press, 1991), p. 247.

38. Plimpton, *Liberator,* pp. 54–55.

39. Karl Evanzz, *The Judas Factor: The Plot to Kill Malcolm X* (New York: Thunder's Mouth Press, 1992), p. 189.

40. Haley, *Autobiography,* p. 472.

41. Report: "Muslim Mosque Inc.," SAC New York to FBI director, June 23, 1964, Section 63, Microfilm Roll 8, FBI file on MMI.

42. Taylor Branch, *Pillar of Fire: America in the King Years, 1963–65* (New York: Simon and Schuster, 1998), p. 254.

43. "Malcolm X Tells of Death Threat," *Amsterdam News,* March 21, 1964.

44. Karim, Skutches, and Gallen, *Remembering Malcolm,* p. 163.

45. Ibid., p. 165.

46. Paul Lee, interview by author, March 1, 1999.

Chapter 7

1. M.S. Handler, "Malcolm X Splits With Muhammad," *Washington Post,* March 9, 1964.

2. Report: "Nation of Islam," Special Agent in Charge (SAC) Phoenix to Federal Bureau of Investigation (FBI) director, March 12, 1964 Section 8, Microfilm Roll 2, FBI file on Elijah Muhammad, Scholarly Resources, Wilmington, Delaware.

3. Report: "Malcolm K. Little," SAC New York to FBI director, April 20, 1964, Section 10, Microfilm Roll 2, FBI file on Malcolm X, Scholarly Resources.

4. Peter Goldman, *The Death and Life of Malcolm X* (Urbana, Ill.: University of Illinois Press, 1979), p. 191.

5. Report: "Muslim Mosque Inc.," (MMI), SAC New York to FBI director, March 13, 1964, Section 1, Microfilm Roll 1, FBI file on MMI, Scholarly Resources.

6. M.S. Handler, "Malcolm X Claims Strategy Role in African Attack on U.S. in U.N." *New York Times,* January 2, 1965.

7. William Worthy, "Why X Quit Muslims," *Afro-American* (Washington), March 13, 1964.

8. Gertrude Samuels, "Feud Within the Black Muslims," *New York Times,* March 22, 1964.

9. Ibid.

10. Report: "Nation of Islam," SAC

Chicago to FBI director, March 27, 1964, Section 1, Microfilm Roll 1, FBI file on MMI.

11. Samuels, *New York Times.*

12. Marc Crawford, "The Ominous Malcolm X Exits from the Muslims," *Life,* March 20, 1964, p. 40.

13. Report: "Nation of Islam," SAC Phoenix to FBI director, March 23, 1964, Section 8, Microfilm, Roll 2, FBI file on Elijah Muhammad, Scholarly Resources.

14. "To Arms With Malcolm X," *New York Times,* March 14, 1964.

15. "Malcolm X," *The Evening Sun* (Baltimore), March 15, 1964.

16. Max Lerner, "White Devils," *New York Post,* March 9, 1964.

17. Dick Schaap, "The Paradox That is Malcolm X: All Charm and All Contradiction," *New York Times,* March 14, 1965.

18. "Black Nationalism," *Washington Post,* March 15, 1964.

19. Donald R. Flynn, "Jolt to Rights Leaders: Muslim's Call to Arms," *New York Journal American,* March 13, 1964.

20. "Negroes Want No Shooting War for Justice," *The New Crusader* (Chicago), March 21, 1964.

21. Flynn, *New York Journal American.*

22. Crawford, *Life,* p. 40.

23. Fred Powledge, "Negroes Ponder Malcolm's Move," *New York Times,* March 15, 1964.

24. Ibid.

25. Ibid.

26. Ibid.

27. George Todd, "Malcolm X Explains His Rifle Statement," *New York Amsterdam News,* March 28, 1964.

28. Milt Freudenheim, "Negro Has Right to Protection," *Chicago Daily News,* March 21, 1964.

29. Dick Schaap, "The Paradox That is Malcolm X: All Charm and All Contradictions," *New York Herald Tribune,* March 22, 1964.

30. Crawford, *Life,* p. 42.

31. Robert Laird, "Malcolm X: In Life, As in Death, the Center of Violence," *New York World Telegram and Sun,* February 22, 1965.

32. Benjamin Karim, Peter Skutches, and David Gallen, *Remembering Malcolm* (New York: Carroll and Graf, 1992), p. 141.

33. Dick Schaap, "Hatred Was His Pitch and Hatred His Undoing," *New York Herald Tribune,* February 22, 1965.

34. Goldman, *Death and Life,* pp. 92–93.

35. Bayard Rustin, "Making His Mark," *Washington Post,* November 14, 1965.

36. Crawford, *Life,* p. 42.

37. Stan Putnam, "Malcolm Negro Awake Now," *The Detroit Free Press,* April 13, 1964.

38. Donald Flynn and Stanley Roberts, "The

Malcolm X Murders: Expected Death Not by His Own," *New York Times,* February 22, 1965.

39. Report: "Malcolm K. Little," SAC New York to FBI director, April 10, 1964, Section 59, Microfilm Roll 8, FBI file on Malcolm X.

40. Ibid.

41. "Blast Fire Sweep New York Muslim Center," *Chicago Daily News,* February 23, 1965.

42. "Malcolm X Interview," *New York Amsterdam News,* March 14, 1964.

43. Report: "Muslim Mosque Inc.," SAC New York to FBI director, April 3, 1964, Section 1, Microfilm Roll 1, FBI file on MMI.

44. "Malcolm Maps Negro Vote Drive," *New York Post,* March 30, 1964.

45. Freudeheim, *Chicago Daily News,* March 21, 1964.

46. George Todd, "Malcolm X Explains His Rifle Statement," *Amsterdam News,* March 28, 1964.

47. Report: "Malcolm K. Little," SAC New York to FBI director, April 10, 1964, Section 59, Microfilm Roll 8, FBI file on Malcolm X.

48. Malcolm X, "The Ballot or the Bullet," in *Malcolm X Speaks: Selected Speeches and Statements,* ed. George Breitman (New York: Pathfinder Press, 1989), p. 39.

49. Report: "Muslim Mosque Inc.," SAC Cleveland to FBI director, April 14, 1964, Section 1, Microfilm Roll 1, FBI file on MMI.

50. M.S. Handler, "Assertive Spirit Stirs Negroes, Puts Vigor in Civil Rights Drive," *New York Times,* April 23, 1963.

51. Junius Griftin, "Malcolm X Plans Muslim Crusade," *New York Times,* April 3, 1964.

52. Linn Allen, "Brother Bitterly Condemns Malcolm X," *Chicago Sun Times,* March 27, 1964.

53. Report: "Muslim Mosque Inc.," SAC New York to FBI director, April 3, 1964, Section 1, Microfilm Roll 1, FBI file on MMI.

54. Report: "Muslim Mosque Inc.," SAC Cleveland to FBI director, April 17, 1964, Section 1, Microfilm Roll 1, FBI file on MMI.

55. Report: "Malcolm K. Little," SAC Detroit to FBI director, April 14, 1964, Section 10, Microfilm Roll 2, FBI file on Malcolm X.

56. Philbert Little, in *Malcolm X: Make It Plain,* ed. Cheryll Y. Greene (New York: Viking Penguin, 1994), p. 174.

57. James W. Sullivan, "The X Brothers: Malcolm, Philbert," *New York Herald Tribune,* March 28, 1964.

58. "Malcolm X in Gallery, Sees Rights' Con Game," *The Evening Star* (Washington), March 27, 1964.

59. "King and Malcolm X Join in Protest Vow," *New York Journal American,* March 27, 1964.

60. Ted Knap, "Malcolm Outflanks Dr. King on Capital Battleground," *New York World Telegram and Sun*, March 27, 1964.

61. Clayborne Carson, ed., *Malcolm X: The FBI File* (New York: Carroll and Graf, 1991), p. 37.

62. Report: "Malcolm K. Little," SAC New York to FBI director, April 20, 1964, Section 10, Microfilm Roll 2, FBI file on Malcolm X.

63. Editorial, "On My Own," *Muhammad Speaks*, April 10, 1964.

64. Wallace Muhammad, in Greene, *Malcolm X*, p. 175.

65. Haley, *Autobiography*, p. 474.

66. Bayard Rustin, "Making His Mark," *Washington Post*, November 14, 1965.

Chapter 8

1. Report: "Malcolm K. Little," Special Agent in Charge (SAC) Boston to Federal Bureau of Investigation (FBI) director, May 5, 1964, Section 15, FBI file on Malcolm X, in *Malcolm X: The FBI file*, ed. Clayborne Carson (New York: Carroll and Graf, 1991), p. 30.

2. Jesse W. Lewis, Jr., "Man Who Tamed Malcolm is Hopeful," *Washington Post*, May 25, 1964.

3. Report: "Muslim Mosque Inc." (MMI), SAC New York to FBI director, April 20, 1964, Section 1, Microfilm Roll 10, FBI file on Malcolm X, Scholarly Resources, Wilmington, Delaware.

4. Ella Collins, in *Malcolm X: Make It Plain*, ed. Cheryll Y. Greene (New York: Penguin Books, 1994), p. 178.

5. "Paper's Already Filed in Court," *New York Amsterdam*, April 18, 1964.

6. Alex Haley, *The Autobiography of Malcolm X* (New York: Ballantine Books, 1992), pp. 369–370.

7. Ibid., pp. 374–375.

8. Ibid., p. 381.

9. Ibid., pp. 382–383.

10. Louis A. DeCaro, Jr., *On the Side of My People: A Religious Life of Malcolm X* (New York: New York University Press, 1996), p. 217.

11. Report: "Muslim Mosque Inc.," SAC New York to FBI director, April 20, 1964, Section 1, Microfilm Roll 10, FBI file on Malcolm X.

12. DeCaro, *Side of the People*, p. 203.

13. Victor Wolfenstein, *The Victims of Democracy: Malcolm X and the Black Revolution* (New York: Guildford Press, 1993), p. 307.

14. Muhammad Al-Faysal, in *Malcolm X: Make It Plain*, prod. and dir. Orlando Bagwell, 136 min., MIP Home Video, 1995, videocassette.

15. DeCaro, *Side of the People*, p. 220.

16. Report: "Malcolm K. Little," SAC Boston to FBI director, March 8, 1965, Section 16, Microfilm Roll 2, FBI file on Malcolm X.

17. M.S. Handler, "Malcolm X Pleased by Whites' Attitudes on Trip to Mecca," *New York Times*, May 13, 1964.

18. Jesse W. Lewis, Jr., "Malcolm X Says Visit to Mecca Turned Him from Race Hatred," *Washington Post*, May 7, 1964.

19. Charles Kenyatta, interview by author, March 6, 1999.

20. Bayard Rustin, "Making His Mark," *Washington Post*, November 14, 1965.

21. Betty Shabazz, "Malcolm X: As Husband and Father," in *Malcolm X: The Man and His Times*, ed. John H. Clarke (Trenton, N.J.: Africa World Press, 1990), p. 141.

22. John H. Clarke, in Greene, *Malcolm X*, p. 179.

23. Yuri Kochiyama, interview by author, March 5, 1999.

24. Peter Goldman, interview by author, February 27, 1999.

25. James Farmer, *Lay Bare the Heart: An Autobiography of the Civil Rights Movement* (New York: Penguin Books, 1985), p. 229.

26. "Negro Moderation Decried by Malcolm X in Lebanon," *New York Times*, May 2, 1964.

27. Alex Haley, *The Autobiography of Malcolm X* (New York: Ballantine Books, 1992), pp. 400–401.

28. Bruce Perry, *Malcolm: The Life of a Man Who Changed Black America* (New York: Station Hill Press, 1991), pp. 268–269.

29. Haley, *Autobiography*, pp. 400–401.

30. Victor Riesel, "Malcolm X Gives Africa Twisted Look," *New York Journal America*, July 25, 1964.

31. Peter Goldman, *The Death and Life of Malcolm X* (Urbana, Ill.: University of Illinois Press, 1979), p. 174.

32. Heywood, Gould, "Real Malcolm X," *Amsterdam News*, March 20, 1965.

33. Report: "Malcolm X Visits Accra," Daniel A. Britz to U.S. Department of State, May 24, 1964, Section 72, Microfilm Roll 9, FBI file on Malcolm X.

34. Maya Angelou, *All God's Children Need Traveling Shoes* (New York: Vintage Books, 1991), p. 131.

35. Goldman, *Death and Life*, p. 178.

36. Alice Windom to Organization of Afro-American Unity (OAAU), May 19, 1964, Section 1, Microfilm Roll 1, FBI file on Malcolm X.

37. Leslie Alexander Lacy, "Malcolm X in Ghana," in Clarke, *Man and His Times*, p. 218.

38. Britz to Department of State, May 24, 1964, FBI file on Malcolm X.

39. Ibid.

40. Jack Barnes and Barry Sheppard, "Interview with Malcolm X," *Young Socialist*, March–April, 1965.

41. Haley, *Autobiography*, p. 407.

42. Windom to OAAU, May 19, 1964, FBI file on Malcolm X.

43. Ibid.

44. Goldman, *Death and Life*, p. 176.

45. David Gallen, ed. *Malcolm X: As They Knew Him* (New York: Ballantine Books, 1992), p. 41.

46. Lacy, in Clarke, *Man and His Times*, p. 223.

47. Angelou, *God's Children*, p. 130.

48. Ibid., pp. 136–137.

49. Windom to OAAU, May 19, 1964, FBI file on Malcolm X.

50. Ibid.

51. Goldman, *Death and Life*, p. 177.

52. Ruby M. and E.U. Essien-Udom, "Malcolm X: An International Man," in Clarke, *Man and His Times*, p. 250.

53. Angelou, *God's Children*, p. 138.

54. Editorial, "Cassius Raps Malcolm," *New York Post*, May 18, 1964.

55. Angelou, *God's Children*, p. 144.

56. Britz to Department of State, May 24, 1964, FBI file on Malcolm X.

57. Ibid.

58. Malcolm X's 'New Insight,'" *Chicago American*, March 9, 1965.

59. Attallah Shabazz, in Greene, *Malcolm X*, p. 183.

60. Helen Dudar, "The Return of Malcolm X," *New York Post*, May 22, 1964.

61. Milt Freudenheim, "Ex-Muslim Malcolm Returns Praising Muslims," *Chicago Daily News*, May 22, 1964.

62. M.S. Handler, "Cites Jews' Progress," *New York Times*, May 24, 1964.

63. Dudar, *New York Post*.

64. Dick Gregory, in *The Real Malcolm X: An Intimate Portrait of the Man*, prod. and dir. Andrew Lack and Brett Alexander, 60 min., CBS Video, 1992, videocassette.

Chapter 9

1. Herman Ferguson, interview by author, September 6, 1997.

2. Zak A. Kondo, *Conspiracys: Unraveling the Assassination of Malcolm X* (Washington, D.C.: Nubia Press, 1993), p. 70.

3. Claude A. Clegg III, interview by author, September 6, 1997.

4. Ferguson, interview.

5. Louis DeCaro, Jr., interview by author, March 4, 1999.

6. Wallace Muhammad, in *Malcolm X: Make It Plain*, prod. and dir. Orlando Bagwell, 136 min., MPI Home Video, 1995, videocassette.

7. Peter Goldman, "Malcolm X: An Unfinished Story?" *New York Times Magazine*, August 19, 1979, pp. 26–32.

8. Report: "Malcolm K. Little," Special Agent in Charge (SAC) New York to SAC Chicago, June 20, 1964, Section 65, Microfilm Roll 9, FBI file on Malcolm X, Scholarly Resources, Wilmington, Delaware.

9. Report: "Malcolm K. Little," SAC New York to Federal Bureau of Investigation (FBI) director, June 20, 1965, Section 14, Microfilm Roll 2, FBI file on Malcolm X.

10. Report: "Malcolm K. Little," SAC New York to FBI director, January 20, 1965, Section 14, FBI file on Malcolm X.

11. Malcolm X, in Bagwell, *Make It Plain*.

12. Report: "Malcolm K. Little," SAC New York to FBI director, July 8, 1964, Section 1, Microfilm Roll 9, FBI file on Malcolm X.

13. Report: "Malcolm K. Little," SAC New York to FBI director, October 5, 1964, Section 6, Microfilm Roll 2, FBI file on Muslim Mosque Inc. (MMI), Scholarly Resources.

14. George Murry, "Muslim Insiders Tell Power Flight of Malcolm," *Chicago American*, February 22, 1965.

15. Kondo, *Conspiracys*, pp. 145–146.

16. Benjamin Karim, Peter Skutches, and David Gallen, *Remembering Malcolm* (New York: Carroll and Graf, 1992), pp. 145–146.

17. "Malcolm X: Man Marked for Death," *New York World Telegram and The Sun*, June 18, 1964.

18. Report: "Malcolm K. Little," SAC New York to FBI director, October 5, 1964, Section 6, Microfilm Roll 2, FBI file on MMI.

19. Peter Goldman, *The Death and Life of Malcolm X* (Urbana, Ill.: University of Illinois Press, 1979), p. 195.

20. Report: "Malcolm K. Little," SAC New York to FBI director, July 8, 1964, Section 2, Microfilm Roll 9, FBI file on Malcolm X.

21. Goldman, *Death and Life*, p. 195.

22. "Malcolm X Ordered to Vacate Home," *New York World Telegram and Sun*, June 3, 1964.

23. Report: "Malcolm K. Little," SAC New York to FBI director, June 20, 1965, Section 14, Microfilm Roll 2, FBI file on Malcolm X.

24. Report: "Nation of Islam," SAC Cleveland to FBI director, June 16, 1964, Section 3, Microfilm Roll 1, FBI file on MMI.

25. Report: "Malcolm K. Little," SAC New York to FBI director, June 20, 1964, Section 14, Microfilm Roll 2, FBI file on Malcolm X.

26. Goldman, *Life and Death*, pp. 198–199.

27. Report: "Malcolm K. Little," SAC New

York to FBI director, October 5, 1964, Section 6, Microfilm Roll 2, FBI file on MMI.

28. "Malcolm X: Man Marked for Death," *New York World Telegram and Sun,* June 18, 1964.

29. Report: "Nation of Islam," SAC Phoenix to SAC New York, June 24, 1964, Section 64, Microfilm Roll 8, FBI file on Malcolm X.

30. "Malcolm X to Elijah; Let's End the Fighting," *New York Post,* June 22, 1964.

31. Report: "Malcolm K. Little," SAC New York to FBI director, January 20, 1965, Section 14, Microfilm Roll 2, FBI file on Malcolm X.

32. Ferguson, interview.

33. George Breitman, *The Last Year of Malcolm X: The Evolution of a Revolutionary* (New York: Pathfinder Press, 1967), p. 77.

34. "Malcolm X to Elijah: Let's End the Fighting," *New York Post,* June 26, 1964.

35. William McCullan, "Malcolm vs. Elijah: Muslim Showdown," *New York Journal American.*

36. Report: "Malcolm K. Little," SAC New York to FBI director, June 20, 1965, Section 14, Microfilm Roll 3, FBI file on Malcolm X.

37. Ted Poston, "Malcolm and the Muslims," *New York Post,* February 22, 1965.

38. Report: "Muslim Mosque Inc.," F.J. Baumgardner to W.C. Sullivan, June 30, 1964, Section 3, Microfilm Roll 1, FBI file on MMI.

39. David Herman, "Malcolm Launches a New Organization," *The Militant,* July 30, 1964.

40. Report: "Muslim Mosque Inc.," SAC New York to FBI director, June 29, 1964, Section 3, Microfilm Roll 1, FBI file on Malcolm X.

41. Report: "Nation of Islam," SAC Chicago to SAC New York, August 10, 1964, Section 67, Microfilm Roll 9, FBI file on Malcolm X.

42. "Muslims Forecast Malcolm's Failure," *The New Crusader,* November 28, 1964.

43. "Clifton DeBerry, Socialist Workers Party Candidate," *The Militant,* July 29, 1964.

44. Report: "Organization of Afro-American Unity," FBI director to SAC New York, July 20, 1964, Section 1, Microfilm Roll 1, FBI file on Malcolm X.

45. Charles Bartlett, "In Search of Armageddon," *Chicago Sun Times,* July 29, 1964.

46. Report: "Organization of Afro-American Unity," (OAAU), SAC New York to FBI director, July 15, 1964, Section 1, Microfilm Roll 1, FBI file on Malcolm X.

47. Report: "Malcolm K. Little," SAC New York to FBI director, October 5, 1964, Section 6, Microfilm Roll 2, FBI file on MMI.

48. Report: "Malcolm K. Little," SAC New York to FBI director, September 30, 1965, Section 87, Microfilm Roll 3, FBI file on Malcolm X.

49. Report: "Organization of Afro-American Unity," SAC New York to FBI director, September 23, 1964, Section 2, Microfilm Roll 1, FBI file on OAAU, Scholarly Resources.

50. Goldman, *Death and Life,* p. 14.

51. Report: "Malcolm K. Little," SAC New York to FBI director, January 20, 1965, Section 14, Microfilm Roll 3, FBI file on Malcolm X.

52. Clarence Hunter, "Guerrilla Warfare is Next," *The Evening Star,* June 14, 1964.

53. "Malcolm Favors a Mau Mau in U.S.," *New York Times,* December 21, 1964.

54. Report: "Nation of Islam," SAC Chicago to FBI director, June 19, 1964, Section 63, Microfilm Roll 8, FBI file on Malcolm X.

55. Malcolm X, "Educate Our People in the Science of Politics," in *February 1965: The Final Speeches, Malcolm X,* ed. Steve Clark (New York: Pathfinder Press, 1992).

56. Timothy Lee, "Malcolm X and His Enemies," *New York Post,* February 23, 1965.

57. Malcolm X, "The Second Rally of the OAAU," in *By Any Means Necessary: Malcolm X,* ed. George Breitman (New York: Pathfinder Press, 1992), pp. 83–84.

58. Hunter, *The Evening Star.*

59. Malcolm X, "Final Views," in *Malcolm X: As They Knew Him,* ed. David Gallen (New York: Ballantine Books, 1992), pp. 169–170.

60. Roy Wilkins, "The Violent Ones," *New York Post,* January 3, 1965.

61. Victor Wolfenstein, *The Victims of Democracy: Malcolm X and the Black Revolution* (New York: Guilford Press, 1993), p. 317.

62. Report: "Malcolm K. Little," SAC New York to FBI director, February 4, 1965, Section 14, Microfilm Roll 2, FBI file on Malcolm X.

63. Malcolm X, "At a Meeting in Paris," in Breitman, *By Any Means Necessary,* p. 119.

64. "Malcolm X Back to Hard Line in Talk to Haryou-Act," *New York Herald Tribune,* December 13, 1964.

65. "Malcolm X Sees End of Muslims," *The Evening Star* (Chicago), August 30, 1964.

66. Malcolm X, interview by Marlene Nadle, February 4, 1965, in Clark, *Final Years,* p. 243.

67. Peter Goldman, interview by author, February 27, 1999.

68. "Malcolm X's 'New Insight,'" *Chicago American,* March 9, 1965.

69. Report: "Malcolm K. Little," SAC New York to FBI director, February 4, 1965, Section 14, Microfilm Roll 2, FBI file on Malcolm X.

70. Malcolm X, "Confrontation With an 'Expert'" February 18, 1965, in *Malcolm X Speaks: Selected Speeches and Statements,* ed. George Breitman (New York: Grove Press, 1965), p. 190.

71. Hans J. Massaquoi, "Mystery of Malcolm X," *Ebony,* September 1964, pp. 38–46.

72. Marlene Nadle, "Malcolm X: The Complexity of a Man in the Jungle," *Village Voice,* February 25, 1965, p. 5.

73. Report: "Malcolm K. Little," SAC New York to FBI director, January 20, 1965, Section 14, Microfilm Roll 2, FBI file on Malcolm X.

74. Report: "Malcolm K. Little," SAC New York to FBI director, January 14, 1965, Section 73, Microfilm Roll 9, FBI file on Malcolm X.

75. Nadle, *The Village Voice,* p. 7.

76. Milt Freudenheim, "Myth Already Springing Up: Malcolm X, Martyred Hero," *Chicago Daily News,* February 23, 1965.

77. Breitman, *Last Year of Malcolm X,* p. 83.

78. Herman Ferguson, interview by author, March 5, 1999.

79. "Malcolm Rejects Race Separation," *New York Times,* May 24, 1964.

80. Malcolm X, "The Second Rally of the OAAU," July 5, 1964, in Breitman, *By Any Means Necessary,* pp. 78–79.

81. Ferguson, interview.

82. Report: "Malcolm K. Little," SAC New York to FBI director, February 8, 1965, Section 15, Microfilm Roll 2, FBI file on Malcolm X.

83. Haley, *Autobiography,* p. 419.

84. Bayard Rustin, "Making His Mark," *Washington Post,* November 14, 1965.

85. Yuri Kochiyama, interview by author, March 5, 1999.

86. Bryce B. Miller, "Malcolm X, Angriest Muslim, Changes Mind," *New York World Telegram and Sun,* July 3, 1964.

87. Massaquoi, *Ebony,* p. 39.

88. Malcolm X, "With Fannie Lou Hamer," in *Malcolm X Speaks: Selected Speeches and Statements* (New York: Pathfinder Press, 1989), p. 112.

89. Goldman, *Death and Life,* pp. 225–226.

90. Nadle, *The Village Voice,* p. 6.

91. Malcolm X, interview by Marlene Nadle, February 4, 1965, in Breitman, *Malcolm X Speaks,* p. 213.

92. Nadle, *The Village Voice,* p. 6.

93. Haley, *Autobiography,* pp. 432–433.

94. "Malcolm X Article Favors Goldwater," *New York Times,* September 8, 1964.

95. "Turner Raps Malcolm X," *Newark Evening News,* September 9, 1964.

96. Editorial, "The Confession of Malcolm X," *New York Post,* September 9, 1964.

97. Malcolm X, interview by Jack Barnes and Barry Sheppard, January 18, 1965, in Breitman, *By Any Means Necessary,* p. 165.

98. Nadle, *The Village Voice,* p. 7.

Chapter 10

1. Peter Goldman, interview by author, February 27, 1999.

2. Herman Ferguson, interview by author, March 5, 1999.

3. Benjamin 2X, in *Malcolm X: Make It Plain,* prod. and dir. Orlando Bagwell, 136 min., MPI Home Video, 1995, videocassette.

4. Peter Goldman, "Malcolm X: An Unfinished Story?" *New York Times Magazine,* August 19, 1979, pp. 26–32.

5. Charles W. Wiley, "Who Was Malcolm X?" *National Review,* March 23, 1965, pp. 239–240.

6. Theodore Jones, "Malcolm Knew He Was a Marked Man," *New York Times,* February 22, 1965.

7. Malcolm X, "The Second Rally of the OAAU," in *By Any Means Necessary: Malcolm X* (New York: Pathfinder Press, 1992), p. 102.

8. Leonard Shecter, "Malcolm X: A Year Later," *New York Post,* February 21, 1966.

9. Joseph X, in *The Real Malcolm X: An Intimate Portrait of the Man,* prod. and dir. Andrew Lack and Brett Alexander, 60 min., 1992, videocassette.

10. Report: "Malcolm K. Little," SAC Los Angeles to FBI director, September 2, 1965, Section 18, Microfilm Roll 3, FBI file on Malcolm X, Scholarly Resources, Wilmington, Delaware.

11. "Ex-Sweetheart of Malcolm X Accuses Elijah," *New York Amsterdam News,* July 11, 1964.

12. Ibid.

13. Balm L. Leavell, "False Charges Made Against Muhammad," *The New Crusader,* July 11, 1964.

14. Karl Evanzz, *The Judas Factor: The Plot to Kill Malcolm X* (New York: Thunder's Mouth Press, 1992), p. 249.

15. "Malcolm X Gets Guard," *The Washington Post and Times Herald,* July 5, 1964.

16. John Mallon, "Malcolm X Family Bombed Out of Home," *New York Daily News,* February 15, 1965.

17. Dave Potter, "Elijah's Kin Echoes Charge," *Chicago Daily Defender,* July 8, 1964.

18. Report: "Nation of Islam," SAC Chicago to FBI director, June 10, 1964, Section 65, Microfilm Roll 5, FBI file on Malcolm X.

19. "Malcolm X in Cairo Says He'll See African Leaders," *New York Times,* August 17, 1964.

20. Peter Goldman, *The Death and Life of Malcolm X* (Urbana, Ill.: University of Illinois Press, 1979), pp. 210–211.

21. M.S. Handler, "Malcolm X Seeks U.N. Negro Debate," *New York Times,* August 17, 1964.

22. Malcolm X, "Appeal to African Heads of State," July 17, 1964, in *Malcolm X Speaks: Selected Speeches and Statements,* ed. George Breitman (New York: Grove Press, 1965), p. 84.

23. Goldman, *Death and Life,* p. 209.

24. Malcolm X, "After the Bombing," February 14, 1965, in Breitman, *Malcolm X Speaks,* pp. 166–167.

25. "Malcolm X's New Insights," *Chicago American,* March 9, 1965.

26. Bruce Perry, *Malcolm: The Life of a Man Who Changed Black America* (New York: Station Hill Press, 1991), p. 320.

27. Ferguson interview.

28. Malcolm X, interview by Presence Africaine, December 7, 1964, in Breitman, *By Any Means Necessary,* p. 112.

29. Report: "Malcolm K. Little," John Edgar Hoover to Central Intelligence Agency (CIA) director, November 23, 1964, Section 13, Microfilm Roll 2, FBI file on Malcolm X.

30. Victor Reisel, "Malcolm X and the Red Chinese," *New York Journal American,* August 5, 1964.

31. Samuel Schreig, "From Everywhere," *The Sentinel,* August 6, 1964.

32. Report: "Malcolm K. Little," SAC New York to FBI director, June 20, 1965, Section 14, Microfilm Roll 2, FBI file on Malcolm X.

33. Report: "Malcolm K. Little," SAC New York to FBI director, October 5, 1964, Section 6, Microfilm Roll 2, FBI file on Malcolm X.

34. Report: "Malcolm K. Little," SAC New York to FBI director, September 8, 1965, Section 18, Microfilm Roll 3, FBI file on Malcolm X.

35. Alex Haley, *The Autobiography of Malcolm X* (New York: Ballantine Books, 1992), p. 428.

36. Michael Friedly, *Malcolm X: The Assassination* (New York: Ballantine Books, 1992), pp. 70–71.

37. Report: "Muslim Mosque Inc." (MMI) October 22, 1964, Section 6, Microfilm Roll 2, FBI file on MMI, Scholarly Resources.

38. "Order Eviction of Malcolm X," *New York Amsterdam News,* September 5, 1964.

39. M.S. Handler, "Malcolm Rejects Racist Doctrine," *New York Times,* October 4, 1964.

40. Report: "Malcolm K. Little," SAC New York to FBI director, January 20, 1965, Section 14, Microfilm Roll 2, FBI file on Malcolm X.

41. "Malcolm Home Blasts U.S. Congo Policy," *The Philadelphia Independent,* December 4, 1964.

42. John Lewis, in *Malcolm X: Make It Plain,* ed. Cheryll Y. Greene (New York: Penguin Books, 1994), p. 1994.

43. James B. Wechsler, "About Malcolm X," *New York Post,* February 23, 1965.

44. Alice Windom, in Greene, *Malcolm X,* p. 194.

45. Leslie Alexander Lacy, "Malcolm X in Ghana," in *Malcolm X: The Man and His Times* (Trenton, N.J.: Africa World Press, 1993), p. 225.

46. Report: "Muslim Mosque Inc.," Legot, Tokyo to FBI director, December 8, 1964, Section 72, Microfilm Roll 9, FBI file on Malcolm X.

47. George Murray, "New Threats Stir Muslim Turmoil," *Chicago American,* February 24, 1965.

48. Shirley Graham DuBois, "The Beginning, Not the End," in Clarke, *Man and His Times,* p. 127.

49. Claude A. Clegg III, interview by author, September 9, 1997.

50. Ferguson, interview.

51. Yuri Kochiyama, interview by author, March 5, 1999.

52. Charles Kenyatta, interview by author, March 6, 1999.

53. Report: "Malcolm K. Little," SAC Report to FBI director, February 4, 1965, Section 13, Microfilm Roll 2, FBI file on Malcolm X.

54. Robert W. White, "Malcolm X Slain by Gunmen," *New York Herald Tribune,* February 22, 1965.

55. Yvonne Woodward, in Greene, *Malcolm X,* p. 195.

56. Roger Prots, "Millions of Britons See Malcolm X in T.V. Broadcast of Debate at Oxford," *The Militant,* December 14, 1964.

57. "Africans Call Malcolm X the 'American Lumumba,'" *New York Herald Tribune,* February 24, 1965.

58. "Elijah Losing Muslim Following Says Son," *Chicago American,* September 15, 1964.

59. "Muhammad's Son Says Muslims Threaten His Life," *Chicago Daily Defender,* July 8, 1964.

60. Report: "Afro-Descendant Upliftment Society," SAC Philadelphia to FBI director, October 8, 1964, Section 72, Microfilm Roll 10, FBI file on Malcolm X.

61. Report: "Nation of Islam," SAC New York to FBI director, August 17, 1964, Section 8, Microfilm Roll 2, FBI file on Elijah Muhammad, Scholarly Resources.

62. Report: "Organization of Afro-American Unity," (OAAU), SAC Los Angeles to FBI director, February 4, 1965, Section 3, Microfilm Roll 1, FBI file on OAAU, Scholarly Resources.

63. Major Robinson, "Muhammad's Son Favors Malcolm X," *New York Courier,* December 26, 1964.

64. Goldman, *Death and Life,* p. 247.

Chapter 11

1. Peter Goldman, *The Death and Life of Malcolm X* (Urbana, Ill.: University of Illinois Press, 1979), p. 246.

2. Theodore Jones, "Malcolm Knew He Was a Marked Man," *New York Times*, February 22, 1965.

3. George Breitman, *The Last Year of Malcolm X: The Evolution of a Revolutionary* (New York: Pathfinder Press, 1967).

4. Alex Haley, in *Malcolm X: Make It Plain*, ed. Cheryll Y. Greene (New York: Penguin Books, 1994), p. 202.

5. Herman Ferguson, interview by author, March 5, 1999.

6. Charles Kenyatta, interview by author, March 6, 1999.

7. Yuri Kochiyama, interview by author, March 6, 1999.

8. Benjamin Karim, Peter Skutches, and David Gallen, *Remembering Malcolm* (New York: Carroll and Graf, 1992), pp. 187–188.

9. Kenyatta, interview.

10. Kochiyama, interview.

11. Louis A. DeCaro, Jr., interview by author, March 4, 1999.

12. Louis X, "Boston Minister Tells of Malcolm, Muhammad's Biggest Hypocrite," *Muhammad Speaks*, December 4, 1964.

13. Raymond Sharrieff, "Nation of Islam, Warns Malcolm X," *The Crusader* (Chicago), December 15, 1964.

14. Karim, Skutches, and Gallen, *Remembering Malcolm*, p. 183.

15. "Foil Plot to Murder Malcolm X in Philly," *New York Courier*, January 9, 1965.

16. Peter Goldman, *The Death and Life of Malcolm X* (Urbana, Ill.: University of Illinois Press, 1979), p. 252.

17. Zak A. Kondo, *Conspiracys: Unraveling the Assassination of Malcolm X* (Washington, D.C.: Nubia Press, 1993), p. 74.

18. Peter Kihiss, "Hunt for Killers in Malcolm Case 'On Right Target,'" *New York Times*, February 25, 1965.

19. Goldman, *Death and Life*, pp. 233–234.

20. Report: "Malcolm K. Little," Special Agent in Charge (SAC) New York to Federal Bureau of Investigation (FBI) director, September 8, 1965, Section 18, Microfilm Roll 3, FBI file on Malcolm X, Scholarly Resources, Wilmington, Delaware.

21. Kenyatta, interview.

22. James W. Sullivan, "Didn't Kill Malcolm, Defendant Testifies," *New York Tribune*, February 26, 1966.

23. Report: "Muslim Mosque Inc.," SAC New York to FBI director, September 30, 1964, Section 66, Microfilm Roll 9, FBI file on Malcolm X.

24. George Breitman, *The Last Year of Malcolm X: The Evolution of a Revolutionary* (New York: Pathfinder Press, 1967), pp. 50–51.

25. Kochiyama, interview.

26. Herman Ferguson, interview by author, March 5, 1999.

27. Kenyatta, interview.

28. Paul Lee, interview by author, March 1, 1999.

29. James H. Cone, *Martin and Malcolm and America: A Dream or a Nightmare* (Maryknoll, N.Y.: Orbis Books, 1991), p. 285.

30. Theodore Jones, "Malcolm Knew He Was a Marked Man," *New York Times*, February 22, 1965.

31. James Booker, "Malcolm X Speaks," *New York Amsterdam News*, February 6, 1965.

32. Report: "Organization of Afro-American Unity," (OAAU) SAC Los Angeles to FBI director, February 4, 1965, Section 25, Microfilm Roll 6, FBI file on Malcolm X.

33. Sam Crowther, "The Last Desperate Days of Malcolm X Pursued by Death," *New York Journal*, February 28, 1965.

34. Seymour Korman, "Reveals Malcolm's Role in Elijah Paternity Suit," *Chicago Tribune*, February 25, 1965.

35. Karl Evanzz, *The Judas Factor: The Plot to Kill Malcolm X* (New York: Thunder's Mouth Press, 1992), p. 287.

36. Crowther, *New York Journal*.

37. John G. Trezevant, "Reveal Police Guard Given Malcolm X On Visit Here," *Chicago Sun Times*, February 24, 1965.

38. Edward Bradley, "Driver Tells How Malcolm X Escaped Death in Chase," *Washington Evening Star*, February 24, 1965.

39. Report: OAAU, February 4, 1965, FBI file on Malcolm X.

40. Trezevant, *Chicago Sun Times*.

41. Report: "Organization of Afro-American Unity," February 16, 1965, Section 15, Microfilm Roll 2, FBI file on Malcolm X.

42. Crowther, *New York Journal*.

43. Ibid.

44. Report: "Malcolm K. Little," SAC Chicago to FBI director, February 4, 1965, Section 3, Microfilm Roll 1, FBI file on OAAU, Scholarly Resources.

45. Report: "Young Socialist Alliance," SAC New York to SAC Boston, September 8, 1964, Section 69, Microfilm Roll 9, FBI file on Malcolm X.

46. Report: "Malcolm K. Little," SAC Mobile to FBI director, February 8, 1965, Section 15, Microfilm Roll 2, FBI file on Malcolm X.

47. Don McKee, "Malcolm X Warns Vio-

lence May Come," *Chicago American,* February 4, 1965.

48. Lewis V. Baldwin, "Malcolm X and Martin Luther King Jr.: What They Thought of Each Other," *Islamic Studies,* Vol. 25 (4), Winter 1986, p. 398.

49. George Carmack, "Malcolm X's Road to Violence," *Washington Daily News,* February 5, 1965.

50. Report: "Malcolm K. Little," February 8, 1965, FBI file on Malcolm X.

51. Baldwin, *Islamic Studies,* p. 399.

52. David J. Garrow, *Bearing The Cross: Martin Luther King Jr., and the Southern Christian Leadership Conference* (New York: William Morrow, 1986), pp. 393.

53. Baldwin, *Islamic Studies,* p. 398.

54. Peter Goldman, interview by author, February 27, 1999.

55. Malcolm X, "Speech to Council of African Organization Congress," February 8, 1965, in *February 1965: The Final Speeches, Malcolm X,* ed. Steve Clark (New York: Pathfinder Press, 1992), p. 33.

56. Jack Monet, "France Bars Malcolm X to Avoid 'Trouble' at Meeting," *New York Herald Tribune,* February 10, 1965.

57. "Malcolm Enjoyed Privileges at U.N.," *New York Times,* February 26, 1965.

58. Zak A. Kondo, *Conspiracys: Unraveling the Assassination of Malcolm X* (Washington, D.C.: Nubia Press, 1993), p. 78.

59. Jack Monet, "France Bars Malcolm X to Avoid 'Trouble' at Meeting," *New York Herald Tribune,* February 10, 1965.

60. Malcolm X, "There's a Worldwide Revolution Going On," February 15, 1965, in *Malcolm X: The Last Speeches* (New York: Pathfinder Press, 1989), p. 113.

61. Monet, *New York Herald Tribune.*

62. Malcolm X, in Clark, *Final Speeches,* p. 40.

63. Taylor Branch, *Pillar of Fire: America in the King Years 1963–65* (New York: Simon and Schuster, 1998), pp. 585–586.

64. "BBC Assailed for Conducting Malcolm X on Smethwick Tour," *New York Times,* February 14, 1965.

65. "Aid to Malcolm X by BBC Assailed," *New York Times,* February 14, 1965.

66. Goldman, *Death and Life,* p. 255.

67. Malcolm X, "Remarks to the Press in Smethwick and Birmingham," February 12, 1965, in Clark, *Final Speeches,* pp. 66–67.

68. Ibid., p. 67.

Chapter 12

1. William M. Kunstler, *My Life as a Radical Lawyer* (New York: Carol Publishing Group, 1996), pp. 381–382.

2. Report: "Malcolm K. Little," Special Agent in Charge (SAC) to Federal Bureau of Investigation (FBI) director, February 16, 1965, Section 15, Microfilm Roll 2, FBI file on Malcolm X, Scholarly Resources, Wilmington, Delaware.

3. Report: "Interview of Malcolm X," Commanding Officer, Bureau of Special Services (BOSS) to Chief of Detectives, February 16, 1965, New York Police Department (NYPD) Legal Bureau, File 99PL100576, New York City, New York.

4. John Mallon, "Malcolm X, Family Bombed Out of Home," *New York Daily News,* February 15, 1965.

5. Fletcher Knebel, "A Visit With the Widow of Malcolm X," *Look,* March 4, 1969, p. 76.

6. Mallon, "A New Bomb Hits Malcolm: Eviction Writ," *New York Daily News,* February 16, 1965.

7. Commanding Officer BOSS to Chief of Detectives, NYPD File 99PL100576.

8. "Malcolm X Moves, Averting City Writ," *New York Times,* February 19, 1965.

9. Milton Lewis, "Members of City's Secret Police Unit Saw Malcolm Shot," *New York Herald Tribune,* February 23, 1965.

10. Alfred Robbins, "Malcolm X Slain to Silence Him: The Reason Why," *Journal American,* February 23, 1965.

11. Mallon, "Malcolm X, Family Bombed Out of Home," *New York Daily News,* February 15, 1965.

12. Alex Haley, in *Malcolm X: Make It Plain,* prod. and dir. Orlando Bagwell, 136 min., MPI Home Video, 1995, videocassette.

13. Report: "Organization of Afro-American Unity," (OAAU), SAC Philadelphia to FBI director, February 22, 1965, Section 3, Microfilm Roll 1, FBI file on OAAU, Scholarly Resources, Wilmington, Delaware.

14. Mallon, *New York Daily News,* February 18, 1965.

15. Earl Grant, "The Last Days of Malcolm X," in *Malcolm X: The Man And His Times,* ed. John H. Clarke (Trenton, N.J.: Africa World Press, 1990), p. 87.

16. Taylor Branch, *Pillar of Fire: America in the King Years 1963–65* (New York: Simon and Schuster, 1998), p. 590.

17. Malcolm X, "After the Bombing," February 14, 1965, in *Malcolm X Speaks: Selected Speeches and Statements* (New York: Pathfinder Press, 1989), pp. 157–158.

18. Mallon, *New York Daily News,* February 18, 1965.

19. Commanding Officer BOSS to Chief of Detectives, NYPD File 99PL100576.

20. Peter Goldman, *The Death and Life of Malcolm X* (Urbana, Ill.: University of Illinois Press, 1979), p. 265.

21. Gene Roberts, in *Malcolm X: Make It Plain,* ed. Cheryll Y. Greene (New York: Viking Penguin, 1994), p. 202.

22. Spike Lee, *By Any Means Necessary: The Trials and Tribulations of the Making of Malcolm X* (New York: Hyperion Press, 1992), p. 49.

23. Archie Epps, ed. *Malcolm X: Speeches at Harvard* (New York: Paragon House, 1991), p. 45.

24. Benjamin Karim, Peter Skutches, and David Gallen, *Remembering Malcolm* (New York: Carroll and Graf, 1992), p. 181.

25. Betty Shabazz, "Malcolm X as a Husband and Father," in *Malcolm X: The Man and His Times* (Trenton, N.J.: Africa World Press, 1990), p. 142.

26. Malcolm X, "Not Just an American Problem, but a World Problem," February 16, 1965, in Clarke, *Man and His Times,* p. 143.

27. Sam Crowther, "The Last Desperate Days of Malcolm X, Pursued by Death," *New York Journal,* February 28, 1965.

28. Theodore Jones, "Malcolm Knew He Was a Marked Man," *New York Times,* February 22, 1965.

29. Michael Friedly, *Malcolm X: The Assassination* (New York: Ballantine Books, 1992), p. 8.

30. Richard D. Peters, "Malcolm Applies for Gun Permit," *New York World Telegram and the Sun,* February 19, 1965.

31. Lee, Trials and Tribulations," p. 66.

32. Gordon Parks, "The Violent End of the Man Called Malcolm," *Life,* March 5, 1965, p. 28.

33. Alan Morrison, "Who Killed Malcolm X?" *Ebony,* October 1965, pp. 137–138.

34. Earl Grant, "The Last Days of Malcolm X," in Clarke, *Man and His Times,* pp. 91–92.

35. John Mallon, "Gunned Down as He Addresses Rally; 3 Men Wounded," *New York Daily News,* February 22, 1965.

36. Alfred Robbins, Mike Pearl, and Richard Barr, "Malcolm X Slain to Silence Him: The Reason Why," *New York Journal American,* February 22, 1965.

37. Attallah Shabazz, in *Malcolm X: Make It Plain,* ed. Cheryll Y. Greene (New York: Penguin Books, 1994), p. 203.

38. Grant, in Clarke, *Man and His Times,* p. 92.

39. David Murry and Ralph Blumenfeld,

"Cops Seek Muslim Link in Killing," *New York Post,* February 22, 1965.

40. Bruce Perry, *Malcolm: The Life of a Man Who Changed Black America* (New York: Station Hill Press, 1991), p. 362.

41. Dick Gregory, in Malcolm X: Biography, prod. and dir. Lisa Zeff and Ron Steinman, 50 min., New Video Group, 1995, videocassette.

42. Crowther, *New York Journal.*

43. Friedly, *The Assassination,* p. 7.

44. Alex Haley, *The Autobiography of Malcolm X* (New York: Ballantine Books, 1992), p. 496.

45. Gene Roberts, in *Brother Minister: The Assassination of El-Hajj Malik Shabazz,* prod. and dir. Jack Baxter and Jefri Aal Muhammad, 115 min., X-ceptional Productions Inc., 1997, videocassette.

46. Claude A. Clegg III, interview by author, September 6, 1999.

47. Peter Goldman, *The Death and Life of Malcolm X* (Urbana, Ill.: University of Illinois Press, 1979), p. 269.

48. Friedly, *The Assassination,* p. 16.

49. Charles Kenyatta, in Baxter and Aal Muhammad, *Brother Minister.*

50. William Federici and Henry Lee, "Malcolm Double-Xd From Within: 37X," *New York Times,* February 25, 1965.

51. Friedly, *The Assassination,* p. 13.

52. Grant, in Clarke, *Man and His Times,* p. 94.

53. Karim, Skutches, and Gallen, *Remembering Malcolm,* pp. 188–189.

54. Haley, *Autobiography,* p. 497.

55. Karim, Skutches, and Gallen, *Remembering Malcolm,* pp. 188–189.

56. Haley, *Autobiography,* pp. 498–499.

57. Welton Smith, "The 15 Seconds of Murder: Shots, a Bomb, and Despair," *New York Herald Tribune,* February 22, 1964.

58. John Mallon, "Gunned Down as He Addresses Rally: 3 Men Wounded," *New York News,* February 22, 1965.

59. Benjamin Karim, in Greene, *Malcolm X,* p. 206.

60. Jimmy Breslin, "As 400 in Ballroom Watch," *New York Herald Tribune,* February 22, 1965.

61. Zak A. Kondo, *Conspiracys: Unraveling the Assassination of Malcolm X* (Washington, D.C.: Nubia Press, 1993), p. 87.

62. Breslin, *New York Herald Tribune.*

63. Tom Collins and Paul Meskil, "Fear Revenge for Malcolm X," *New York World Telegram and the Sun,* February 22, 1965.

64. Friedly, *The Assassination,* p. 232.

65. Muriel Feelings, in Greene, *Malcolm X,* p. 205.

66. Grant, in Clarke, *Man and His Times*, p. 96.

67. Friedly, *The Assassination*, p. 16.

68. Breslin, *New York Herald Tribune*.

69. Smith, *New York Herald Tribune*.

70. Breslin, *New York Herald Tribune*.

71. Report: "Malcolm K. Little," SAC New York to FBI director, February 22, 1997, Section 15, Microfilm Roll 2, FBI file on Malcolm X.

72. Report: "Malcolm K. Little," John C. Sullivan to FBI director, September 8, 1965, Section 18, Microfilm Roll 2, FBI file on Malcolm X.

73. Alfred Robbins, Mike Pearl, and Richard Barr, "Malcolm X Slain to Silence Him: The Reasons Why," *Journal American*, February 22, 1965.

74. Editorial, "Malcolm X," *New York Times*, February 22, 1965.

75. Crowther, *New York Journal*.

76. Robert Laird, "Malcolm X: In Life, As in Death, The Center of Violence," *New York World Telegram*, February 22, 1965.

77. Dick Shaap, "Hatred Was His Pitch ... And Hatred His Undoing," *New York Herald Tribune*, February 22, 1965.

78. Walter Winchell, "Man Reading the Papers," *New York Journal American*, February 28, 1965.

79. James A. Wechsler, "About Malcolm X," *New York Post*, February 23, 1965.

80. Jim Powell, "Malcolm X, Nat King Cole: Two Men," *The New Crusader*, February 27, 1965.

81. "Africans Call Malcolm X the 'American Lumumba,'" *New York Herald Tribune*, February 24, 1965.

82. Henri Dumoulin, "African Reactions to Malcolm X's Assassination," *Washington Daily News*, March 29, 1965.

83. Report: "Nation of Islam," SAC New York to FBI director, February 25, 1965, Section 15, Microfilm Roll 2, FBI file on Malcolm X.

84. E.W. Kenworthy, "Malcolm Called Martyr Abroad," *New York Times*, February 26, 1965.

85. "Malcolm X Called Martyr in Africa," *Chicago Daily News*, February 26, 1965.

86. "Africans Call Malcolm X the 'American Lumumba,'" *New York Herald Tribune*, February 24, 1965.

87. Peter Kihss, "Hunt for Killers in Malcolm Case 'On Right Track,'" *New York Times*, February 25, 1965.

88. "World Pays Little Attention to Malcolm Slaying," *New York Times*, February 27, 1965.

89. Whitney M. Young, Jr., "Malcolm's Death Solves Nothing," *New York World Telegram and the Sun*, March 4, 1965.

90. Austin C. Wehrwein, "Muhammad Says Muslims Played No Part in Slaying," *New York Times*, February 23, 1965.

91. Bayard Rustin, "Making His Mark," *Washington Post*, November 14, 1965.

92. Robert Penn Warren, *Who Speaks for the Negro?* (New York: Random House, 1965), p. 267.

93. Paul Meskil, "Probe Red Dope Tie to Malcolm Murder," *New York World Telegram and the Sun*, February 25, 1965.

94. Roy Wilkins, "Malcolm X," *New York Post*, March 7, 1965.

95. Cy Egan, "Widow Under Police Guard," *New York Journal American*, February 25, 1965.

96. Alfred Robbins, Mike Pearl, and Richard Barr, "Malcolm X Slain to Silence Him: The Reason Why," *New York Journal American*, February 22, 1965.

97. Ibid.

98. Robert Jackson, "Muhammad's Son Pleads to Rejoin Black Muslims," *New York Times*, February 25, 1965.

99. David Murry and Ralph Blumenfeld, "Cops Seek Muslim Link in Killing," *New York Post*, February 22, 1965.

100. Report: "Malcolm K. Little," SAC New York to FBI director, February 21, 1965, Section 15, Microfilm Roll 2, FBI file on Malcolm X.

101. Report: "Organization of Afro-American Unity" (OAAU), February 26, 1965, Section 3, Microfilm Roll 1, FBI file on OAAU, Scholarly Resources.

102. Wehawein, *New York Times*.

103. Norman Glubok, "Elijah Isn't Worried But Guards Are," *Chicago Daily News*, February 23, 1965.

104. Robert Wiedbich, "Close Guard Kept on Muhammad Home Here," *Chicago Tribune*, February 23, 1965.

105. Report: "Nation of Islam," SAC Chicago to FBI director, February 27, 1965, Section 16, Microfilm Roll 2, FBI file on Malcolm X.

106. Murry and Blumenfeld, *New York Post*.

107. Karim, Skutches, and Gallen, *Remembering Malcolm*, p. 193.

108. Tom Collins and Paul Meskil, "Cops Blanket Harlem," *New York World Telegram and Sun*, February 22, 1965.

109. Maurice C. Carroll, "Fear, Tension Call for Probe," *New York Herald Tribune*, February 24, 1965.

110. Ibid.

111. Kenneth Gross and Ralph Blumenfeld, "Blast Wrecks Muslim HQ Here," *New York Post*, February 23, 1965.

112. Carroll, *New York Herald Tribune*.

113. Paul L. Montgomery, "Muslims Enraged by 'Sneak Attack,'" *New York Times*, February 24, 1965.

114. Ibid.

115. Grant, in Clarke, *Man and His Times*, p. 102.

116. Donald R. Flynn, Richard Barr, and Gus Engleman, "Vengeful Blow for Malcolm X, 5 Firemen Hurt," *New York Times*, February 23, 1965.

117. Ibid.

118. Friedly, *The Assassination*, pp. 21–22.

119. George Murray, "New Threats Stir Muslim Turmoil," *Chicago American*, February 24, 1965.

120. Thomas Fitzpatrick, "Heavy Guard Readied for Muslim Chief," *New York Times*, February 25, 1965.

121. Helen Dubar, "A Look at Elijah Muhammad," *New York Post*, February 28, 1965.

122. Friedly, *The Assassination*, p. 28.

123. Louise A. DeCaro, Jr., *On the Side of My People: A Religious Life of Malcolm X* (New York: New York University Press, 1996), p. 275.

124. Peter Kihas, "Mosque Fires Stir Fear of Vendetta in Malcolm Case," *New York Times*, February 24, 1965.

125. Gross and Blumenfeld, "The People Who Came to Mourn," *New York Post*, February 24, 1965.

126. Ibid.

127. Ibid.

128. Grant, in Clarke, *Man and His Times*, p. 102.

129. Mallon, "Close in on Third Man in Malcolm X Killing," *New York Daily News*, February 27, 1965.

130. Paul Hathaway, "Harlem Shops Bare Boycott Threats," *New York World Telegraph and the Sun*, February 25, 1965.

131. Grant, in Clarke, *Man and His Times*, p. 103.

132. "Harlem Tense Funeral is Held for Malcolm X," *Chicago American*, February 27, 1965.

133. Dick Schaap, "Malcolm X: Quiet Dignity," *New York Herald Tribune*, February 28, 1965.

134. John G. Mitchell, "All Quiet and 'X' in a Grave Facing Mecca," *New York Journal American*, February 28, 1965.

135. Report: "Malcolm K. Little," SAC New York to FBI director, February 28, 1965, Section 16, Microfilm Roll 2, FBI file on Malcolm X.

136. Mitchell, *New York Journal American*.

137. Mburumba Kerina, "Malcolm X: The Apostle of Defiance—An African View," in Clarke, *Man and His Times*, p. 119.

Chapter 13

1. Peter Goldman, *The Death and Life of Malcolm X* (Urbana, Ill.: University of Illinois Press, 1979), p. 288.

2. Report: "Malcolm K. Little," SAC New York to FBI director, March 12, 1965, Section 16, Microfilm Roll 2, FBI file on Malcolm X, Scholarly Resources, Wilmington, Delaware.

3. "About to Name His Killers," *Chicago American*, February 22, 1965.

4. Heywood Gould, "Two Malcolm Aides Seized With Shotgun," *New York Post*, March 2, 1965.

5. Goldman, *Death and Life*, p. 312.

6. William McFadden, "Muslim Overlords Here Named," *New York Journal American*, February 26, 1965.

7. "2nd Muslim Seized in Malcolm Killing," *New York World Telegram and the Sun*, February 26, 1965.

8. Benjamin Karim, Peter Skutches, and David Gallen, *Remembering Malcolm* (New York: Carroll and Graf, 1992).

9. Goldman, *Death and Life*, p. 298.

10. Report: "Malcolm K. Little," SAC New York to FBI director, March 12, 1965, Section 16, Microfilm Roll 2, FBI file on Malcolm X.

11. Edward Dillon and Sidney Kline, 3d Man Jailed in the Slaying of Malcolm X," *New York Daily News*, March 4, 1965.

12. Thomas 15X Johnson, in *Brother Minister: The Assassination of El-Hajj Malik Shabazz*, prod. and dir. Jack Baxter and Jefri Aal Muhammad, 115 min., X-ceptional Productions Inc., 1997, videocassette.

13. Goldman, *Death and Life*, pp. 420–421.

14. Baxter and Aal Muhammad, *Brother Minister*.

15. Herman Ferguson, interview by author, March 5, 1999.

16. Peter Goldman, "Malcolm X: An Unfinished Story?" *New York Times Magazine*, August 29, 1979, p. 63.

17. "4 Are Indicted Here in Malcolm X Case," *New York Times*, March 11, 1965.

18. Thomas Buckley, "Daily Drama of Malcolm X Trial is Nearing End," *New York Times*, February 21, 1966.

19. Joseph Mancini, "The Malcolm X Puzzle: Who Planned the Killing?" *New York Post*, March 1, 1966.

20. Thomas Buckley, "Witness Recalls Malcolm Killing," *New York Times*, January 22, 1966.

21. Zak A. Kondo, *Conspiracys: Unraveling The Assassination of Malcolm X* (Washington, D.C.: Nubia Press, 1993), pp. 98–99.

22. Thomas Buckley, "Witness Recalls Malcolm Killing," *New York Times*, January 22, 1966.

23. James W. Sullivan, "Malcolm's Guard Admits Record, Sticks to Story," *New York Herald Tribune,* January 25, 1966.

24. Sullivan, "Unanswered Motive in Malcolm X Murder," *New York Herald Tribune,* January 26, 1966.

25. Goldman, *Death and Life,* p. 324.

26. Kondo, *Conspiracys,* p. 101.

27. "Witness Puts 15X Holding a Shotgun Near Malcolm," *New York Daily News,* February 8, 1966.

28. Kondo, *Conspiracys,* pp. 104–105.

29. Friedly, *The Assassination,* pp. 46–47.

30. Bayard Rustin, "Making His Mark," *Washington Post* November 14, 1965.

31. "Shells Linked to Murder Gun," *The Record* (Newark, N.J.), February 24, 1966.

32. "Defendant Denies Shooting Malcolm," *New York Times,* February 24, 1966.

33. "Wife Alibis Suspect in Malcolm Killing," *New York World Telegram,* February 26, 1966.

34. Evelyn Leopold, "Paid to Kill Hayer Reveals," *The Record,* March 7, 1966.

35. Ibid.

36. Ibid.

37. Thomas Buckley, "An Order to Kill Malcolm Hinted," *New York Times,* March 3, 1966.

38. Buckley, "Defense Sums Up in Malcolm Case," *New York Times,* March 8, 1966.

39. Sullivan, "Malcolm Trial: Don't Believe Confession," *New York Herald Tribune,* March 11, 1966.

40. Murry Kempton, "A Lawyer's Honor," *New York Times,* March 11, 1966.

41. Thomas Buckley, "Malcolm Slaying Called a 'Lesson,'" *New York Times,* March 9, 1966.

42. David Levin, "What Tipped Jury Scale to Guilty in 'X' Case," *New York Journal American,* March 11, 1966.

43. Jack Roth, "3 Get Life Terms in Malcolm Case," *New York Times,* April 15, 1966.

44. Dan Rather, in *The Real Malcolm X: An Intimate Portrait of the Man,* prod. and dir. Andrew Lack and Brett Alexander, 60 min., CBS Video, 1992, videocassette.

45. Peter Goldman, interview by author, February 27, 1999.

46. Yuri Kochiyama, interview by author, March 5, 1999.

47. Herman Ferguson, interview by author, March 5, 1999.

48. William Kunstler, *My Life as a Radical Lawyer* (New York: Carol Publishing Group, 1966), p. 383.

49. Friedly, *The Assassination,* p. 92.

50. Paul Lee, interview by author, March 1, 1999.

51. Kunstler, *Radical Lawyer,* pp. 382–383.

52. Karl Evanzz, *The Judas Factor: The Plot to Kill Malcolm X* (New York: Thunder's Mouth Press, 1992), p. 3.

53. "About to Name His Killer," *Chicago American,* February 22, 1965.

54. Peter Goldman, "Malcolm X: An Unfinished Story?" *New York Times Magazine,* August 19, 1979, p. 28.

55. Sullivan, *New York Herald Tribune,* January 26, 1966.

56. George Breitman, "Malcolm X's Murder and the N.Y. Police," *The Militant,* June 12, 1965.

57. Goldman, *Death and Life,* pp. 365–366.

58. James Farmer, *Lay Bare the Heart: An Autobiography of the Civil Rights Movement* (New York: Penguin Books, 1985), p. 238.

59. Allan Morrison, "Who Killed Malcolm X?" *Ebony,* October 1965, pp. 138–139.

60. Charles Kenyatta, interview by author, March 6, 1999.

61. Karim, Skutches, and Gallen, *Remembering Malcolm,* p. 187.

62. Spike Lee and Ralph Wiley, *By Any Means Necessary: The Trials and Tribulations of the Making of Malcolm X* (New York: Hyperion Press, 1992), p. 64.

63. Peter Goldman, "Who Killed Malcolm?" *Newsweek,* May 7, 1979, p. 39.

64. David Bruder, "Farrakhan Shares Blame in Malcolm X Murder," *The Charleston Gazette* (West Virginia), May 11, 2000.

65. Paul Lee, interview by author, March 1, 1999.

66. Goldman, *Newsweek,* p. 39.

67. Jack Newfield, in Baxter and Aal Muhammad, *Brother Minister.*

68. Ibid.

69. Goldman, *New York Times Magazine,* p. 64.

70. Friedly, *The Assassination,* pp. 107–108.

71. Talmadge Hayer, in Baxter and Aal Muhammad, *Brother Minister.*

72. Kunstler, *Radical Lawyer,* p. 384.

73. Talmadge Hayer, in *The Real Malcolm X: An Intimate Portrait of the Man,* prod. and dir. Andrew Lack and Brett Alexander, 60 min., CBS Video, 1992, videocassette.

74. Peter Goldman, interview by author, February 27, 1999.

75. Ibid.

76. Goldman, *New York Times Magazine,* p. 28.

77. Goldman, *Newsweek,* p. 39.

78. Kunstler, *Radical Lawyer,* pp. 384–385.

Bibliography

Reports, Interviews, and Videocassettes

Clegg, Claude A. III. Interview by author, September 6, 1997.

DeCaro, Louis A., Jr. Interview by author, March 4, 1999.

Federal Bureau of Investigation. *FBI's War on Black America,* prod. and dir. Waleed B. Ali and Malik B. Ali, 50 min., MPI Home Video, 1990, videocassette.

Ferguson, Herman. Interview by author, March 5, 1999.

Goldman, Peter. Interview by author, March 5, 1999.

Kenyatta, Charles. Interview by author, March 6, 1999.

Kochiyama, Yuri. Interview by author, March 6, 1999.

Lee, Paul. Interview by author, March 1, 1999.

Malcolm X. *Brother Minister: The Assassination of El-Hajj Malik Shabazz.* Produced and directed by Jack Baxter and Jefri Aal Muhammad. 115 min. X-ceptional Productions Inc., 1997. Videocassette.

_____. Federal Bureau of Investigation File on Malcolm X, Microfilm (10 rolls). Scholarly Resources, Wilmington, Delaware.

_____. *The Life and Death of Malcolm X.* Produced and directed by Dan Dalton. 90 min. Simitar Entertainment Inc., 1996. Videocassette.

_____. *Malcolm X.* Produced and directed by Marvin Worth and Arnold Perl. 92 min. Marvin Worth Productions, 1972. Videocassette.

_____. *Malcolm X.* Produced and directed by Rhonda Fabian and Jerry Baber. 30 min. Schlessinger Video Productions, 1994. Videocassette.

_____. *Malcolm X: Biography.* Produced and directed by Lisa Zeff and Ron Steinman. 50 min. New Video Group, 1995. Videocassette.

_____. *Malcolm X: In My Case Music.* Produced and directed by Marvin Worth and Arnold Perl. 92 min. Warner Bros. and Marvin Worth Productions, 1972. Videocassette.

_____. *Malcolm X: Make It Plain.* Produced and directed by Orlando Bagwell. 136 min. MPI Home Video, 1995. Videocassette.

_____. New York City Police Department, Bureau of Special Services, Malcolm X File 99PL100576 New York City.

_____. *The Real Malcolm X: An Intimate Portrait of the Man.* Produced and directed by Andrew Lack and Brett Alexander, 60 min. CBS Video, 1992. Videocassette.

_____. *The Speeches of Malcolm X.* Produced and directed by Denis Mueller and Jeff Sismelich. 41 min. MPI Home Video, 1997. Videocassette.

_____. Transcripts of the Malcolm X Assassination Trial. *The People of the State of New York vs. Thomas Hagan, Thomas 15X Johnson, and Norman 3X Butler,* Microfilm (3 Rolls), Scholarly Resources, Wilmington, Delaware.

Martin Luther King: A Historical Perspective. Produced and directed by Rhonda Fabian and Jerry Baber, 30 min. Schlesinger Video Productions Inc., 1997. Videocassette.

Muhammad, Elijah. Federal Bureau of Investigation File, Microfilm (3 Rolls), Scholarly Resources, Wilmington, Delaware.

_____. *Elijah Muhammad.* Produced and directed by Rhonda Fabian and Jerry Baber. 30 min. Schlessinger Video Productions, 1994. Videocassette.

Muslim Mosque Inc. Federal Bureau of Investigation File, Microfilm (3 Rolls) Scholarly Resources, Wilmington, Delaware.

Organization of Afro-American Unity. Federal Bureau of Investigation File Microfilm (1 Roll), Scholarly Resources, Wilmington, Delaware.

U.S. Department of Justice, Nation of Islam File 146–28–264, Record group 60, National Archives, College Park, Maryland.

Memoirs, Biographies, Special Studies, and Articles

Alfredsson, Gudmundur, Robert Jabara, and Kumar Rupesinghe. *The Word: The Liberation Analects.* Atlanta, Ga.: Clarity Press, 1992.

Anderson, Jervis. *Bayard Rustin: Troubles I've Seen.* New York: HarperCollins, 1997.

Angelou, Maya. *All God's Children Need Traveling Shoes.* New York: Vintage Books, 1991.

_____. *The Heart of a Woman.* New York: Bantam Books, 1981.

Baldwin, Lewis V. "Malcolm X and Martin Luther King Jr.: What They Thought About Each Other." *Islamic Studies,* Vol. 25 (4), Winter, 1986, pp. 395–416.

Bethune, Lebert. "Malcolm X in Europe." In *Malcolm X: The Man and His Times.* Edited by John H. Clarke. Trenton, N.J.: Africa World Press, 1990, pp. 226–234.

Blackstock, Nelson. *Cointelpro: The FBI's Secret War on Political Freedom.* New York: Pathfinder Press, 1988.

Boulware, Marcus H. "Minister Malcolm Orator Profundo." *Negro History Bulletin,* Vol. 30, November 1967, pp. 12–14.

Branch, Taylor. *Parting the Waters: America in the King Years 1954–63.* New York: Simon and Schuster, 1988.

Breitman, George. *The Last Year of Malcolm X: The Evolution of a Revolutionary.* New York: Pathfinder Press, 1967.

_____, Herman Porter, and Baxter Smith. *The Assassination of Malcolm X.* New York: Pathfinder Press, 1976.

Brown, Kevin. *Malcolm X: His Life and Legacy.* Brookfield, Connecticut: Millbrook Press, 1995.

Buitrago, Ann M., and Leon A. Immerman. *Are You Now or Have You Ever Been in the FBI Files? How to Secure and Interpret Your FBI Files.* New York: Grove Press, 1981.

Carew, Jan. *Ghosts in Our Blood: With Malcolm X in Africa, England, and the Caribbean.* Chicago: Lawrence Hill Books, 1994.

Carson, Clayborne. *In Struggle, SNCC and the Black Awakening of the 1960s.* Cambridge, Mass: Harvard University Press, 1981.

_____, ed. *Malcolm X: The FBI File.* New York: Carroll and Graf, 1991.

Clarke, John H., ed. *Malcolm X: The Man and His Times.* Trenton, N.J.: Africa World Press, 1990.

Cleage, Albert. "Myths About Malcolm X," in *Malcolm X: The Man and His Times,* edited by John H. Clarke. Trenton, N.J.: Africa World Press, 1990, pp. 13–26.

Cleaver, Eldridge. *Soul on Ice.* New York: Dell Publishing, 1968.

Clegg, Claude A. III. *An Original Man: The Life and Times of Elijah Muhammad.* New York: St. Martin's Press, 1997.

Collins, Rodnell P., and Peter Bailey. *Seventh Child: A Family Memoir of Malcolm X.* Secaucus, N.J.: Birch Lane Press, 1998.

Cone, James H. *Martin and Malcolm and America: A Dream or a Nightmare?* Maryknoll, N.Y.: Orbis Books, 1991.

Corson, William R. *The Armies of Ignorance: The Rise of the American Intelligence Empire.* New York: Dial Press/James Wade Books, 1977.

Crawford, Marc, "The Ominous Malcolm X Exits from the Muslims," *Life,* March 20, 1964, pp. 40–42.

Cushmeer, Bernard. *This is the One: Messen-*

ger *Elijah Muhammad.* Phoenix, Ariz.: Truth Publications, 1970.

Davis, Ossie. "Why I Eulogized Malcolm X," in *Malcolm X: The Man and His Times,* edited by John H. Clarke. Trenton, N.J.: Africa World Press, 1990.

DeCaro, Louis A., Jr. *Malcolm and the Cross: The Nation of Islam, Malcolm X, and Christianity.* New York: New York University Press, 1998.

_____. *On the Side of My People: A Religious Life of Malcolm X.* New York: New York University Press, 1996.

Doctor, Bernard A. *Malcolm X for Beginners.* New York: Writers and Readers Publishers, 1992.

Draper, Theodore. *The Rediscovery of Black Nationalism.* New York: Viking Press, 1970.

DuBois, David G. *And Bid Him Sing.* Palo Alto, Calif.: Ramparts Press, 1975.

DuBois, Shirley G. "The Beginning, Not the End," in *Malcolm X: The Man and His Times,* edited by John H. Clarke. Trenton, N.J.: Africa World Press, 1990, pp. 125–127.

Dyson, Michael E. *Making Malcolm: The Myth and Meaning of Malcolm X.* New York: Oxford University Press, 1995.

Essien-Udom, E.U. *Black Nationalism: A Search for an Identity in America.* Chicago: University of Chicago Press, 1992.

Essien-Udom, Ruby M., and E.U. Essien-Udom. "Malcolm X: An International Man," in *Malcolm X: The Man and His Times,* edited by John H. Clarke. Trenton, N.J.: Africa World Press, 1990, pp. 235–267.

Evanzz, Karl. *The Judas Factor: The Plot to Kill Malcolm X.* New York: Thunder's Mouth Press, 1987.

_____. *The Messenger: The Rise and Fall of Elijah Muhammad.* New York: Pantheon Books, 1999.

Everett, Susanne. *History of Slavery.* Edison, N.J.: Chartwell Books, 1996.

Farmer, James. *Lay Bare the Heart: An Autobiography of the Civil Rights Movement.* New York: Penguin Books, 1985.

Fletcher, Knebel. "A Visit With the Widow of Malcolm X." *Look,* March 4, 1969, pp. 74–80.

Flick, Hank, and Larry Powell. "Animal Imagery in the Rhetoric of Malcolm X." *Journal of Black Studies,* Vol. 8 (4) June 1988, pp. 435–451.

Friedly, Michael. *Malcolm X: The Assassination.* New York: Ballantine Books, 1992.

Gallen, David. *Malcolm A to X: The Man and His Ideas.* New York: Carroll and Graf, 1992.

_____, ed. *Malcolm X: As They Knew Him.* New York: Carroll and Graf, 1992.

Gardell, Mattias. *In the Name of Elijah Muhammad: Louis Farrakhan and the Nation of Islam.* Durham, N.C.: Duke University Press, 1996.

Garrow, David J. *Bearing the Cross: Martin Luther King, Jr., and the Southern Christian Leadership Conference.* New York: Vintage Books, 1986.

Gates, Henry L., Jr., and Spike Lee. "Generation X." *Transition: An International Review,* Vol. 56, Winter 1992, pp. 176–190.

Gentry, Curt. *J. Edgar Hoover: The Man and His Secrets.* New York: W.W. Norton, 1991.

Glanville, Brian. "Malcolm X." *New Statesman,* Vol. 6, June 12, 1964, pp. 901–902.

Goldman, Peter. *The Death and Life of Malcolm X.* Urbana, Ill.: University of Illinois Press, 1979.

_____. "Malcolm X: An Unfinished Story?" *New York Times Magazine.* August 19, 1979, pp. 26–32.

_____. "Who Killed Malcolm?" *Newsweek,* May 7, 1979, p. 39.

Grant, Earl. "The Last Days of Malcolm X." In *Malcolm X: The Man and His Times,* edited by John H. Clarke. Trenton, N.J.: Africa World Press, 1990, 83–105.

Greene, Cheryll Y. ed. *Malcolm X: Make It Plain.* New York: Viking Penguin, 1994.

Haley, Alex. *The Autobiography of Malcolm X.* Ballantine Books, 1992.

_____. "Malcolm X: A Candid Conversation With the Militant Major-Domo of the Black Muslims." *Playboy,* May 1963, pp. 53–63.

_____ "Mr. Muhammad Speaks." *Reader's Digest,* March 1969, pp. 100–104.

Hill, Robert A. "The Foremost Radical Among His Race: Marcus Garvey and the Black Scare, 1918–1921." *Prologue: The Journal of the National Archives,* Vol. 16, Winter 1984, pp. 215–231.

Jamal, Hakim A. *From the Dead Level: Malcolm X and Me.* New York: Random House, 1972.

Johnson, Timothy V. *Malcolm X: A Compre-*

hensive Annotated Bibliography. New York: Garland Publishing, 1986.

Karim, Benjamin, Peter Skutches, and David Gallen. *Remembering Malcolm.* New York: Carroll and Graf, 1992.s

Kly, Y.N. *The Black Book: The True Political Philosophy of Malcolm X.* Atlanta, Ga.: Clarity Press, 1986.

Knebel, Fletcher. "A Visit With the Widow of Malcolm X." *Look,* March 4, 1969, pp. 74–80.

Kondo, Zak A. *Conspiracys: Unraveling the Assassination of Malcolm X.* Washington, D.C.: Nubia Press, 1993.

Kunstler, William M., and Sheila Isenberg. *My Life as a Radical Lawyer.* New York: Carol Publishing Group, 1996.

Lacy, Alexander L. "Malcolm X in Ghana." In *Malcolm X: The Man and His Times,* edited by John H. Clarke. Trenton, N.J.: Africa World Press, 1990, pp. 217–234.

Lawler, Mary. *Marcus Garvey: Black Nationalist Leader.* Los Angeles: Melrose Square, 1988.

Lee, Spike, and Ralph Wiley. *By Any Means Necessary: The Trials and Tribulations of the Making of Malcolm X.* New York: Hyperion Press, 1992.

Lemelle, Sid. *Pan-Africanism for Beginners.* New York: Writers and Readers, 1992.

Lewis, David L. *King: A Critical Biography.* New York: Praeger, 1970.

Lincoln, Eric C. *The Black Muslims in America.* Boston, Mass.: Beacon Press, 1961.

_____. "The Meaning of Malcolm X." *Christian Century.* April 7, 1965, pp. 431–433.

_____. *My Face Is Black.* Boston, Mass.: Beacon Press, 1964.

Lomax, Louis E. *The Negro Revolt.* New York: Harper and Row, 1962.

_____. *To Kill a Black Man,* Los Angeles: Holloway House, 1987.

_____. *When the Word is Given.* Cleveland: World Publishing, 1963.

Magida, Arthur J. *Prophet of Rage: A Life of Louis Farrakhan and His Nation.* New York: HarperCollins, 1996.

Maglangbayan, Shawna. *Garvey, Lumumba, and Malcolm: National-Separatists.* Chicago, Ill.: Third World Press, 1972.

Malcolm X. *Malcolm X: By Any Means Necessary,* edited by George Breitman. New York: Pathfinder Press, 1970.

_____. *Malcolm X: February 1965, The Final Speeches.* Edited by Steve Clark. New York: Pathfinder Press, 1992.

_____. *Malcolm X Speaks: Selected Speeches and Statements.* Edited by George Breitman. New York: Pathfinder Press, 1989.

_____. *Malcolm X: The Last Speeches.* Edited by Bruce Perry. New York: Pathfinder Press, 1989.

_____. *Malcolm X on Afro-American History.* Edited by Steve Clark. New York: Pathfinder Press, 1991.

_____. *Malcolm X: Speeches at Harvard.* Edited by Archie Epps. New York: Paragon House, 1991.

_____. *Malcolm X Talks to Young People: Speeches in the U.S., Britain, and Africa.* Edited by Steve Clark. New York: Pathfinder Press, 1991.

Malik, Michael A. *From Michael de Freitas to Michael X.* Great Britain: Andre Deutsch, 1968.

Marsh, Cliften E. *From Black Muslims to Muslims: The Transition From Separatism to Islam, 1930–1980.* Metuchen, N.J.: Scarecrow Press, 1984.

Massaquoi, Hans. "Mystery of Malcolm X." *Ebony.* September 1964, pp. 38–48.

Mealy, Rosemari. *Fidel and Malcolm X: Memories of a Meeting.* Melbourne, Australia: Ocean Press, 1993.

Morrison, Allan. "Who Killed Malcolm X?" *Ebony.* October 1965, pp. 135–142.

Muhammad, Elijah. *Message to the Black Man in America.* Chicago: Muhammad Mosque of Islam No. 2, 1965.

_____. *Our Savior Has Arrived.* Chicago: Muhammad Mosque of Islam No. 2, 1965.

_____. *The Supreme Wisdom: Solution to the So-Called Negroes' Problem.* Chicago: University of Islam, 1934.

Muhammad, Wallace. *As the Light Shineth From the East.* Chicago: WDM Publishing, 1980.

_____. *Fard, Secret Ritual of the Nation of Islam.* Chicago: Zakat Publications, 1988.

Myers, Walter D. *Malcolm X: By Any Means Necessary.* New York: Scholastic, 1993.

Nadle, Marlene. "Malcolm X: The Complexity of a Man in the Jungle." *Village Voice,* February 1965, pp. 1–6.

Ohmann, Carol. "The Autobiography of Malcolm X: A Revolutionary Use of the Franklin Tradition." *American Quarterly,* Vol. 22 (2) 1970, pp. 131–149.

Parks, Gordon, "Malcolm X: The Minutes of Our Last Meeting." In *Malcolm X: The Man and His Times.* Edited by John H. Clarke. Trenton, N.J.: Africa World Press, pp. 120–124.

_____. "The Violent End of the Man Called Malcolm X." *Life,* March 1965, pp. 26–31.

_____. *Voices in the Mirror: An Autobiography.* New York: Doubleday, 1990.

Perry, Bruce. *Malcolm: The Life of a Man Who Changed Black America.* New York: Station Hill Press, 1991.

Powell, Adam C., Jr. *Adam by Adam: The Autobiography of Adam Clayton Powell Jr.* New York: Dial Press, 1971.

Rainwater, Lee, ed. *Black Experience Soul.* New Brunswick, N.J.: Transaction Books, 1970.

Rashad, Adib. *Elijah Muhammad: The Ideological Foundation of The Nation of Islam.* Newport News, Va.: U.B. and U.S. Communications Systems, 1994.

Remnick, David. *King of the World: Muhammad Ali and the Rise of an American Hero.* New York: Random House, 1998.

Rowan, Carl T. *Breaking Barriers: A Memoir.* New York: Little, Brown, 1991.

Rummel, Jack. *Malcolm X.* New York: Chelsea House, 1989.

Salmond, John A. *My Mind Set on Freedom: A History of the Civil Rights Movement, 1954–1968.* Chicago, Ill.: Ivan R. Dee, 1997.

Shabazz, Betty. "The Legacy of My Husband, Malcolm X." *Ebony,* June 1969, pp. 172–182.

_____. "Malcolm X as a Husband and Father." In *Malcolm X: The Man and His Times,* edited by John H. Clarke. Trenton, N.J.: Africa World Press, 1990, 132–143.

Shepard, Ray. *Autobiography of Malcolm X: Notes.* Lincoln, Neb.: Cliff Notes, 1992.

Smith, Baxter. "FBI Memos Reveal Repression Scheme," *The Black Scholar,* Vol. 5, April 1974, pp. 43–48.

Wade, Wyn G. *The Fiery Cross: The Ku Klux Klan in America.* New York: Oxford University Press, 1987.

Wallace, Mike, and Gary P. Gates. *Close Encounters: Mike Wallace's Own Story.* New York: William Morrow, 1984.

Warren, Robert P. "Malcolm X: Mission and Meaning." In *Malcolm X: As They Knew Him.* Edited by David Gallen. New York: Carroll and Graf, 1992, pp. 201–211.

_____. *Who Speaks for the Negro?* New York: Random House, 1965.

Weiss, Samuel. "The Ordeal of Malcolm X." *South Atlantic Quarterly,* Vol. 76 (4), 1977, pp. 53–63.

West, Cornel. *Race Matters.* New York: Vintage Books, 1994.

Wiley, Charles W. "Who Was Malcolm X?" *National Review,* March 23, 1965, pp. 239–240.

Wilkinson, Brenda. *The Civil Rights Movement: An Illustrated History.* Avenel, N.J.: Crescent Books, 1997.

Wise, David. *The American Police State: The Government Against the People.* New York: Vintage Books, 1976.

Wish, Harvey, ed. *The Negro Since Emancipation.* Englewood Cliffs, N.J.: Prentice-Hall, 1964.

Wolfenstein, Victor. *The Victims of Democracy: Malcolm X and the Black Revolution.* New York: Guilford Press, 1993.

Wood, Joe, ed. *Malcolm X: In Our Own Image.* New York: St. Martin's Press, 1992.

Index

219